"Higher education finance is a classic research topic in the economics of education. The book makes a systematic and in-depth exploration on the future of China's higher education finance in the "post-4%" era, which presents the latest research progress of Chinese scholars in relevant fields and shares China's efforts to provide adequate and equitable financial support for the sustainable development of higher education. It is for sure that international colleagues in the economics of education can have a new understanding of China's higher education fiscal policy and practice through this book."

Weifang Min, *Former Dean of Graduate School of Education at Peking University, China*

"Great academic work should be based on theory and practice, and combine methods and policies. This book is the most distinctive one I have seen in higher education finance in recent years. On the one hand, the book carefully combs the relevant theories of higher education finance, as well as China's practical experience in higher education finance, and systematically shows the achievements and challenges of China's higher education finance. On the other hand, this book summarizes the major econometric forecasting methods applying on the forecast of the scale and allocation structure of financial investment in Chinese higher education. Meanwhile, the book not only gives the adjustment coefficient of average student financial allocation in colleges and universities based on the different characteristics of cultivation cost per student but also creatively puts forward the allocation standard of average teacher research funds in different disciplines. It can be foreseen that the publication of the book will make an important contribution to promoting the internationalization of Chinese research on higher education finance."

Xibin Jin, *Beijing Normal University, China*

"Public universities are the main body of China's higher education, government financial funds are the main revenue source of Chinese public universities, so the scale and allocation of government financial funds are closely related to the development of each public university in China. The book is a meaningful attempt and exploration of Chinese scholars in this respect, covering the critical issues in higher education finance. This book will be of reference value for university administrators and higher education policymakers in China and many other countries."

Fanhua Meng, *Secretary of the Party Committee at Capital Normal University, China*

Research on Investment Scale and Allocation Structure of Chinese Higher Education Finance

Based on a systematic literature review, the book aims to forecast the investment scale of Chinese higher education and the allocation structure of different types of higher education institutions in the next decade.

The authors first introduce the complex setting of Chinese higher education finance, including the background and theoretical foundation, as well as an in-depth literature review. Via international comparative data, they explore the adequacy and equity of the financial resources. By applying quantitative methods, such as panel data analysis and time series analysis, they forecast the public investment scale in higher education and the allocation structure and proportion among different types of higher education institutions. In addition, the book investigates the standards of teaching funding and teacher research funding, which are considered the main funding resources of Chinese universities and individual teachers.

As China has become the world's largest country of higher education, "how to provide adequate and equal funds to meet the increasing demand" is of great interest to scholars and policymakers both from China and abroad. The book will also appeal to postgraduate students who would like to know the overall status of Chinese higher education finance.

Yongmei Hu is a professor of the Faculty of Education at Beijing Normal University, Beijing, China. Since 2016, she has been a vice editor-in-chief of the editorial board of *China Economics of Education Review* and a member of the executive board of the Association of China Education and Economics. Her research interests focus on the educational production function, school efficiency analysis, and educational finance policy. She has published more than 140 papers in Chinese and international journals.

Yipeng Tang is an associate professor with the Faculty of Education, East China Normal University, Shanghai, China. He received his PhD in economics of education from Beijing Normal University. He was granted Young Researcher Funds by the National Natural Sciences Foundation of China. He has published more than 40 research articles in academic journals. His research interests include higher education finance, teacher policy, and student development.

China Perspectives

The *China Perspectives* series focuses on translating and publishing works by leading Chinese scholars, writing about both global topics and China-related themes. It covers Humanities & Social Sciences, Education, Media and Psychology, as well as many interdisciplinary themes.

This is the first time any of these books have been published in English for international readers. The series aims to put forward a Chinese perspective, give insights into cutting-edge academic thinking in China, and inspire researchers globally.

To submit proposals, please contact the Taylor & Francis Publisher for China Publishing Programme, Lian Sun (Lian.Sun@informa.com)

Titles in education currently include:

Investment and Interventions to Improve the Quality of Education Systems
Jin Chi and Eduardo Velez Bustillo

Elasticity and Toughness
Ethnography of *Minban* Teachers' Policy Implementation in Rural Chinese Society
Feng Wei

Understanding Professional Agency of Female Language Teachers in a University of China
The Rhetoric and Reality
Xiaolei Ruan

Research on Investment Scale and Allocation Structure of Chinese Higher Education Finance
Yongmei Hu and Yipeng Tang

For more information, please visit https://www.routledge.com/China-Perspectives/book-series/CPH

Research on Investment Scale and Allocation Structure of Chinese Higher Education Finance

Yongmei Hu and Yipeng Tang

LONDON AND NEW YORK

This book is published with financial support from National Natural Science Foundation of China (No.71573020)

First published 2022
by Routledge
2 Park Square, Milton Park, Abingdon, Oxon OX14 4RN

and by Routledge
605 Third Avenue, New York, NY 10158

Routledge is an imprint of the Taylor & Francis Group, an informa business

© 2022 Yongmei Hu and Yipeng Tang

The right of Yongmei Hu and Yipeng Tang to be identified as authors of this work has been asserted in accordance with sections 77 and 78 of the Copyright, Designs and Patents Act 1988.

All rights reserved. No part of this book may be reprinted or reproduced or utilised in any form or by any electronic, mechanical, or other means, now known or hereafter invented, including photocopying and recording, or in any information storage or retrieval system, without permission in writing from the publishers.

Trademark notice: Product or corporate names may be trademarks or registered trademarks, and are used only for identification and explanation without intent to infringe.

British Library Cataloguing in Publication Data
A catalogue record for this book is available from the British Library

Library of Congress Cataloging in Publication Data
A catalog record for this book has been requested

ISBN: 978-1-032-16489-2 (hbk)
ISBN: 978-1-032-16842-5 (pbk)
ISBN: 978-1-003-25052-4 (ebk)

DOI: 10.4324/9781003250524

Typeset in Times New Roman
by Deanta Global Publishing Services, Chennai, India

Contents

List of figures		viii
List of tables		x
Preface		xiii
1	Introduction	1
2	Basic methods of financial forecasting research in higher education	30
3	The adequacy and equity of the financial resources of higher education	48
4	Forecasting the scale of public investment in higher education	68
5	Forecasting the allocation structure and proportion of public investment for different types of higher education institutions	97
6	Research on the standard for teaching funding and average student funding in higher education	120
7	Research on the standard of average teacher research funding for university teachers	160
	Index	225

Figures

1.1	Technical route of the study	23
3.1	Government expenditure per tertiary student (international dollars) 2001–2011	51
3.2	Fiscal expenditure on higher education in various countries as a percentage of GDP 2001–2011	52
3.3	Fiscal expenditure (%) for all types of national higher education, 2001–2011	53
3.4	Correlation coefficient between the government expenditure per tertiary student and GDP per capita	57
3.5	The elasticity coefficient of the government expenditure per tertiary students to GDP per capita	58
3.6	Atkinson index of government expenditure per tertiary student	61
4.1	Predictive accuracy of the student size and investment ratio in higher education	75
4.2	Forecasted values of gross enrollment ratio and student size for 2021–2025	78
4.3	Forecasted values of the proportion and scale of public investment in higher education for 2021–2025	79
5.1	The changes in the proportion of government funding for CHEIs and LHEIs in 1995–2014	99
5.2	The changes in the average student budgetary expenditure for CHEIs and LHEIs in 1995–2014	100
5.3	The change of enrollment of HEIs offering degree programs and HVCs, and the proportion of HEIs' enrollment to the total in 2005–2014	102
5.4	The change of average student budgetary expenditure of centrally administered HEIs offering degree programs and local HVCs and their ratio in 2005–2014	103
5.5	Autocorrelation and partial autocorrelation functions	111
5.6	The feasible interval of the proportion of public investment in HEIs offering degree programs in 2016–2020	113
7.1	China's university research funding system	167

7.2	Comparison of the teacher age structure between the statistics of China's Ministry of Education (MOE) and the sample of this study	182
7.3	The comparison of the teacher title structure between the statistics of China's Ministry of Education (MOE) and the sample of this study	183
7.4	The distribution of the types of research projects obtained by teachers in the survey sample, 2013–2015	185
7.5	The distribution of the types of research projects obtained by teachers in samples of different disciplines, 2013–2015	185
7.6	The type distribution of research projects obtained by university teachers at different institutional levels, 2013–2015	187
7.7	The type distribution of the research project obtained by teachers with different titles, 2013–2015	189
7.8	The distribution of research project funds received by sample university teachers	193
7.9	The distribution of university teachers' attitudes toward noncompetitive research funds	200

Tables

1.1	Content and definition of China's higher education budget expenditure	11
2.1	Literature of higher education financial forecasting and main methods used	43
A2.1	Summary of Stata commands for forecasting method	44
3.1	Government expenditure per tertiary student in 2001–2011 (international dollars)	50
3.2	The correlation coefficients between the proportion of public investment in higher education, GDP, and total public expenditure	55
3.3	Atkinson index of government expenditure per tertiary student	60
3.4	Absolute convergence of government expenditure on higher education	63
3.5	Conditional convergence for government expenditure on higher education	64
4.1	Descriptive statistics on the main variables	72
4.2	Estimates of the structural equation model	74
4.3	Forecasted results of the higher education student size in China from 2021 to 2025	77
4.4	Forecast of the proportion and scale of public investment in higher education in China for 2021–2025	79
A4.1	Results of lower limit models (full sample)	87
A4.2	Results of lower limit models (the Chinese sample)	89
A4.3	Forecasted values of the proportion and scale of public investment in higher education in China (lower limit) for 2016–2020	90
A4.4	Results of the upper limit model	91
A4.5	Forecasted values of the proportion and scale of public investment in higher education in China for 2016–2020 (upper limit)	92
A4.6	Results of models with the per capita GDP (full sample)	92
A4.7	Forecasted values of China's gross enrollment rate, student size, and proportion of tuition fees	93

Tables xi

5.1	Forecast model result of the proportion of public investment in HEIs offering degree programs	108
5.2	Forecast results of the trend model, exponential smoothing, Holt–Winters nonseasonal smoothing, and combination model	110
5.3	Forecast results for the proportion of student size variable GSTUR in 2015–2020 with combination model	111
5.4	Results for ADF unit root test	111
5.5	Forecast results of combination model for GVEXPP (the ratio of centrally administered HEIs' per student budgetary expenditure to local HVCs' per student budgetary expenditure) in 2015–2020	112
5.6	Forecast values of Y_f in 2015–2020	113
5.7	Descriptive statistics for variables (2005–2014)	114
5.8	Forecast results for the public investment in local higher education institutions offering degree programs (HEIs) as a percentage of total public investment in higher education, 2015–2020 by province (fixed effect model)	115
6.1	Average student comprehensive quota standard of undergraduates in central universities after the 2008 reform	125
6.2	Cost items of higher education appropriations in Texas, United States	132
6.3	Standard of HEFCE funding for price groups per student FTE (in pounds)	136
6.4	Standard for the targeted allocations per student of HEFCE (in pounds)	137
6.5	Overview of the econometric methods for average student cultivation cost	143
6.6	List of sampled MOE-administered universities	149
6.7	Variable definitions in the model of influencing factors	151
6.8	Descriptive statistics	152
6.9	Estimated results of the influencing factor model for the average student cultivation cost	153
6.10	Average student cultivation costs in MOE-administered universities and the adjustment factor of the average student funding in universities with different characteristics	154
6.11	Results for robustness check	155
6.12	Comparison of adjustment factors	156
7.1	The Chinese government's funding system for scientific research in colleges and universities	164
7.2	Management measures for the fundamental research funds for central universities, selected cases	175
7.3	Sample distribution	181
7.4	Age distribution of teachers with different titles	183
7.5	Comparison of distribution characteristics of the two samples	184

7.6	Distribution of national-level projects among teachers in different disciplines and different age groups	186
7.7	The type distribution of research projects obtained by teachers in different disciplines at different institutional levels	188
7.8	Type distribution of research projects obtained by teachers in different disciplines and with different titles	191
7.9	Overall situation of university teachers' research funds (10,000 yuan)	192
7.10	Distribution of research funds for teachers in different disciplines (%)	194
7.11	Distribution of age and title structures of teachers with research funds under 50,000 yuan (%)	195
7.12	Distribution of research funds for teachers in different types of universities (%)	197
7.13	Concentration of research funds for teachers in different disciplines (%)	198
7.14	Distribution of teacher characteristics at the bottom 20% of funds (%)	199
7.15	Percentage of teachers with different characteristics who agreed with the establishment of noncompetitive research funding (%)	200
7.16	Description of the main variables and their descriptive statistics	202
7.17	Results for logistic models	203
7.18	Classification and content of HEFCE research grants	206
7.19	Quality and research volume in UoA X_1 in REF	207
7.20	Research volume of three universities in units of assessment X_1, X_2, X_3	207
7.21	Allocation shares of each unit of assessment (UoA)	208
7.22	Allocation results for mainstream QR funding	209
7.23	Standard for the average teacher research funds (10,000 yuan/year)	211
A7.1	Management methods for basic research funds in some universities	219

Preface

During the 21st century, China's higher education has been in a period of rapid development, with 36.47 million students in 2015, ranking first in the world; there are 2852 universities, ranking second in the world; and the gross enrollment rate is 40%, which has achieved the goal of "reaching 40% by 2020", proposed in the national education planning outline ahead of schedule, exceeding the average level of middle- and high-income countries. After the implementation of higher education projects like the "211 Project", "985 Project", "2011 Collaborative Innovation Plan" and "double first-class" construction, China has invested enormous financial funds to support the development of universities, which has also made the reputation and influence of Chinese universities in the world rise rapidly. According to the 2018 Global University Rankings released by *U.S. News & World report*, there are 136 Chinese universities on the list (including Hong Kong and Macao), ranking second in the world, which fully reflects the remarkable achievements of major construction projects of higher education in China. President Xi Jinping pointed out in the report of the 19th National Congress of the Communist Party of China that the intensified development and double first-class construction will be the top priority of China's higher education development in the future.

However, the gross domestic product (GDP) growth rate in China was first less than 8% in 2012, and since then it has been falling to a "new normal" of economic development. Meanwhile, the government's financial support for higher education declined relative to that of other educational levels. According to the 2016 National Statistical Bulletin on the Implementation of Education Funds, among the indicators of average student budgetary educational expenditure and average student operational expenditure at various educational levels, the growth rate of average student budgetary educational expenditure for higher education was the smallest (only 3.33%), and the average student operational expenditure for higher education even had a negative growth rate, which would undoubtedly affect the steady development of higher education in China in the future. Therefore, whether the Chinese government can continue to provide adequate financial support for higher education has become an urgent question to be studied. This requires researchers to carry out scientific and reasonable prediction research according to the historical data of China's higher education and economic development to provide a reference for the government to formulate higher education financial policy.

This book focuses on four aspects: the scale of financial investment in higher education, the allocation structure of financial investment in different types of higher education, the standard of average student funding, and the standard of average teacher research funds. The relevant conclusions can be used to formulate higher education for the Chinese government during the 14th Five-Year Plan period. The scale of educational financial appropriation provides a basis for decision-making; provides a reference for the central and local education authorities to adjust the average student financial appropriation standards; and proposes alternative plans for relevant decision-making agencies to ensure basic scientific research funds for college teachers.

In the process of writing this monograph, we have read through and referred to a large number of related papers and books. We would like to express our sincere thanks to the relevant authors! In addition, we have received help and support from many colleagues and students during the writing of this monograph and benefited from discussions with them. These people include Professor Yuhong Du, Professor Xiaoyu Chen, Professor Yuxiang Li, Professor Zhijun Sun, Professor Zeyun Liu, Professor Yaozong Hu, Dr. Gang Cheng, Dr. Wenyan Liang, and Dr. Weiyi Wang. At the same time, we would like to thank Dr. Huixia Yi, Dr. Ran Zhao, and Mr. An'an Liang for participating in the writing of some chapters.

We appreciate the great support from Routledge, including Ms. Lian Sun, Mr. Feichi Gao, and Ms. Zixu Fan. We would like to thank the reviewers for their valuable comments, which help refine our work. This research is funded by the National Natural Sciences Foundation of China (71573020) "Research on Investment Scale and Allocation Structure of Chinese Higher Education Finance in the Post-4% Era".

Last but not the least, it is also a great honor for us to have recommendations for this new book from three leading scholars: Professor Weifang Min, Professor Xibin Jin, and Professor Fanhua Meng.

Due to our limited research ability, mistakes and omissions are inevitable. We sincerely ask for criticism and correction from all scholars and readers if mistakes are found.

Yongmei Hu and Yipeng Tang

1 Introduction

1.1 Research background

The "Outline of China's Education Reform and Development" issued in July 1993 clearly pointed out that by the end of the 20th century, China's fiscal education expenditures will account for the important goal of 4% of the gross domestic product (GDP). This index was set by the domestic academic circles with reference to the level of government investment in education in major developed countries. But it was not until 20 years later that the proportion of national fiscal expenditure on education in GDP exceeded 4% for the first time. However, the tardy 4% puts the formulation of China's public education fiscal policy into a new dilemma. Some domestic scholars begin to focus on the topic of "post-4% era" to discuss the trend of China's public education fiscal expenditure in the future, as well as the establishment of a long-term guarantee mechanism for education investment (Bao, 2012; Zeng & Long, 2013; Zhang & Lan, 2014; Hu & Tang, 2014). The scale and allocation structure of financial investment in higher education is a very important research topic.

Through reading the existing relative research papers, we find that there are three main problems in the financial investment system of higher education in China: First, the allocation of investment in different "identity" universities is unbalanced, and the operating cost of local colleges and universities is far higher than the standard of financial allocation per student. Second, the internal funding structure of colleges and universities has not reached the optimization state, and the lack of quota of teachers' average in the financial allocation based on the average student comprehensive quota leads to the lack of stable sources for basic scientific research activities of teachers. Third, the university should make beneficial practical exploration and personnel training system reform in accordance with the changes of the demand specification of talents in accordance with the economic and social development under the "new normal" in economic development, which needs the support and guarantee of the government financial funds.

2 *Introduction*

1.1.1 Imbalance of investment allocation in colleges and universities with different "identities"

The "211 Project" and "985 Project" debate in the media around 2015 reflects the imbalance of government investment in different "identity" universities in the era of popular higher education. On August 18, 2015, the meeting of the central leading group for comprehensively deepening reform deliberated and approved the "Overall Plan for Promoting the Construction of World-Class Universities and First-Class Disciplines", including the 211 Project, 985 Project, and "Innovation Platform for Advantageous Disciplines" into the construction of world-class universities and first-class disciplines. In January 2017, the Ministry of Education, the Ministry of Finance, and the National Development and Reform Commission issued "The Implementation Measures for Promoting the Construction of World-Class Universities and First-Class Disciplines as a Whole (Provisional)". On September 21, 2017, the Ministry of Education, the Ministry of Finance, and the National Development and Reform Commission jointly issued the notice on publishing the university lists of world-class universities construction (hereafter WCUC) and world-class discipline construction (hereafter WCDC), officially announcing the list of 140 "double first-class" construction universities, including 42 WCUC universities and 95 WCDC universities. In October 2018, the Riseqi Think Tank published statistics on the annual budget of 42 WCUC universities from 2016 to 2018. More than 60% of the double first-class universities had a budget of more than 5 billion yuan, and Tsinghua University ranked first. The budget of Tsinghua University in 2018 was close to 27 billion yuan. The budget of most colleges and universities increased significantly, especially for Tongji University, Lanzhou University, Ocean University of China, and Yunnan University in 2018 showed a larger increase than the previous year, and the total budget for Tongji University and Yunnan University even doubled, which is related to the local government's support for the double first-class policy (Wang, 2018).

Not only is there a huge difference between the central and local finance in the financial allocation of double first-class and non–double first-class universities, but also the gap between the central and local universities has been widening for a long time. Through sorting the data of higher education funds from 1998 to 2015, Xu (2018) found that compared with the central universities, local universities are seriously insufficient in average funding and average student funding. In 1998, there were 263 central universities and 759 local universities. The average funding of central universities was 4.28 times that of local universities. By 2015, there were only 111 central colleges and universities, while the number of local colleges and universities had increased to 2734. However, the average funding of central colleges and universities had expanded to 10.52 times that of local colleges and universities. From the perspective of average student funding, before 2011, the gap between central universities and local universities had been expanding, from 1.75 times to 2.5 times. The data of 2015 shows that the average student funding of central universities is 51,600 yuan, while that of local universities is only 24,500 yuan, and the gap is still very obvious.

Under the situation that the average funding level of local colleges and universities is at a low level, the budget expenditure of local colleges and universities is constantly improving, and the financial allocation is far lower than the actual operating cost of colleges and universities, which has become an obstacle for ordinary colleges and universities to improve the quality of higher education.[1] In fact, some researchers have noticed the operating cost of local colleges and universities and pointed out that the operating cost of local colleges and universities far exceeds the average student funding level from the finance. For example, Fan's (2015) analysis shows that the income and expenditure of education funds in local colleges and universities are becoming increasingly unbalanced, and many colleges and universities even try to seek loans from banks to alleviate the problem of funds shortage. Li (2016) pointed out that the original limited financial support cannot be fully realized. About 27.38% of local universities said that the government funding is difficult to fully meet, which further improves the difficulty of raising education funds. On the other hand, based on the principle of educational equity, colleges and universities also need to ensure that poverty does not keep students from low-income families out of school. The communique of the 2009 World Conference on Higher Education put forward that

> while expanding the enrollment opportunities of higher education, higher education must pursue the three goals of fairness, appropriateness and quality at the same time. Equity is not just a simple issue of access — it also means that to ensure the smooth participation and completion of the goals of their studies, while ensuring the treatment of students, it is necessary to provide appropriate financial assistance to poor and marginalized groups.
>
> (Xiong, 2009)

According to the research of Jin and Lou (2019), the average tuition fees of Zhejiang University in 2017 reached 27.8% of the disposable income of rural residents and 18.32% of the disposable income of urban residents. It can be seen that the tuition fees of local colleges and universities still exceed the affordability of some rural families. In addition, the study also points out that the tuition fee of public colleges and universities in Zhejiang Province has only increased by 15.4% in the past ten years, which is very limited compared with the increase of average student expenditure (102.7%). However, we still need to pay attention to the design of a tuition fee reduction system for rural and urban low-income students while maintaining a reasonable increase in tuition fees. Therefore, in the process of improving the financial system of higher education, we need to pay attention to improving the tuition standard setting and student financial assistance system.

1.1.2 The internal funding structure of colleges and universities has not been optimized

At present, the investment allocation of finance at all levels to different "status" universities is not balanced, and the financial funds obtained by central universities and local universities are quite different.[2] There is also a big gap in the average financial allocation of colleges and universities students in different provinces. Moreover, the internal funding structure of colleges and universities has not been optimized, and the financial allocation based on the average student comprehensive quota lacks the quota per teacher, which leads to the lack of a stable source of teachers' basic scientific research activities.

Yingsheng Zhao, director of the Department of Comprehensive Reform of the Ministry of Education, pointed out at the first National Symposium on University Development, Fund Raising and Investment that "in recent years, the central government has increased the investment in per student funds, and the scientific research funds have also increased by a large margin. It seems that our universities are not short of money, but it seems that the fund structure hasn't been optimized" (Li, 2014). This kind of unreasonable structure not only exists in the large difference between the aforementioned universities under the administration of China's Ministry of Education (MOE) and local universities in the proportion of financial allocation but also in the universities directly under the Ministry of Education based only on the average student comprehensive quota (the average student comprehensive quota does not cover teachers' scientific research expenses, only teachers' wages and welfare expenses). Lacking the average teacher quota, as a result, there is no stable source for teachers to carry out basic scientific research activities. At present, among the six categories of "project expenditure budget" implemented by the universities directly under the Ministry of Education, the "basic research business expenses of Central Universities and special funds for top innovative talents in basic disciplines" in the "other categories" are also competitive funds in the internal allocation of universities, rather than noncompetitive funds to guarantee all teachers to engage in basic scientific research activities.[3]

1.1.3 Under the "new normal" of China's economic development, the support of financial funds for talent cultivation in colleges and universities is insufficient

As China moves toward becoming a high-income country, its economic development depends on industrial upgrading, technological progress, and talent dividends. This puts forward higher requirements for higher education. Colleges and universities have a long way to go in the work of high-quality talent cultivation and scientific and technological innovation. In 2010, the "Excellent Engineer Education and Cultivation Plan" was implemented. In August 2012, the Ministry of Education promulgated the "Basic Requirements for Entrepreneurship Education for Ordinary Undergraduate Students (Trial)", comprehensively promoting the scientific, institutionalized and standardized construction of entrepreneurship education in colleges and universities. In November 2013, the Ministry of Education, together with the Ministry of Human Resources and Social Security, formulated and promulgated the "Opinions on Further Promoting the Reform of the Cultivation Mode of Professional Degree Postgraduates". The "opinions" proposed to establish a cultivation mode of professional degree postgraduates with Chinese characteristics, which is suitable for economic and social development. The basic principles include guided by professional needs, focusing on the training of practical ability, and taking the combination of production and learning as the way. The "5 + 3" mode of the comprehensive reform of clinical medical education in China, jointly implemented by Fudan University, Shanghai Jiaotong University, Tongji University, Shanghai University of Traditional Chinese Medicine, and the Second Military Medical University, and the "three-three system" undergraduate talent cultivation system reform of Nanjing University are beneficial practical explorations made by colleges and universities to adapt to the changes in the talent demand specifications of economic and social development. In recent years, the construction of "New Engineering" has become an important starting point of engineering talent cultivation. Under the guidance of the Ministry of Education, it has successively carried out many discussions and formed the "Fudan Consensus", "Tianda Action", and "Beijing Guide", aiming at speeding the construction of New Engineering. In 2017, the Ministry of Education issued the notice on carrying out New Engineering research and practice, and in 2018 issued the notice on publishing the first batch of New Engineering research and practice projects, which identified the first batch of 202 comprehensive reform projects and 410 professional reform projects. By the end of 2019, nine engineering universities (Harbin Institute of Technology, Tianjin University, Southeast University, Tongji University, Beijing Institute of Technology, Chongqing University, Dalian University of Technology, South China University of Technology, and Northwest Polytechnical University) jointly issued the "New Engineering Education Quality Declaration of Excellent Universities Alliance", forming the excellent universities alliance, to explore the New Engineering talent cultivation system of "three complete education" and "five education simultaneously" with the New Engineering construction as the carrier. The rapid development and reform of China's higher education need sufficient funds. However, in the context of China's overall economic growth slowing down, the possibility of a substantial increase in education funding is very small. Therefore, under the background of the economic new normal in the post-4% era, the government's guarantee of the scale of higher education investment matching with the development of China's higher education and how to optimize the allocation of financial resources in the higher education system are important issues related to the smooth progress of the development and reform of higher education.

1.2 Research significance

Under the background of the economic new normal in the post-4% era, it is of great academic value to carry out theoretical and applied research on the prediction of financial investment scale and allocation structure of higher education. The research on financial investment in higher education has always been an important field of educational economics at home and abroad. However, due to the limitations of theory, method, and data, the angle and depth of the existing research are limited to varying degrees. This study will use the econometric model analysis method based on long-term time series data to predict the scale and proportion of China's higher education financial investment, as well as the investment proportion of general higher education and higher vocational education, the standard of average student comprehensive quota allocation, etc., and strive to make contributions to the theoretical model construction, analysis method, and research design improvement.

At the same time, this study based on the prediction of higher education financial scale and the estimation of allocation structure will also have important policy reference value for the formulation and improvement of related higher education development planning and financial policy. This study focuses on the scale and allocation structure of China's higher education financial investment in the post-4% era. It mainly explores how to formulate the scale of higher education financial investment to meet the needs of economic and social development, and how to reasonably allocate public education financial resources in the higher education system, so as to ensure the quality of all kinds of higher education personnel cultivation and the sustainable development of scientific research. The solution of these two problems can provide a decision-making basis for the government to create the scale of higher education financial allocation in the next few years. It provides a reference for the Ministry of Education and relevant decision-making departments to reasonably allocate the proportion of public financial investment in different types of colleges and universities (ordinary higher education institutions and higher vocational education institutions), to set the adjustment coefficient of the average student quota standard, and to put forward alternative plans for the formulation of basic research funds for university teachers.

In a word, the research on the aforementioned issues not only provides a theoretical basis for the government to further improve and perfect the macro-control policy of higher education finance, but also has great significance for ensuring the sustainable development of China's higher education, and will expand and enrich the theoretical research of China's higher education finance, as well as improve and perfect the theoretical model, method, and technology of the financial investment scale and allocation structure of higher education.

1.3 Theoretical basis of higher education finance research

The research of higher education finance is to use the theories and methods of economics and finance to study the financial problems in higher education, focusing on the financing, distribution, and use of higher education funds, which is closely related to the education financial policy. The research on the financing, distribution, and use of higher education funds involves the source channel and sharing mechanism of education funds, especially the role of the government, society, and individuals in higher education finance.

1.3.1 Cost-sharing theory of higher education

The cost-sharing theory of higher education was put forward by D. Bruce Johnstone, an American educational economist. According to this theory, the various costs of higher education should be borne by the government or taxpayers, students' parents, students themselves, and private or social donors (Johnstone, 2004). Since then, the financial allocation policies of higher education formulated by governments and the related revenue and expenditure systems of tuition and miscellaneous fees formulated by colleges and universities have been taken as an important theoretical basis.

The cost of higher education is reasonably shared by the beneficiaries in the main body of higher education, that is, the beneficiaries compensate the cost of higher education according to their respective income and ability to pay. According to the cost-sharing theory of higher education, the beneficiaries need to pay. As a kind of educational service and product with investment and income, higher education can meet the needs of the state, government, educatees, taxpayers, enterprises, families, and colleges and universities, and they are also the real beneficiaries. Therefore, the government, students' parents, students themselves, and enterprises or social donors need to share the cost of higher education.

Samuelson put forward the theory of public goods in 1954 that all social goods and services can be divided into public goods, quasi-public goods, and private goods. Among them, public goods should be provided by the government, quasi-public goods should be provided by the government and the relevant beneficiaries, and private goods should be provided by the beneficiaries. As a quasi-public product between private products and public products, higher education products have great positive external effects, especially in promoting economic growth, improving national living standards, and narrowing the gap between the rich and the poor. Obviously, the products should be provided by the government and relevant beneficiaries. This also provides a theoretical and practical basis for the government to share the cost of higher education. Based on this theory, most countries in the world resolve the contradiction between the demand and supply of higher education funds by establishing a diversified higher education investment mechanism. The United States, Canada, the United Kingdom, Australia, the Netherlands, and other countries have also formulated a series of related policies on the revenue and expenditure of higher education and put them into practice (He, 2016).

With the continuous expansion of the scale of China's higher education and the continuous improvement of the overall level of higher education, the average cost of students in colleges and universities is also gradually increasing. Coupled with the limited national financial resources, after more than 30 years of rapid economic growth, China has entered a relatively stable period of medium- and low-speed development, that is, it is in the new normal of economic development, and the growth rate of national fiscal revenue is low, the sustainable development of higher education is facing challenges, and the financial guarantee of double-first-class construction is also facing greater pressure. At the same time, all kinds of universities need a lot of financial support for their own development, and the distribution of higher education resources in China is seriously unbalanced. Therefore, it is necessary to build a reasonable higher education cost-sharing mechanism, which can effectively solve the aforementioned problems.

The cost of higher education institutions refers to the value of educational resources consumed by higher education activities in a certain period according to certain educational service standards. According to the payment subject, the cost of higher education can be divided into school subject and individual subject. The cost of the university includes the cost of education and management, the cost of land used by the university, the cost of fixed assets used in teaching and scientific research, and other costs related to the overall operation of the university. The individual cost of higher education refers to the sum of various expenses paid by the family and individual for receiving higher education, also known as private costs, including tuition, miscellaneous expenses, accommodations, living expenses, and other private expenses.

The sources of education funds of ordinary high schools in China mainly include five parts: national financial allocation, tuition fees and miscellaneous fees, school-run industry and social service funds for education, social donation funds, and other income. For a long time, financial allocation and tuition have been the main sources of education funds in colleges and universities in China, but the pattern of diversified education funds has not yet formed (Wu et al., 2018).

According to the experience of financial allocation and tuition pricing in the United Kingdom, the United States, and other countries, they usually carry out differential allocation and tuition pricing for students of different quality levels and different disciplines. At the same time, according to "the principle of ability to pay", college students from different income families will be charged differently or tuition fee reduction policies will be formulated, so as to ensure the fairness of higher education admission opportunities. Therefore, China's colleges and universities can also refer to the experience of the United Kingdom, the United States, and other countries. The Ministry of Education and the Ministry of Finance organize experts and scholars in the field of higher education finance to calculate the national average teaching cost of different disciplines and divide all disciplines into different price groups according to the cost level. Each group sets an average student funding standard and, according to the principle of cost sharing, determines the tuition standard of each subject as the reference line of tuition pricing for different cost subjects in colleges and universities. In addition, colleges and universities need to consider factors such as region and economic status of students' families to formulate different tuition standards, especially for students from remote areas in Western China, rural areas, and poor families, according to the specific family income of students, the tuition should be reduced appropriately, and the tuition standard should be controlled within their economic affordability.

1.3.2 Financial allocation mode of higher education

The research group at Shanghai Academy of Educational Sciences summarized the existing ways of government funding for higher education into four types:[4]

1. Incremental funding – Incremental funding is a way of base plus development. In the 1970s and 1980s, many countries adopted this method of funding, which just conforms to the trend of the development of higher education from elite education to popular education in this period, so as to meet the needs of the government and universities for the growth of funding. However, now many countries no longer use the incremental allocation method, because the incremental allocation method is contrary to the principles of fairness and efficiency.
2. Formula funding – Replacing incremental funding with formula funding is a major change in the funding system of higher education in industrialized countries in the last century. Formula allocation means that the government allocates funds according to the total cost per student and gives different weights to different factors that constitute the cost per student. For example, Germany, the Netherlands, Denmark, Norway, and other countries have implemented the formula funding model after the 1980s, which takes the learning time, professional type, and level as the weight factors of the average cost of students. Since 1986, the average student comprehensive quota allocation implemented in China has belonged to this type.
3. Contract funding – Contract funding is a university research funding model formed in the 1970s. Government funding agencies usually allocate research funding in the form of bidding to ensure the optimal allocation and efficient use of financial funding. France, Denmark, the Netherlands, and other countries have adopted this funding model in order to effectively allocate limited research funds.
4. Tuition funding – This is a kind of direct government funding for students to receive higher education. It can be allocated either to schools or directly to students, either in full or in part, or in balance. The countries implementing full funding are mainly European welfare countries, such as Germany, France, Spain, and Finland. Since the 1980s, many countries have begun to implement a part of the grant, including Australia, Britain, and Singapore. The government subsidizes students with interest-free, low interest, and other ways, which helps to achieve the goal of efficiency and fairness.

Some scholars have studied the composition of higher education financial allocation in the United States, Britain, Japan, and Australia, and found that the higher education financial allocation in these countries is mainly composed of teaching allocation, scientific research allocation, and student funding. The financial allocation of higher education in the United States mainly includes three categories – regular funds, capital funds, and special funds – and it is allocated by the federal government, state government, and local government. The federal government's funding mainly includes research funding and student funding. State funding is the main source of university funding, which is implemented by the higher education management committee of each state. Local government funding is generally limited (Zhao, 2009). The British government's funding for universities mainly involves teaching recurrent funds, research funding, and student funding. The central government, prefectures, and cities of Japan share the responsibility of financial allocation for higher education. The financial allocation of the central government is mainly used for the direct expenditure of national education activities, such as the allocation to national universities. The central government also gives financial subsidies to public and private universities. The specific funding is implemented by the Ministry of Education and Culture of Japan. The scope of funding mainly covers the following aspects: One is for national higher education institutions. Second, it is used to make up the recurrent expenditure of private colleges and universities. Third, there are also competitive grants for scientific research and national strategic and innovative research promotion programs. The fourth is the funding for the scholarship program of cultivating elite talents. Australian higher education funding mainly comes from the federal government; the state government is responsible for the legislative management of higher education in the state and a small amount of funding for universities. The financial allocation of the federal government to universities is mainly implemented through its subordinate Ministry of Education, Science and Training, which has a special higher education funding department that is responsible for teaching, scientific research, and student assistance. Since 1994, the federal government has combined the original recurrent funding and infrastructure funding, which is called "package funding". It mainly includes teaching funding, research funding, and student funding program funding (Zhu, 2004).

Domestic scholars have done a lot of research on the financial allocation mode of higher education in China (Wang & Zhou, 1991; Tao & Sun, 2007; Zhang & Xie, 2008; Sun, 2009; Wang, 2012). Wang (2012) believes that the funding mode of "basic expenditure budget and project expenditure budget" implemented in 2002 has not fundamentally changed from the mode of "comprehensive quota plus special subsidies" implemented from 1986 to 2002, and the funding mode of "average student comprehensive quota plus special subsidies" is still adopted (see Table 1.1). This funding model has the following problems: (1) due to the lack of scientific and accurate cost accounting methods, the determination of student quota standard is often inconsistent with the actual cost needs of colleges and universities; (2) considering a single factor, not considering the differences of cultivation costs of different majors, and not considering the differences of operating costs of different functions of the school; and (3) the lack of an effective growth mechanism makes the quota standard often inconsistent with the actual expenditure demand and financial capacity of colleges and universities. Moreover, with the increase of central and local financial revenue, new funds are more distributed through projects (Deng, 2002).

Led by Central China Normal University and entrusted by the Finance Department of the Ministry of Education, the project "Research on Reforming

Table 1.1 Content and definition of China's higher education budget expenditure

	Interpretation	*Expenditure items*
Average student comprehensive quota	According to the cultivation cost, the financial department and the department in charge of education determine the quota standard of per student education funds, which is different for different levels, majors, and departments.	Salary, subsidy, and welfare of teaching staff; student scholarships; official expenses; operating expenses; equipment purchase cost, repairing charges, and others.
Special grants[a,b]	It is a supplement to the comprehensive quota. According to the national policy guidance and the special development needs of colleges and universities, the financial department and the education department separately approve the special funds allocated to colleges and universities.	New disciplines, key disciplines, and laboratory construction costs (equipment subsidies); training expenses for teachers (such as funds for further study and training abroad for doctors, masters, visiting scholars, etc.); funds for retirees; special project subsidies (such as long-term foreign expert funds), etc.

[a] The total budget of "accounting by item, special fund for special purpose" remains unchanged and can be adjusted within the department.

[b] The "project expenditure budget" in the 2002 funding model is a special fund allocated by the central government to complete its specific tasks or career development goals. The special funds shall be set up according to the national economic and social development strategy, the development needs of higher education and the financial situation. At present, the budget allocation of education projects is divided into six categories: (1) key guidance category, such as 211 Project special funds, 985 Project special funds, "2011" collaborative innovation plan special funds, etc.; (2) infrastructure maintenance for example, the special funds for the improvement of basic school running conditions of central universities; (3) performance guidance, such as performance allocation, donation matching special funds; (4) student financial aid, such as national scholarship, national inspirational scholarship; (5) international exchange, such as international student funds, Confucius Institute funding; (6) other categories, such as special funds for undergraduate teaching engineering, basic scientific research business fees of central universities, special funds for top-notch innovative talents in basic disciplines, etc. (RRIFIMCURG, 2014).

and Improving the Funding Input Mechanism of Central Universities" makes a comprehensive, systematic, and in-depth study on the funding mode of universities directly under the central government (RRIFIMCURG, 2014). The project not only combed and analyzed the characteristics and problems of the three stages of the budget allocation mode of China's colleges and universities since the founding of the people's Republic of China, namely, the "base plus growth" stage from 1955 to 1985, the "comprehensive quota plus special subsidies" stage from 1986 to 2002, and the "basic expenditure budget plus project expenditure budget" stage from 2002 to the present, moreover, it put forth a constructive reform plan of financial allocation mode of universities directly under the central government, that is, to build a budget allocation system of "basic expenditure" with university cost as the core, "project expenditure" with national demand as the guidance, and "performance expenditure" based on university function, which points out the direction for the financial allocation reform of universities directly under the central government. However, the research only gives the factors that need to be considered in the comprehensive quota allocation of students in basic expenditure, such as setting the conversion coefficient according to the student level, discipline (major), and price situation in different regions, but no specific allocation formula is given. The research also proposes that the basic funding for scientific research should be increased in view of the lack of basic funding for teachers in the current comprehensive quota allocation standard. The allocation standard is determined according to the individual income per capita of teachers of centrally administered higher education institutions and the financial resources of the central government, and dynamic adjustment is made considering the changes of individual income and price level. However, this study does not give the specific standard of average teacher research quota in different types of disciplines. This research will try to explore two aspects: the standard design of average student comprehensive quota allocation and the basic quota standard of average teacher research funds in different types of disciplines.

1.4 Empirical research on financial investment in higher education

The research on financial investment in higher education has always been an important field of educational economics at home and abroad. The attention and research on this issue will not only affect the development of higher education and the improvement of social equity but also affect the accumulation of national human resources and the level of economic and cultural development. From the research contents of higher education financial investment at home and abroad, it mainly includes the scale of higher education financial investment (Li, 1988; Lang, 2002; Yang & McCall, 2014; Carnoy et al., 2014), the proportion of higher education financial investment in GDP and the proportion in three-level education investment (Tandberg, 2010; Liu & Yuan, 2007; Cao & Zhang, 2009; Yue, 2011), the relationship between higher education investment and economic growth (Becker, 1975; Baldwin & Borrelli, 2008; Hu & Tang, 2014), the financial allocation model of higher education (Wang & Zhou, 1991; Wang, 2012; Sun & Jing, 2003; Zhang & Xie, 2008; Wang & Shen, 2014; Chowdry et al., 2012), the cost-sharing mechanism of higher education and student subsidy policy (Ding, 1996; Yuan, 2004; Fan, 2010; Shen & Zhao, 2014; Johnstone, 2004; Carpentier, 2012; Chapman & Sinning, 2014), investment risk and income of higher education (Han & Zhu, 2009; Hanushek et al., 2011), economies of scale and economies of scope in higher education (Cohn et al., 1989; Johnes et al., 2008; Ding, 2000; Cheng & Sun, 2008; Hou et al., 2009; Chen & Dong, 2011; Li & Chen, 2013), the efficiency of funds utilization in colleges and universities (Wang & Fu, 2009; Li, 2010; Hillman et al., 2014), and the fundraising mode and fund management system of higher education (Kallison & Cohen, 2010; Maria & Bleotu, 2014; Nagy et al., 2014). Since the 1980s, although the investment in higher education in the world has shown an obvious trend of diversification, the government's investment still plays the main role. The scale and mode of government financial allocation (that is, the scale and mode of government financial investment) directly affect the development of higher education, and the reform of allocation mode also affects the efficiency of running colleges and universities (RRIFIMCURG, 2014). Therefore, research on the scale of financial investment in higher education and its proportion in GDP, funding mode, and so on has been the main field of domestic and foreign scholars' research on higher education finance, while the domestic scholars' research on the structure of financial allocation in higher education is relatively less (Bi, 2008; Hu, 2011).

1.4.1 Empirical study on the scale and proportion of financial investment in higher education

The scale of financial investment in higher education is positively related to economic development. Generally speaking, in the economic take-off stage, government higher education funds increase faster. In an economic downturn, the growth rate of the scale of higher education funding will slow down, sometimes even to negative growth. In a period of high economic growth, the increase of higher education demand will stimulate the government's investment in higher education. For example, in the period of high-speed economic growth in the United States from the 1960s to the mid-1970s, the growth of higher education was rapid, but after the 1980s, due to the economic downturn, the financial allocation of higher education was relatively slow. Britain, Japan, and Australia also have similar experiences (Zhu, 2004).

According to the internationally accepted method of linking the total scale of education investment to the level of economic development in a fixed proportion, Jin (1990) proposed that the total amount of education investment that the country's economic strength may provide should be taken as the upper limit, and the minimum supply of talents required by its economic growth should be taken as the lower limit. According to the historical data of the number of students, Li (1988) constructed an econometric model to predict the scale of investment in higher education. Based on the data of government investment in higher education and gross national product (GNP) from 1990 to 1999, Lang (2002) used various regression models to determine the adaptability between the scale of investment in higher education and the scale of national economic development and predicted the scale of investment in higher education in 2010. Jin (2004) summarized three methods to calculate the investment scale of higher education, namely, the prediction of the demand for social and economic development, the calculation based on the number of students at all levels and the supply of talents to meet the social and economic development goals, and the measurement based on the national standards for education costs.

The scale of education financial investment is closely related to the proportion of public education investment. The proportion of public education investment reflects the government's attention and efforts toward public education. Once the proportion of public education investment is determined, the government's financial investment in public education is also determined. The share of the government to be allocated to education from the amount of financial expenditure is clear.[5] In order to achieve the government's strategic goal of appropriately advancing the development of education, we should ensure that the proportion of education investment is higher than the international average level corresponding to the level of China's economic development. Yue, Xiaohao, Ding, Zeyun, Liu, Liansheng, Yuan, and other scholars all use the econometric model method based on transnational data to predict the proportion of China's education investment in 2010 and 2020, which is about 4–4.5%.[6] Yao's research (Yao & Ma, 2016) also analyzes transnational data and concludes that the proportion of financial education funds in China should reach more than 4.5%, but the research has not made a prediction.

In terms of domestic literature, there are relatively many studies on the proportion of public education investment. However, only Li (1988), Yue (2011), and a few other scholars have carried out research on the proportion of public higher education investment, which is worthy of in-depth study and related to the healthy development of higher education. In fact, although the scale of public investment in higher education continues to expand, in the face of the rapid expansion of the scale of college students after 1999, the per student financial funds are declining year by year, especially in local colleges and universities (Sun, 2009). Yue (2011) found that China's financial investment in higher education has neither reached the supply level of economic development nor met the basic needs of higher education development. From the perspective of supply capacity, the proportion of public higher education investment in China can reach 0.81% in 2012 and 0.90% in 2020. From the perspective of necessary demand, the per student public expenditure index of higher education in China should exceed 70.0 and 53.6 in 2012 and 2020, respectively. Moreover, the proportion of public higher education investment fluctuated from 2000 to 2007. This study is of great reference value in the prediction method, but the sample data period in the econometric model is from 2000 to 2007. After 2008, the economic development speed of many countries in the world, especially the developed countries, is in the stage of slowing or declining, and China's economic growth has slowed since 2014, entering the stage of medium and high-speed growth.[7] Yue (2011) also predicts that the average growth rate of per capita GDP of public higher education investment in China from 2008 to 2020 would be 9%, which is difficult to achieve. Therefore, we need to use new time series data to re-estimate the model coefficient, and then give a more reasonable forecast of the proportion of financial investment in higher education in 2016–2025.[8] The scientific prediction of investment scale and investment proportion of higher education in China from 2016 to 2025 will be the main problem to be solved in this study.

1.4.2 Empirical research on the allocation structure of financial investment in higher education

We believe that the allocation structure of financial investment in higher education can be divided into external allocation structure and internal allocation structure. The external allocation structure refers to the proportion of financial investment (including the ratio of the total amount and the proportion of student average funds) between different regional universities, different types of administrations (central directly affiliated universities, local affiliated universities[9]), and different types of universities (general colleges and universities, vocational colleges[10]). The internal configuration structure refers to the proportion of the expenditure structure of the financial investment in the university. The external configuration structure needs to pay more attention to the issue of balance, while the internal configuration structure needs to pay more attention to the issue of rationality. The rational arrangement and determination of the proportion of the internal funds' allocation structure of colleges and universities restricts the efficiency of the utilization of the investment in education and the efficiency of resource allocation. For a university, under the condition of a certain amount of educational investment, the allocation structure of internal financial input directly affects the development and function of colleges and universities.

The imbalance of the external allocation of higher education financial investment is mainly reflected in the imbalance of the investment allocation of higher education between different types of universities and different provinces. Hu (2011) made an empirical analysis on the allocation structure of financial investment in higher education among different types of universities and different provinces. The research found that the average student expenditure and the budget for average student expenditure of central and local universities are differentiated, and the gap between them is widening. The financial education funds tend to be invested in central universities, and local universities mainly rely on tuition income and bank loans to maintain their operation. This is basically consistent with Sun's (2009) research conclusion. Hu (2011) believes that the higher education finances for central universities is unevenly allocated among provinces and is mainly invested in the institutions directly under the central government and competitive projects. According to the eastern, central, and western regions, the ratio of government public financial input is 1.84:1:1.29, and the ratio of social input per student is 2.23:1:0.68, showing a pattern of "high in the east, low in the west, and collapse in the middle". The public financial input of universities transferred from the central government to local governments is divided, and the public financial allocation of universities transferred from some provinces continues to decline.

Not only is the allocation of higher education financial resources among different types of colleges and universities and different provinces not balanced, but also the average student funding of ordinary undergraduate colleges and higher vocational colleges is quite different. According to data from the China Education Statistics Yearbook and China Education Finance Statistics Yearbook,

16 *Introduction*

we found that the average operating funding of higher vocational college students in China was 3000 yuan per student in 2005, and it increased to 12,404 yuan per student in 2011, a quadruple increase. In the same period, the average institutional funds of undergraduate students doubled from 16,207 yuan per student (2005) to 33,599 yuan per student (2011). However, from the absolute level, the per student operating funding of higher vocational colleges in 2011 still does not reach the level of undergraduate colleges in 2005. It is precisely because there are still some outstanding problems in the investment in higher vocational education: the mechanism of stable investment in multichannel financing and financial students' average funding is not perfect, the overall investment level of higher vocational colleges is still low, and the regional differences are large. The Ministry of Finance issued a document in November 2014 that requires that the annual average financial allocation level of vocational colleges in 2017 should not be less than 12,000 yuan.[11] However, it is still a question worthy of further study whether this funding standard meets the actual needs.

In addition, some studies show that the unreasonable internal allocation structure of China's higher education financial investment is reflected in three aspects: First, the trend of education expenditure structure is unreasonable, and the proportion of official business expenses and personnel funds are in a downward trend (Bi, 2008; Li, 2008; Hu & Ding, 2014; Yuan et al., 2016). Second, the ratio of the average student comprehensive quota allocation to the budget allocation of project expenditure is unreasonable. There are many and miscellaneous special projects that account for a large proportion of the allocation, and the budget allocation of project expenditure cannot better promote the function of the university (RRIFIMCURG, 2014). Third, although universities currently have "basic scientific research business expenses of central universities" in the "project expenditure budget", they not only account for a low proportion, but also belong to competitive scientific research funds in the internal allocation of universities, and the funds for basic scientific research activities of university teachers are not guaranteed (Zhou, 2013). Based on these factors, this study will carry out in-depth and systematic research on the rational allocation of higher education financial resources.

1.5 Comments on the literature research

The contradiction between the expansion of the scale of higher education and the decline of the government's financial investment ability has become increasingly prominent. Since the 1970s, American economist D. Bruce Johnstone proposed the cost-sharing mechanism of higher education based on the quasi-public goods attribute of higher education, which makes the investment in higher education show an obvious trend of diversification, but the government's financial investment still plays a dominant role. The scale of the government's financial investment in higher education and the mode of funding has always been the main fields of domestic and foreign scholars in the research of higher education finance. These research results lay a theoretical and methodological foundation for us to carry out the research on the scale and allocation structure of China's higher education financial investment in the post-4% era, and also provide a reference for policymakers to adjust and issue new higher education financial policies under the new economic, social, and educational development background. However, due to the complexity and sensitivity of higher education finance, it is difficult to obtain comprehensive and reliable index data for scientific quantitative research.[12] Looking at the existing research on the investment scale, funding mode, and allocation structure of higher education, we find that there are the following deficiencies.

First, the research on the scale of financial investment in higher education is mostly based on the needs of social and economic development or the number of students at all levels of higher education and the national standard of per student funds. Few of them combine the two aspects to estimate the elastic range of investment in higher education. Research on the proportion of public education investment mostly adopts the method of international comparison, and uses the econometric model of cross-sectional data to predict the proportion of investment in the next few years or decades. However, the existing research uses the data relatively early, and the economic development situation is constantly changing, so it is necessary to use the new time series data to re-estimate the model coefficient to give a more reasonable prediction of the proportion of financial investment in higher education in 2016–2025. In addition, there are also defects in the selection of econometric models and estimation methods. At present, the model to estimate the scale or proportion of financial investment in higher education usually adopts cross-sectional data model of multiple countries, and gives the model coefficient by the year, and then takes the average or median coefficient as the coefficient of the prediction model to estimate the scale or proportion of financial investment in higher education in the future. With this method it is difficult to reflect the influence of time trends on investment scale or investment proportion, and the influence of economic development level and financial supply capacity on investment scale or investment proportion usually lags behind. Therefore, it is necessary to use the distributed lag model to predict the financial investment scale or investment proportion of higher education.

Second, the research on the mode of financial allocation of higher education mostly focuses on the mechanism of financial allocation of higher education, the mode of financial allocation, and the standard formulation of the average student comprehensive quota. Few of them construct the structure of financial allocation of higher education from the perspective of the function of higher education. Moreover, as mentioned earlier, the current funding model in China does not involve the basic funding for teachers' scientific research, and the determination of the comprehensive quota funding standard for students in different regions, different university types, and different disciplines is still a key problem to be solved. Solving this problem will help to adjust the allocation structure of China's higher education finance, and rationally allocate higher education financial resources in different regions, different levels, and different types of disciplines.

Third, research on the financial allocation structure of higher education is relatively rare, and there is a lack of systematic research. The solution of this problem is closely related to the funding mode and structure of higher education. The current funding model takes the difference between the universities directly under the central government and local universities in terms of per student funding, showing the status quo of "high in the east, collapse in the middle, low in the west", and there is a big difference in per student funding between ordinary universities and higher vocational colleges. Scientifically formulating the minimum standards of per student expenditures for different types of universities and universities in different regions is an important issue in the study of higher education financial allocation. Therefore, according to the current level of economic development and economic structure in China, we need to carry out systematic and in-depth research on how to reasonably allocate higher education financial resources among regions with different levels of economic development, different categories of higher education (universities directly under the central government/local universities) and different types of higher education (ordinary higher education/higher vocational education), and how to ensure that the proportion of operating expenses and infrastructure expenses of different types of universities is reasonable, as well as the reasonable proportion of personnel funds and operational funds in the educational expenditure.

1.6 Research design

1.6.1 Research objectives

Based on the systematic analysis of the existing domestic and foreign researches on the financial scale and allocation structure of higher education, this study uses the longitudinal data and econometric model to explore the scale and allocation structure of financial investment in higher education from multiple perspectives. It provides a theoretical basis for the government to further improve and perfect the macro-control policy of higher education finance. The sub-objectives of this study include the following four aspects.

(1) This study reveals the current situation and trend of financial investment in higher education in developed countries and countries with similar economic development levels to China; analyzes the investment policies and funding modes of higher education in developed countries and developing countries with similar economies and culture to China, and their impact on the development of higher education and economic development; and puts forward some ideas for improving the existing funding mode in China.
(2) This study analyzes the correlation between the scale of financial investment in higher education and the level of economic development and financial supply capacity and builds the prediction model of the proportion of financial investment in higher education from the perspectives of national financial supply capacity and higher education development adapting to the needs of

economic development, so as to predict the scale of financial investment in higher education in China from 2016 to 2025.
(3) This study puts forward the standard setting principle of average student financial allocation in different types and different economic level regions and the minimum standard of average teacher scientific research allocation in different types of disciplines.
(4) This study forecasts the allocation ratio of financial investment in China's regular undergraduate and higher vocational colleges from 2015 to 2020.

1.6.2 Research contents

1.6.2.1 Literature research on the scale and allocation structure of financial investment in higher education

This part first analyzes the theories of higher education investment and the empirical research of investment scale and allocation structure, summarizes the current situation and trend of financial investment in higher education in developed countries and countries with similar economic development levels to China, and analyzes higher education investment policy in developed countries and developing countries with a similar culture and economic development level to China and its impact on higher education development and economic development. On this basis, the study defines the core concepts of the scale and configuration of the financial investment in higher education, analyzes the factors influencing the demand and supply of the financial investment in higher education, and explains the constraints of the scale of the financial investment in higher education. In addition, based on the theory of public economics and finance, the study analyzes the external and internal allocation principles of higher education financial investment, compares the advantages and disadvantages of different allocation modes, analyzes the main defects of the current allocation mode in China, and puts forward ideas to improve the existing allocation mode, which provide a reference for the theoretical model of the subsequent empirical research.

1.6.2.2 Research on the prediction of financial investment scale in higher education

Research on the scale of financial investment in higher education is to answer the question of how big is the portion of government public finance for higher education investment. In this part, the scale of financial investment in higher education in China from 2001 to 2011 is compared with developed countries and countries with similar economic development levels,[13] and the correlation between the scale of financial investment in higher education and the level of economic development and financial supply capacity is analyzed. Based on the international time series data and panel data from 31 provinces, from the perspective of adequacy and fairness, this study investigates the allocation of financial funds for higher education in China, which lays the foundation for the follow-up studies of financial funds for higher education. Second, it builds the prediction model of the proportion of financial investment in higher education. To construct a reasonable prediction model of the proportion of financial investment in higher education, we should not only consider the constraints of the level of economic development and financial capacity but also consider the needs of the development of higher education to adapt to the speed of economic development. The reasonable prediction of the proportion of financial investment in higher education should be flexible, because the demand for funds allocated by higher education development is often different from the financial funds of higher education that can be provided by the government financial capacity expenditure. In addition, the latter is usually lower than the former (Yue, 2011). Therefore, we plan to construct the lower limit prediction model of the higher education financial investment proportion from the perspective of supply capacity and economic development demand.[14] For the lower bound model, we first use multinational data to construct the higher education investment proportion model. One is to consider the perspective of international comparison, and the other is to ensure that China's predicted value is not lower than the average investment proportion of countries with similar economic development levels. Then, according to the growth rate of China's GDP and fiscal expenditure, it gives the forecast value of China's GDP and fiscal expenditure from 2016 to 2025, and then gives the forecast value of the proportion and scale of higher education investment.[15] At the same time, based on the historical data of the scale and speed of higher education development in China (1995–2014), the upper limit prediction model of the proportion of financial investment in higher education is constructed from the perspective of higher education development to meet the needs of economic development.[16] Then, based on the predicted value of investment proportion and the predicted value of economic development level, this study gives the predicted value of China's higher education financial investment scale from 2016 to 2025.

1.6.2.3 Research on the allocation structure of financial investment in higher education

In 1985, "The decision of the Central Committee of the Communist Party of China on the reform of the education system" initially established the three-level school running system of the central government, provinces (autonomous regions, municipalities directly under the central government), and central cities in China's higher education. The basic principle of higher education finance has been gradually established in "The Outline of Medium and Long-Term Development of National Education" issued in 1993 and "The Opinions on the Implementation of the Outline" issued in 1994. Therefore, at present, China's higher education finance presents a situation of "three levels of school running and three levels of burden" (Wang, 2012). Then, how should the financial resources of higher education be allocated in a balanced way among regions with different economic development levels and different types of higher education? How should the financial allocation be designed according to the actual needs of university operation?

Introduction 21

These will be the main questions we need to answer. The answer to these questions is actually to solve the problem of how to reasonably divide the "cake" of higher education finance from different perspectives.

- **The allocation structure of financial investment in different types of higher education**

This part solves the problem of how to divide the higher education financial "cake" according to different types of universities (general higher education/higher vocational education). For example, higher vocational colleges have higher requirements for practical teaching. They not only need equipment and sites for practice but also need double qualified teachers, as well as special plans for joint cultivation of talent with enterprises. Ordinary colleges and universities generally have two major tasks: talent cultivation and scientific research. Most research-oriented colleges and universities also need the allocation of key disciplines, key laboratories, and research bases. Therefore, it is necessary to distinguish the financial investment allocation of these two different types of universities. Based on the financial funds' data of China's regular undergraduate colleges and higher vocational colleges from 2005 to 2014,[17] this study uses the combination model of trend analysis, autoregressive integrated moving average (ARIMA), quadratic exponential smoothing, Holt–Winters nonseasonal model, and other methods to predict the proportion of financial investment allocation of ordinary undergraduate and higher vocational colleges in China from 2015 to 2020 and uses the provincial panel data to predict the proportion of financial investment of local ordinary undergraduate and higher vocational colleges.

- **Design and estimation of average student comprehensive quota and average teacher research funding standard**

The current comprehensive quota allocation model mainly takes the number of students as the allocation policy parameter. Although it also takes into account the differences between different schools and majors, it does not accurately reflect the changes in the actual operating costs of different types of colleges and universities (ordinary colleges and higher vocational colleges) and the differences in the operating costs of different functional activities in different regions with different economic development levels, it is not very consistent with the actual cost of the school. At present, the average comprehensive quota standard of local colleges and universities is set by the provincial financial departments according to the requirements of the Ministry of Education.[18] This way of allocating resources according to the average cost rather than the marginal cost, that is, according to the scale of students, has a strong orientation of extensive development. As a result, some colleges and universities blindly expand the enrollment scale and improve the level of running a school (such as upgrading a junior college to an undergraduate college), which is not conducive to improving the efficiency of running a school and reflecting the characteristics of running a school. It is also not conducive to fair competition among universities of different development stages and scales. In addition, due to the lack of an effective growth mechanism, the quota standard is often inconsistent with the actual expenditure demand and financial capacity of colleges and universities, which makes it difficult to ensure the sustainable development of colleges and universities.

Therefore, this study designs the funding framework of China's future student average comprehensive quota by combing the historical evolution of higher education funding in China and comparing the funding methods of higher education in developed countries. At the same time, this study builds the influencing factor model according to the average student cultivation cost data of universities directly under the Ministry of Education (2015–2018) and estimates the adjustment coefficient of the average comprehensive quota standard of universities at different levels, different scales, different types, and different regions. In addition, this study also carried out a nationwide questionnaire survey on the current situation and demand of university teachers' scientific research funds, and based on this survey data, estimated the average allocation standard of university teachers' scientific research funds.

1.6.3 Key research questions

(1) How does one predict the scale of financial investment in higher education to meet the needs of economic and social development? That is to answer the question of how big is the portion of the government's public finance investment in higher education.
(2) How does one balance the public financial resources of higher education among different regions of economic development and different types of higher education (general higher education and higher vocational education)? How does one estimate the average comprehensive quota of students and the average scientific research funding standard of teachers in colleges and universities? The answer to these questions is actually to solve the problem of how to reasonably divide the "cake" of higher education finance from different perspectives.

1.6.4 Research framework

This research adopts the technical route of the combination of theoretical research and empirical research, and the combination of macro and micro. It uses the relevant data of higher education finance, public finance, and economic level of developed countries and countries similar to China's economy and culture, as well as the data of higher education finance, higher education scale, public finance, and economic level of China. The time series regression model, structural equation model, and other quantitative research methods are used to predict the scale of financial investment in higher education and its proportion in the GDP from 2016 to 2025 in China. The survey data is used to estimate the average scientific research funding standard of different types of disciplines. At the same time,

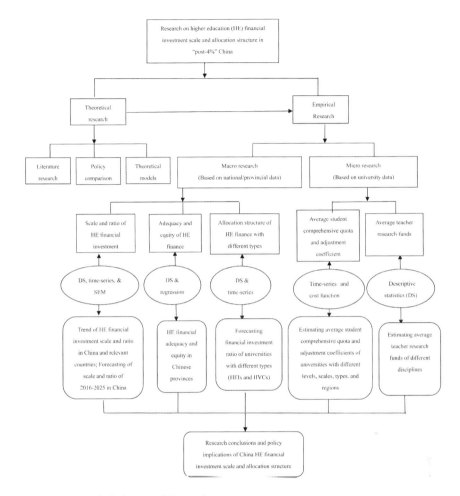

Figure 1.1 Technical route of the study.

the principle of setting the average comprehensive quota standard for students of different disciplines and different levels is given. See Figure 1.1 for the specific technical route.

Notes

1 According to the financial theory of higher education, the cost of higher education institutions is often determined by the income, and its quality improvement is constrained by the cost. In the long run, the cost of colleges and universities should be increasing due to the requirements of quality improvement. The low-cost operation of local colleges and universities in China in the past decade, to a certain extent, shows that the quality of higher education has not changed much, or even decreased (Yuan, 2004).

24 *Introduction*

2 Luo and Ma (2013) reviewed the progress of financing, distribution, and use of general universities in China in the past 20 years, and described and analyzed the income and expenditure structure of education funds. It was found that the gap between the central and local universities' average income from 1994 to 2011 is widening. In 1994, the average income of local colleges and universities was 45% of that of central colleges and universities. After 2000, the average income of local colleges and universities continued to decline. The average income of local colleges and universities was only about 13% of that of central colleges and universities. This difference in income structure is closely related to the preferential investment policy of China's colleges and universities, which makes the situation of insufficient funds of local colleges and universities more severe.
3 See RRIFIMCURG (2014).
4 It should be noted that a country does not only use one of the funding methods, but may use two or more methods at the same time according to different purposes of funding.
5 It is assumed that the ratio of government expenditure to GDP is fixed in the short term. Proportion of public education investment = Proportion of government fiscal expenditure in GDP × Proportion of fiscal education expenditure in government fiscal expenditure.
6 According to the data modeling of 23 middle-income countries, Zeyun Liu and colleagues predicted that the proportion of China's public education investment in 2010 and 2020 would be 3.7% and 4.54%, respectively. Changjun Yue and colleagues predicted that the proportion of China's education investment in 2010 and 2020 would be 4.04% and 4.3%, respectively, according to the GNP average annual growth rate of 7.18%. According to their opinion that the growth rate of education investment should be ahead of schedule, it is suggested that the investment proportion ranges from 4.0% to 4.5% in 2010 and from 4.5% to 5.0% in 2020.
7 In 2012 and 2013, China's economic growth rate was 7.8% and 7.7%, respectively, and the average annual GDP growth rate during the 30 years of reform and opening up was 9.8%.
8 Selecting 2016–2025 as the forecast annual interval, there are two aspects to consider. One is that China usually has a five-year planning cycle, and 2016–2025 is the 13th Five-Year Plan and 14th Five-Year Plan. Second, the forecast period based on the time series model should not be too long, because there will be many uncontrollable intervention factors in the long-term forecast of more than 10 years, which is difficult to ensure the accuracy of the forecast. Therefore, we intend to give the forecast of the scale and proportion of higher education investment in 2016–2025.
9 According to the source of income or expenditure structure, the China Education Finance Statistics Yearbook divides the institutions of higher education into central and local institutions of higher education.
10 According to The International Standard Classification of Education issued by UNESCO in 1997, University Education (Level 5) is divided into academic education (5A) and technical education (5B). The general undergraduate and junior college education in China belong to 5A, and the higher vocational education belongs to 5B. Therefore, we divide the types of colleges and universities into ordinary colleges and universities and higher vocational colleges. According to the statistics of the Ministry of Education, there were 1170 regular colleges and universities in China in 2013, including 548 ordinary colleges and universities with graduate training institutions and 1321 higher vocational colleges.
11 Cai Jiao (2014), "Opinions on establishing and improving the reform and performance oriented average student allocation system and accelerating the development of modern higher vocational education", No. 352. Retrieved February 10, 2015, from http://finance.sina.com.cn/china/20141128/134820948045.shtml.
12 For example, the scale of investment in higher education involves not only the level of economic development and financial supply capacity, but also the scale and quality of

higher education development, as well as the reasonable proportion of higher education finance in three-level education, etc.

13 Due to the different scale of higher education development in different countries, in order to be comparable, we will use the per student budget allocation as the comparison index.

14 Supply capacity and economic development level have a certain lag for financial investment in higher education, and the scale of investment in the previous year will also affect the total investment in the next year, so we will use the autoregressive distributed lag model as the prediction model.

15 Usually, when making the decision of educational financial expenditure, the government should first set the proportion of public education financial investment, and then give the specific investment budget. However, the proportion of public education financial investment is related to the GDP of the previous year. Therefore, when we predict the limit of the scale of financial investment in higher education, we first predict the investment proportion, and then give the investment scale prediction value according to the GDP forecast value.

16 Because the scale of higher education development varies greatly in different countries in different periods, and the speed of economic development of each country is greatly disturbed by external sudden factors, it is not suitable to use the index variable data of other countries to predict the investment scale model of China's higher education development to meet the needs of economic development. Using only domestic historical data cannot only reduce the heteroscedasticity of error terms, but also make the time series variables keep the same order and single integer.

17 In 1985, the "Decision of the CPC Central Committee on the Reform of the Education System" clearly put forward that to "actively develop higher vocational and technical colleges, … Gradually establish a vocational and technical education system from primary to advanced, with supporting industries, reasonable structure and communication with general education". Since the promulgation of the decision, more than 120 vocational universities have been established in China to hold higher vocational education. Therefore, we plan to use the historical data from 2005 to 2014 to establish a prediction model.

18 For example, the average student funding standard of Jiangsu provincial undergraduate universities in 2012 was 7600 yuan, that of Shandong provincial undergraduate universities in 2011 was 9500 yuan and that of 2012 was 12,000 yuan. The average student comprehensive quota standard of Guangdong province from 2003 to 2010 has been 6600 yuan, which has not increased for eight years.

References

Baldwin, N., & Borrelli, S. A. (2008). Education and economic growth in the United States: cross-national applications for an intra-national path Analysis. *Policy Science*, *41*, 183–204.

Bao, C. (2012). Post-4% era: The guarantee and usage of China's education funds. *Journal of the Chinese Society of Education*, *9*, 9–12.

Becker, G. (1975). Front matter, human capital: A theoretical and empirical analysis, with special reference to education. In *Human Capital: A Theoretical and Empirical Analysis, with Special Reference to Education* (2nd ed.). New York: NBER.

Bi, X. Y. (2008). An empirical analysis on the structural characteristics of educational financial investment in Colleges and Universities. *China Higher Education Research*, *7*, 40–42.

Cao, S. J., & Zhang, J. (2009). Research on Influencing Factors of internal distribution proportion of education investment. *China Higher Education Research*, *9*, 26–28.

Carnoy, M., Froumin, I., Loyalka, P. K., & Tilak, J. B. G. (2014). The concept of public goods, the state, and higher education finance: A view from the BRICs. *High Education, 68*, 359–378.

Carpentier, V. (2012). Public-private substitution in higher education: Has cost-sharing gone too far? *Higher Education Quarterly, 66*(4), 363–390.

Chapman, B., & Sinning, M. (2014). Student loan reforms for German higher education: Financing tuition fees. *Education Economics, 22*(6), 569–588.

Chen, X. Y., & Dong, Z. J. (2011). Scale economy and scope economy of higher education in the stage of popularization. *Educational Research, 9*, 14–21.

Cheng, G., & Sun, Z. J. (2008). Research on Chinese higher education efficiency. *China Economic Quarterly, 3*, 1079–1103.

Chowdry, H., Dearden, L., Goodman, A., & Jin, W. C. (2012). The distributional impact of the 2012–13 higher education funding reforms in England. *Fiscal Studies, 33*(2), 211–236.

Cohn, E., Rhine, S. L. W., & Santos, M. C. (1989). Institutions of higher education as multi-product firms: economies of scale and scope. *Review of Economics and Statistics, 71*, 284–290.

Deng, Y. (2002). The development of market economy and the reform of higher education financial system. *Higher Education Research, 4*, 50–54.

Ding, X. H. (1996). Financial crisis and cost compensation of higher education. *Higher Education Research, 2*, 37–45.

Ding, X. H. (2000). *Economics of Scale in Chinese Higher Education*. Beijing: Educational Science Press.

Fan, S. (2015). *A Case Study on the Overall Planning of Education Funds in Local Colleges and Universities in Sichuan Province*. Dissertation, University of Electronic Science and Technology of China.

Fan, X. Z. (2010). Review and reflection on China's student assistance system. *Journal of Central China Normal University (Social Science Edition), 49*(6), 123–132.

Han, C. L., & Zhu, K. L. (2009). The study of returns to private investment in higher education from the point of employment. *Canadian Social Science, 5*(1), 119–125.

Hanushek, E. A., Woessmann, L., & Zhang, L. (2011). *General Education, Vocational Education, and Labor-Market Outcomes over the Life-Cycle*. NBER Working Paper 17504, Cambridge, MA: National Bureau of Economic Research.

He, G. W. (2016). Government public finance must provide financial assistance to non-profit private colleges and Universities: From the perspective of higher education cost sharing theory. *Journal of Yangzhou University (Higher Education Edition), 5*, 12–14+24.

Hillman, N. W., Tandberg, D. A., & Gross, J. P. K. (2014). Market-based higher education: Does Colorado's voucher model improve higher education access and efficiency? *Research in High Education, 55*, 601–625.

Hou, L. L., Li, F. L., & Min, W. F. (2009). Multi-product total cost functions for higher education: The case of Chinese research universities. *Economics of Education Review, 28*(4), 505–511.

Hu, S., & Ding, X. H. (2014). Substitution or complementarity: A study on the expenditure structure of colleges and universities in China from the perspective of elasticity. *Education Research Monthly, 8*, 45–52.

Hu, Y. M., & Tang, Y. P. (2014). Apportion of education budget in the post-4% era: An empirical study based on transnational data. *Journal of Beijing Normal University (Social Sciences), 5*, 13–24.

Hu, Y. Z. (2011). Analysis on financial differences of different universities. *China Higher Education Research, 11*, 17–20.

Johnes, G., Johnes, J. & Thanassoulis. E. (2008). An analysis of costs in institutions of higher education in England. *Studies in Higher Education, 33*(5), 527–549.

Johnstone, D. B. (2004). The economics and politics of cost sharing in higher education: Comparative perspectives. *Economics of Education Review, 23*(4), 403–410.

Jin, F. Y., & Lou, S. Z. (2019). Research on tuition pricing standard and behavior of public colleges and universities in china from the perspective of educational policy sociology: Based on the data analysis of ordinary colleges and universities in Zhejiang province. *Educational Development Research, 39*(19), 25–33+67.

Jin, X. B. (1990). Some issues in determining the ratio of educational investment. *Journal of Beijing Normal University (Social Sciences), 4*, 5–12.

Jin, X. B. (2004). *Economics of Education*. Beijing: People's Education Press.

Kallison, J. M., & Cohen, P. (2010). A new compact for higher education: Funding and autonomy for reform and accountability. *Innovation Higher Education, 35*, 37–49.

Lang Y. (2002). *Study on the Mode of Investment in Higher Education in China*. Doctoral Dissertation, Harbin Engineering University.

Li, F. L., & Chen, X. L. (2013). Economies of scope in distance education: the case of Chinese research universities. *The International Review of Research in Open and Distance Learning, 13*(3), 117–131.

Li, P. S. (2014). The first national symposium on university development, financing and investment was held at Beijing Normal University. Retrieved May 2, 2020, from http://www.cssn.cn/gx/xskx/201411/t20141126_1417143.shtml

Li, W. (2016). *Research on the Dilemma and Countermeasures of Education Financing in Local Colleges and Universities: A Case Study of H University in Hunan Province*. Dissertation, Hunan Agricultural University.

Li, W. L. (2008). *From Scarcity to Adequacy: Research on Higher Education Demand and Supply*. Beijing: Education Science Press.

Li, Y. N. (1988). *Research on Educational Economics*. Shanghai: Shanghai People's Press.

Li, Y. X. (2010). Connotation, measurement index and influencing factors of educational financial efficiency. *Educational Research, 31*(3), 15–22.

Liu, Z. Y., & Yuan, L. S. (2007). An international comparative study on the public ratio of investment in education. *International and Comparative Education, 2*, 32–36.

Luo, J. P., & Ma, L. T. (2013). Analysis on the effectiveness of the allocation of funds in Colleges and universities in China. *Education Exploration, 9*, 22–24.

Maria, T. D., & Bleotu, V. (2014). Modern trends in higher education funding. *Procedia – Social and Behavioral Sciences, 116*, 2226–2230.

Nagy, S. G., Kováts, G., & Némethc, A. O. (2014). Governance and funding of higher education – International trends and best practices. *Procedia – Social and Behavioral Sciences, 116*, 180–184.

RRIFIMCURG ("Research on Reforming and Improving the Funding Input Mechanism of Central Universities" Research Group). (2014). Historical changes and reform ideas of financial allocation mode of universities directly under the central government. *Journal of Central China Normal University (Humanities and Social Sciences), 6*, 149–156.

Shen, H., & Zhao, Y. H. (2014). Reform and effect of student financial aid policy in American colleges and universities. *Research in Higher Education of Engineering, 4*, 135–140.

Sun, Z. J. (2009). Changes in university income in a decade of expansion in China: An interpretation. *Tsinghua Journal of Education, 4*, 72–80.

Sun, Z. J., & Jin, P. (2003). International comparison and enlightenment: The practice of performance allocation in higher education. *Higher Education Research, 6*, 88–92.

Tandberg, D. A. (2010). Politics, interest groups and state funding of public higher education. *Research in High Education, 51*, 416–450.

Tao, C. M., & Sun, Z. J. (2007). Reform and innovation of basic expenditure allocation mode in Colleges and Universities: The reform experience of Beijing since 2004. *Finance & Trade Economics, 10*, 76–78.

Wang, D., & Fu, M. Y. (2009). The evaluation of higher education expenditure performance and investment mechanism reform. *International Education Studies, 2*(1), 18–24.

Wang, J. H., & Shen, H. (2014). Evolution and reform of American higher education funding formula. *Studies in Foreign Education, 41*(10), 109–118.

Wang, S. M. (2012). *Research on Public Education Financing System under Public Finance Framework*. Beijing: Economic Science Press.

Wang, S. M., & Zhou, W. (1991). Higher education funding system in China. *Education and Economics, 4*, 51–55.

Wang, Y. (2018). "Double first class" observation: University's budget and outputs. Retrieved October 26, 2018, from http://gjs.njust.edu.cn

Wu, Y. L., Zhang, T. Y., & Li, Y. L. (2018). Research on the cost sharing mechanism of higher education in China. *Industry and Science Tribune, 17*(19), 106–109.

Xiong, J. H. (2009). Communique of world higher education conference 2009: The new dynamics of higher education and research for in social change and development. *World Education Information, 9*, 23–27.

Xu, Z. Q. (2018). *Research on the Differences and Countermeasures of Financial Expenditure in Colleges and Universities in China*. Dissertation, Chinese Academy of Fiscal Sciences.

Yang, L. J., & McCall, B. (2014). World education finance policies and higher education access: A statistical analysis of World Development Indicators for 86 countries. *International Journal of Educational Development, 35*, 25–36.

Yao, J. J., & Ma, L. L. (2016). An analysis on the amount and structure of educational finance investment in "Post 4% age". *Research in Educational Development, 36*(5), 17–21.

Yuan, L. S. (2004). Analysis on the change of average cost per student in Chinese Universities. *Educational Research, 6*, 23–27.

Yuan, L. S., Liao, Z. Z., Li, Z. Y., & He, T. T. (2016). Why is the proportion of personnel expenditure in Colleges and universities seriously low in China. *Journal of Beijing Normal University (Social Sciences), 3*, 26–37.

Yue, C. J. (2011). International comparative study on the supply and demand of higher education funds. *Peking University Education Review, 9*(3), 92–104.

Zeng, X. D., & Long, Y. (2013). How to walk the road of post-4%? *Guangming Daily*, March, 19.

Zhang, H. F., & Xie, A. B. (2008). Classification, comparison and reflection on investment modes of higher education. *China Higher Education Research, 5*, 24–27.

Zhang, X. M., & Lan, Z. Y. (2014). Post-4% era-a research on public financial system for education in China. *Journal of National Academy of Education Administration, 4*, 19–26.

Zhao, L. N. (2009). International comparison of financial policies in higher education. *Journal of Central China Normal University (Social Science Edition)*, *48*(5), 135–140.

Zhou, C. (2013). The government needs to further increase the investment of research funds in colleges and universities. *Studies in Science of Science*, *10*, 1450–1452.

Zhu, C. F. (2004). International comparative research on higher education funding systems. *Review of Economic Research*, *60*, 8–20.

2 Basic methods of financial forecasting research in higher education

Forecasting is to take account of historical data to econometrically analyze and predict changing trends in the future. In the field of education finance research, the traditional forecasting method is basically conducted by using the standard of funding per student and the change in student number. There are volumes of studies in this respect that have provided valuable reference for the financial work of higher education in China in a certain period (Hu & Wang, 2010; Luo, 2004; Wang et al., 2003; Yue, 2008). However, in the coming of the big data era, the science of forecasting is on the path of development and methods are improving along the way (Wang, 2018; Feng, 2008). Many of them have been applied in the studies of forecasting educational finance (Tang & Hu, 2015; Zhao & Hu, 2017). Therefore, it is of great importance to systematically review the existing literature and those highly used methods. Considering that panel data and time series data are the two main types of data in the modern economics of forecasting, this chapter gives a brief introduction to the methods used in processing and modeling panel data and time series data.

2.1 Forecasting methods based on panel data

Early studies of forecasting research have mostly used the ordinary least squares (OLS) method to estimate cross-sectional data. However, classical textbooks in econometrics have pointed out that BLUE (best linear unbiased estimation) is too ideal to meet in practice, and there are various compounding factors in real-life settings that make traditional econometric methods full of challenges. In terms of data, given that the shortcomings of cross-sectional data are being more and more recognized by researchers, panel data plays an increasingly important role in econometrics and has been widely used in forecasting research, especially fixed effect models and random effect models.

2.1.1 Overview of panel data

Panel data, also known as longitudinal data, is a combination of cross-sectional data and time series data. Early studies in economic forecasting have mostly used the OLS technique to model cross-sectional data. However, there are various

DOI: 10.4324/9781003250524-2

compounding factors in real-life circumstances, especially the issue of unobservable heterogeneities, that cannot be solved by modeling cross-sectional data or pooled data. In this situation, all kinds of methods for panel data have been developed to overcome the weaknesses of cross-sectional data. The advantage of panel data is that the same individual is observed repeatedly multiple times, so the individual's multiperiod data can be used to control or eliminate the effects of some unobservable heterogeneities made on the dependent variable.

Depending on the missing pattern of samples, panel data can be divided into two types: balanced panel data and unbalanced panel data. The first type refers to those data that has observations for each individual in every period, while the second type allows individuals to have missing values in certain periods. Depending on the size of cross-section n and the length of time T, panel data can also be divided into two types: microscopic panel data and large dimensional panel data. The former has a larger n (hundreds or thousands) and smaller T (generally two to ten), which more often shows up in areas where microlevel data is more frequently used, such as labor economics and economics of education (Jin & Jin, 2011). It is worth noting that most of the data used in this study is microbalance panel data.

Simply combining data of multiple periods for all individuals can make a pooled regression, but this is not a standard panel data method. It does not establish a link between multiple periods of data from the same individual, but simply treats data from different periods as different individuals. The pooled model in the most concise form can be represented as follows:

$$y_{it} = b_0 + b_1 x_{it} + e_{it} \tag{2.1}$$

where y_{it} indicates the observation of a dependent variable at the time t of individual i, and x_{it} indicates the observation of an independent variable at the time t of individual i. In Equation 2.1, b_1, the coefficient of the independent variable x_{it}, contains no subscript (i or t), which means that the regression coefficient does not change with the characteristics of individuals or over time. This assumes that the effect of x_{it} on y_{it} is kept constant for all individuals at any time. Thus, the model shown in Equation 2.1 is not fundamentally different from an ordinary linear regression, but merely a pooled model by combing cases at different periods.

The pooled model ignores the nature of panel data, which often assumes that there are no differences between different individual characteristics and different periods. However, issues such as heteroscedasticity and correlations with error terms in actual data tend to bring estimation bias to the pooled model, especially the biased estimate of standard errors will reduce the reliability of the hypothesis test (Hill et al., 2018). Therefore, it is necessary to modify the aforementioned models from two classical methods in panel data analysis: the fixed effect model and random effect model.

2.1.2 Fixed effect model

How does one use the characteristics of panel data to overcome the shortcomings of the pooled model? One choice is to relax the assumption of unchanged

32 Basics of financial forecasting research

coefficient as shown in Equation 2.1, which results in the following model expressed in Equation 2.2:

$$y_{it} = b_0 + b_{1i}x_{it} + e_{it} \tag{2.2}$$

This new equation is different from Equation 2.1 in one respect: the coefficient of x_{it} is changed to b_{1i}, indicating that the coefficient of x_{it} is no longer fixed but related to individual i, thus containing the individual characteristics. Though this new model shown in Equation 2.2 appears to be able to capture the characteristics of different individuals, in practice it can be affected by the length of the panel and bring in the issue of estimation bias, especially in the case of $N \gg T$ (e.g., 500 individuals but only 5 periods). Thus, to overcome this problem, economists make modifications to Equation 2.2 to obtain a standard fixed effect model as shown in Equation 2.3:

$$y_{it} = b_{0i} + b_1 x_{it} + e_{it} \tag{2.3}$$

The difference between Equation 2.3 and Equation 2.2 is the change of subscript i, from the regression coefficient x_i to the intercept b_{0i}. This new model uses a changing intercept to capture the characteristic differences between individuals. In this form, the intercept changes with different individuals to control for the individual heterogeneity and time-invariant characteristics.

The fixed effect model shown in Equation 2.3 has two typical methods of estimation: the least squares dummy variable (LSDV) and first difference (FD) estimator. The LSDV method sets a dummy variable for each individual (D_i, $i = 1, \ldots, n$), which decomposes the intercept into each individual. For example, the following model is estimated:

$$y_{it} = b_{01}D_1 + \cdots + b_{0n-1}D_{n-1} + b_1 x_{it} + e_{it} \tag{2.4}$$

where $b_{01}, \ldots, b_{0n-1}$ are regression coefficients for the dummy variables from the first individual to the $n-1$th individual, respectively. Because adding all n dummy variables in the same equation would bring about full collinearity, the model 2.4 contains only $n-1$ dummy variables.

When n is very small, it is convenient to use the LSDV method, but when n is large, the LSDV method will not only lose too many degrees of freedom but also be complicated. For a better choice, the FD method is more applicable. The FD method uses first differencing to eliminate variables that do not change over time, as shown in Equation 2.5:

$$y_{it} - \bar{y}_i = b_1 (x_{it} - \bar{x}_i) + (e_{it} - \bar{e}_i) \tag{2.5}$$

In Equation 2.5, $\bar{y}_i$, $\bar{x}_i$, and $\bar{e}_i$ indicate the averages of individual i for all periods. Virtually, Equation 2.5 can be obtained by first differencing all variables in Equation 2.3 by subtracting the averages for each individual at all periods.

Through first differencing, we can eliminate all variables that do not change over time, such as b_{0i}, and then obtain the estimate of the regression coefficient b_1.

2.1.3 Random effect model

On the other side of the fixed effect model is the random effect model. In the fixed effect model, we assume that all individual differences are captured by differences in intercept, which are considered to be "fixed" parameters, so they can be estimated using the OLS method. In the random effect model, individual differences are still assumed to exist in intercept, but they are no longer considered to be individual fixed effects and contain random individual differences. Alternatively, the intercept b_{0i} consists of two parts: a fixed part b_0 indicating the sample mean and a random part u_i indicating individual deviation from the sample mean. Meanwhile, the typical specification of the random effect model can be written as

$$y_{it} = b_0 + b_1 x_{it} + e_{it} + u_i \tag{2.6}$$

In Equation 2.6, e_{it} and u_i are random terms, and the former indicates random error terms, while the latter indicates individual random effects. Because the regression error of the random effect model consists of two parts, one for the individual and one for the regression, the random effect model is also known as the error components model.

In general, random error terms for regression should be satisfied with the condition $E(e_{it}) = 0$, and random error terms for individuals should be satisfied with $\sigma_u^2 \neq 0$. The latter condition means that there are differences among individuals, otherwise, the error term can be merged with the regression error term, and the random effect model is reduced to a pooled model. It can be seen that the key to establish a random effect model is whether the individual error term is constant, that is, whether the hypothesis of $\sigma_u^2 = 0$ is true. If this assumption holds, then there is no variation in the random error, namely, no random effect. If this assumption does not hold, there exists a random effect.

There are generally two techniques to estimate random effect models: one is feasible generalized least squares (FLGS) and the other is maximum likelihood (ML) estimator. The results of the two techniques are almost the same regarding the results of coefficients, but differ regarding results of statistical tests. The FGLS technique still reports the explained variance R^2, but the ML estimator reports only a likelihood ratio.

Regarding the essential differences between fixed effect and random effect models, econometrist Greene (2011) made a classical explanation. The major difference is that with the correlation between the unobservable heterogeneity and the included explanatory variables, the fixed effect model assumes certain correlations and controls for the unobservable heterogeneity by technically adding individual dummies (i.e., controlling for the individual difference by including a dummy variable for each).

34 Basics of financial forecasting research

2.1.4 Fixed effect model or random effect model

For panel data, if both fixed effect and random effect models can be used, then a natural question is how to decide which model to be used at what time. In other words, which model is better for a particular analysis? Currently, no agreement has been reached between economists on this issue. Some economists believe that as long as the existence of random effects is true, then the random effect model is certainly better than the fixed effect model. There are mainly three reasons (Woodbridge,2001): First, the random effect model takes into account the random sampling process of data collection. Second, the random effect model can be used to estimate time-invariant variables, but the fixed effect model is sometimes unable to do so (especially the first difference estimator). Third, the estimation technique for the random effect model is GLS, whereas the fixed effect model is more reliant on OLS, and in a large sample, the GLS technique tends to produce a smaller variance than the OLS technique. In fact, the random effect model can be more precise because of its ability to include time-invariant variables. The fixed effect model uses only information about the changes over time for each individual, but not the information about changes between individuals, which can be attributed to the differences among them. However, this information can be used by the random effect model.

However, for other economists, the random effect model should not be simply considered to be better than the fixed effect model, and the decision should be based on the hypothesis test. In the condition that error items (u_i) and independent variables (x_{it}) are independent and identically distributed, namely, u_i and x_{it} are uncorrelated (the null hypothesis H_0), the random effect model would be fully efficient. This is because the fixed effect model is always uniform, regardless of the null hypothesis H_0. If H_0 holds, the random effect model is more efficient than the fixed effect model. Otherwise, if H_0 does not hold, the random effect model is not a uniform estimation. Therefore, if H_0 holds, the estimation results of both the fixed effect model and random effect model will converge to the true parameter values. Conversely, if the estimation results of the fixed effect model significantly differ from the results of the random effect model, the H_0 tends to be rejected This statistical hypothesis test was proposed by Durbin, Wu, and Hausman, and is also known as the Hausman specification test.

Supposing that the estimation result of coefficients of the fixed effect model is b_{FE}, and the estimation result of coefficients of the random effect model is a vector b_{RE}, the null hypothesis to be tested is H_0: $b_{FE} = b_{RE}$, and the alternative hypothesis is H_1: $b_{FE} \neq b_{RE}$. The t-test can then be performed by constructing the following t-statistic:

$$t = \frac{b_{FE} - b_{RE}}{\left[se(b_{FE})^2 - se(b_{RE})^2 \right]^{1/2}} \tag{2.7}$$

In Equation 2.7, se indicates the standard error of the coefficient. By comparing the t-statistic calculated from Equation 2.7 with the critical value of the t-distribution, one can determine whether to accept or reject the null hypothesis. If the null hypothesis is accepted, which means no significant differences between b_{FE} and b_{RE}, then the estimates of the two models are consistent. Therefore, the random effect model is more appropriate. If the null hypothesis is rejected, which means there are significant differences between b_{FE} and b_{RE}, then the estimates of the two models are inconsistent. Since the estimation results of the fixed effect model tend to converge to true values in a large sample, the fixed effect model is more suitable.

The disadvantage of the Haussmann test is that it assumes that random effect estimates are fully efficient when H_0 holds. However, if there is heteroscedasticity for the random error, the random effect estimator will not be fully efficient. Therefore, the Haussmann test does not apply in the condition of heteroscedasticity. In the case of heteroscedasticity, the bootstrap method can be used to calculate var($b_{FE} - b_{RE}$).

Nevertheless, both the fixed effect model and the random effect model have certain limitations. For the fixed effect model, the main limitation is the overexplanation of the intercept term. For the random effect model, it is difficult to satisfy the assumption that the individual error component is independent of explanatory variables. The econometrist Greene (2005) pointed out that neither the fixed effect model nor the random effect model can completely solve the issue of heterogeneity, especially for highly heterogeneous panel data (interprovincial or cross-national panel data) and some high-quality panel data (e.g., different provinces, different countries). How to overcome heterogeneity has become the focus of econometrists, and the panel time series model with heterogeneous slopes is proposed. This method plays a very positive role in enhancing the scientific nature of forecasting higher education finance.

2.1.5 Panel data model with heterogeneity

Forecasting higher education finance is usually conducted by using cross-provincial or cross-national data. Therefore, compared with microlevel individual panel data, this kind of macroeconomic data is more heterogeneous. As a result, the panel times series model with heterogeneous slopes yields more accurate estimates. The general form of the model is as follows:

$$y_{it} = \beta_i x_{it} + u_{it} \tag{2.8}$$

$$u_{it} = \alpha_{1i} + \lambda_i f_t + \varepsilon_{it} \tag{2.9}$$

$$x_{it} = \alpha_{2i} + \lambda_i f_t + \gamma_i g_t + e_{it} \tag{2.10}$$

In Equations 2.8 to 2.10, i indicates a unit, and t indicates the time periods. In Equation 2.8, y_{it} and x_{it} are observable dependent variables and independent variables for the ith unit in the ith year. β_i is the slope of the ith observable independent variable, and u_{it} indicates the unobservable part, including the unobservable variable and error term. In Equation 2.9, the unobservable part u_{it} consists of a group fixed effect α_{1i} and an unobservable common factor f_t. The group fixed effect is mainly used to control for the cross-group heterogeneity that does not change over time, while f_t is mainly used to control for the time-varying heterogeneity and cross-section dependence.[1] In Equation 2.10, α_{1i} and f_t are still used to indicate group fixed effects and unobservable common factors. Also, g_t is added to Equation 2.10 to control for other factors that f_t does not include. u_{it}, ε_{it}, and e_{it} are white noises.

For the model shown in Equations 2.8 to 2.10, there are generally three types of estimators: the mean group (MG) estimator proposed by Pesaran and Smith (1995), the common correlated effects mean group (CCEMG) estimator by Pesaran (2006), and the augmented mean group (AMG) estimator proposed by Eberhardt and Teal (2010). Among these three estimators, the MG estimator does not control for cross-sectional dependence. The CCEMG estimator controls for cross-sectional dependence by adding sectional means ($\bar{y}_t$ and $\bar{x}_t$) for each variable (including dependent and independent variables) to the equation. The AMG estimator uses an additional explanatory variable common dynamic process (c.d.p.) to indicate the dynamic process that all units share. There are both advantages and disadvantages to these estimators. Considering that CCEMG and AMG estimators include cross-sectional means in the current period and other current-period variables reflecting the dynamic process of the common macroeconomics across different countries, they are not fully appropriate for out-of-sample forecasting for future periods.

2.2 Forecasting methods based on time series data

Actually, forecasting is modeling the relationships between variables, so the characteristics of the data are important for forecasting research, and choosing a suitable econometric model is also key. The critical issue for time series analysis to address is the effect of one variable x on another variable y over time. In other words, what is the dynamic effect of x change on y? Owing to the development of macroeconomic forecasting, financial data analysis, and other fields, the methods of time series data analysis have been very fruitful, and a series of important forecasting methods, including the finite distributed lag (FDL) model, serial correlation, autoregression integrated distribution (ARID) model, cointegration model, vector error correction, and vector autoregression, have been developed. This section focuses on several methods frequently used in higher education financial forecasting, including time series trend models, single-exponential smoothing model, and autoregressive integrated moving average (ARIMA) model.

2.2.1 Overview of time series data

Time series data is the data collected by a single unit at multiple points in time. Time series data has some characteristics that are different from other types of data. First, there may be correlations between observations, so the testing and modeling regarding correlations have become one of the main tasks for time series analysis. Second, all observations of time series data are sorted by time, and if the time order is wrongly processed, the dynamic relationship between variables may be disturbed, i.e., the change at one time period of one variable will result in changes at the next time period or more, in itself or even other variables. Third, an important assumption in time series analysis is that the future is similar to the past (i.e., stationarity). If the probability distribution of a time series does not change over time, it is called a stationary time series; otherwise, it is classed a nonstationary series. Stationary time series data has good statistical characteristics, and robust estimations can be obtained by simply using OLS, whereas a nonstationary time series requires more complex methods to converse it to a stationary one.

The essential of time series analysis is on processing observations from different time periods, so lags and differences are two of the most basic terminologies. Supposing the observation on the time series variable y at period t is y_t, and the total number of periods is T, for the observation at period t, y_{t-1} indicates the first-lagged value, also known as lag 1 value. And y_{t-j} indicates the jth lagged value, also known as the lag j value. For the change in value between different periods, it can be measured by differences. $y_t - y_{t-1}$ indicates the first difference of y_t; it can also be written as $\Delta y_t = y_t - y_{t-1}$.

The "trend" is another important terminology in time series analysis, which refers to the persistent long-term movement of a variable over time. In time series data, there are two types of trends: deterministic trends and stochastic trends. A deterministic trend is a nonstochastic function of time, whereas a stochastic trend changes over time. For a deterministic trend, you can generally control it by inserting time dummy variables. The stochastic trend is more complex, resulting in a series of estimation bias, so stochastic trend testing, such as the Dickey–Fuller test, is required.

2.2.2 Forecasting with univariate time series

A univariate time series is time series data consisting of observations of a single unit at different periods. Since no other covariates exist, univariate time series data can only be modeled and analyzed according to its own pattern of changes. A smoother is a kind of technique for modeling univariate time series data. In general, there are three types of smoothers: moving average smoothers, nonlinear smoothers, and recursive smoothers. Among these, the moving average smoothers and nonlinear smoothers are only suitable for analyzing in-sample observations, thus they are usually used to extract the trend by filtering the noise components, which is not suitable for forecasting. The recursive smoothers are suitable for forecasting univariate time series. Therefore, this section focuses on several frequently used recursive smoothers, including the single-exponential smoother, double-exponential smoother, nonseasonal H–W smoother, and seasonal H–W smoother.

2.2.2.1 Exponential smoothing

Exponential smoothing is a special form of weighted moving average filter. Its basic idea is that the value of any period is the weighted average of the actual observation value of the current period and the smoothed value of the previous period. The feature of weighting is to give large weights to the values near the forecasting period and smaller weights to the values far from the forecasting period. The weights decline geometrically, so this method is called exponential smoothing. Exponential smoothing includes single-exponential smoothing and double-exponential smoothing, which are described next.

Single-exponential smoothing can be viewed either as an adaptive forecasting algorithm or as a geometrically weighted moving average filter. It is most appropriate when the time series data exhibit low velocity, aperiodic variation in the mean (e.g., no linear or higher-order trends). The basic formula for this smoothing is as follows:

$$S_t = \alpha x_t + (1-\alpha)S_{t-1} \tag{2.11}$$

where S_t indicates the smoothed value of the period t, x_t indicates the true value of the period t, and S_{t-1} is the smoothed value of the period $t-1$. a is set to be the smoothing parameter (or smoothing constant) with a range of values from 0 to 1.

Based on single-exponential smoothing, double-exponential smoothing (also known as secondary smoothing) can be performed. The series obtained after single-exponential smoothing can be smoothed again, as follows:

$$S_t^{(2)} = aS_t^{(1)} + (1-a)S_{t-1}^{(2)} \tag{2.12}$$

In Equation 2.12, $S_t^{(1)}$ is the same as S_t in Equation 2.11, indicating the results of single-exponential smoothing, while $S_t^{(2)}$ and $S_{t-1}^{(2)}$ indicate the smoothed smoothing results of period t and $t-1$, respectively. a is still the smoothing parameter, and its range of values also lies in the interval of [0,1].

When double-exponential smoothing is applied, its predicted values consist of two parts: one is a constant part (the linear part of the last observation in the smoothed series), and the other is about the time. It is worth noting that double-exponential smoothing is closely related to the Holt–Winters (H–W) method and ARIMA model, which will be described in the next sections. Double-exponential smoothing can be viewed as a restricted version of the H–W method (Gardner, 1985) or as the ARIMA (0,2,2) model with equal roots (Chatfield, 2001).

2.2.2.2 Holt–Winters smoothing

Holt–Winters (H–W) smoothing is a frequently used method for forecasting univariate time series. This method can be applied to different types of data and is further categorized into H–W seasonal smoothing and H–W nonseasonal smoothing according to the existence of a seasonal component. H–W seasonal smoothing is a method to forecast univariate time series that have a seasonal component. The basic principle of this method is to minimize the in-sample sum-of-squares forecast errors. When the beginning of the series has missing values, the H–W method

Basics of financial forecasting research 39

automatically starts with the first nonmissing value and then fills the missing values with forecasted values. Considering the pattern of the amplitudes of the seasonal component, the H–W seasonal method can be further categorized into the H–W multiplicative method, which should be applied if the amplitude of seasonal component grows with the series, and the H–W additive method, which should be applied if the amplitude of seasonal component is not growing with the series.

The general form of the H–W multiplicative method is as follows:

$$x_{t+j} = (\mu_t + \beta_j) s_{t+j} + e_{t+j} \tag{2.13}$$

In Equation 2.13, x_{t+j} indicates the original values of the series at time $t+j$, s_t indicates seasonal component at time $t+j$, μ_t indicates time-varying mean at time t, β_j indicates the smoothing parameter, and e_{t+j} indicates an idiosyncratic error at time $t+j$. As can be seen from Equation 2.13, the H–W multiplication method actually divides the value in the series into two parts: one part is the seasonal component and the other part is the average trend. And there is a non-linear relationship between the two parts.

Similarly, changing the multiplicative relationship in Equation 2.13 to the additive relationship will result in the general form of the H–W additive method as follows:

$$x_{t+j} = (\mu_t + \beta_j) + s_{t+j} + e_{t+j} \tag{2.14}$$

All notations in Equation 2.14 are as in Equation 2.13; the only change is the relationship between $\mu_t + \beta_j$ and s_{t+j} is from multiplication to addition, which turns the two terms into a linear additive relationship.

H–W nonseasonal models are suitable for predicting time-varying linear trends in intercepts and coefficients, and their general form can be presented as

$$\hat{x}_{t+1} = a_t + b_t t \tag{2.15}$$

In Equation 2.15, $\hat{x}_{t+1}$ indicates the predicted value, a_t indicates the mean that changes over time, and b_t is the coefficient on time that also changes. The two parameters a_t and b_t can be estimated through formulas as follows:

$$a_t = \alpha x_t + (1-\alpha)(a_{t-1} + b_{t-1}) \tag{2.16}$$

$$b_t = \beta(a_t - a_{t-1}) + (1-\beta) b_{t-1} \tag{2.17}$$

In the preceding equations, α and β are the smoothing parameters of a_t and b_t, respectively. As a result, the H–W nonseasonal smoother is also considered as double-exponential smoothing with two parameters.

2.2.3 Autoregressive (AR) and moving average (MA) models

2.2.3.1 pth-Order autoregressive models

One of the characteristics of time series data is the time dependence between values in the series, and the autoregressive model is featured for its ability to depict, model, and predict the series based on this time dependence. In the autoregressive model, the simplest form is the linear relation between the time $t-1$ and t, which can be specified as

$$y_t = b_1 y_{t-1} + e_t \tag{2.18}$$

In Equation 2.18, y_t and y_{t-1} indicate the values of time t and $t-1$ in the series. b_1 is the autoregressive coefficient, which also demonstrates the degree of dependency between values in time $t-1$ and t. e_t is a random error term. It is worth noting that the necessary condition for the establishment of the first-order autoregressive model is that the time series is stationary, i.e., the autoregressive coefficient b_1 satisfies the condition $|b_1| < 1$.

Equation 2.18 depicts the relation between y_t and its lag -1 value y_{t-1}, and is therefore also known as the first-order self-regressive model, or briefly AR(1). Equation 2.18 can be extended to be a function of more lagged values, resulting in a more general form of the pth-order autoregressive model, or AR(p), as follows:

$$y_t = a_1 y_{t-1} + \cdots + a_p y_{t-p} + e_t \tag{2.19}$$

In Equation 2.19, p indicates the number of lags or the lag length. y_t is the observed value in time t; and y_{t-1}, ..., y_{t-p} are its lagged values in the series. a_1, ..., a_p are the autoregressive coefficients, also known as the weighted coefficients, which represent the effect of the lagged values' change on the y_t. e_t is a random error term.

2.2.3.2 Moving average models

The establishment of the autoregressive models depends on a functional relationship that exists between the value in time t and its lags in the same series. Similarly, if we assume that there is a functional relationship between the value in time t and its random error terms in previous times, we can also analyze the time series using the equation

$$y_t = e_t + b_1 e_{t-1} + \cdots + b_q e_{t-q} \tag{2.20}$$

In Equation 2.20, q indicates the number of lags or the order of the model. e_{t-1} and e_{t-q} are the random error terms in time $t-1$ and $t-q$, respectively, and b_1 and b_q are their corresponding coefficients of moving average.

According to the preceding equation, if we only consider the relationship between the value in time 1 and lag 1 random error term, the model is called the first-order moving average model, or briefly denoted as MA(1). If more lags of random error terms are included in the model, for example, e_{t-q}, the model is called the qth-order moving average model, or briefly denoted as MA(q).

2.2.3.3 Autoregressive moving average models

The autoregressive models assume that there is a certain functional relationship between the value in time t and its lags in the series, while the moving average models assume that there is a certain functional relationship between the value in time t and the random error terms of its lags. In practice, the aforementioned assumptions are both too strong, because the value in time t is not only related to the lagged values but also their random error terms. Therefore, combining the two techniques together bring about the method called the autoregressive moving average (ARMA) model. The general form of a typical ARMA model is as follows:

$$y_t = a_1 y_{t-1} + \cdots + a_p y_{t-p} + e_t + b_1 e_{t-1} + \cdots + b_q e_{t-q} \qquad (2.21)$$

In Equation 2.21, y_t is the observed value in time t; $y_{t-1}, \ldots, y_{t-p}$ are its lagged values in the series; and a_1 and a_p are the autoregressive coefficients. Similarly, e_{t-1} and e_{t-q} are the lag -1 and lag $-q$ random error terms, and b_1 and b_q are their coefficients of moving averages. Equation 2.21 is actually a combination of Equations 2.19 and 2.20, so the equation can be divided into two parts: the autoregression part and the moving average part, where p and q are the order of the autoregressions and the moving averages, respectively. Therefore, the model can also be briefly denoted as ARMA(p,q). A time series that follows the pattern of these ARMA models are considered to obey the (p,q) order of autoregressive moving average models.

No matter whether autoregressive models, moving average models, or autoregressive moving average models, they all build on the assumption that the time series is stationary. For nonstationary time series, these methods cannot be used directly for modeling the data and forecasting future values. It is necessary to first process the nonstationary time series, and then apply these modeling techniques. With regard to how to process the nonstationary time series data, differencing is a frequently used method, and, consequently, the ARMA models are extended to autoregressive integrated moving average (ARIMA) models to deal with nonstationary time series. The next section will introduce this method.

2.2.3.4 Autoregressive integrated moving average models

After conducting tests to the time series, if the time series belongs to a nonstationary one, we can make differences to the time series and at the same time analyze the differenced series to examine its stationarity until a stationary series is obtained. In general, the most used values for the parameters of differenced series are 0, 1, and 2.[2]

ARIMA models were proposed by Box and Jenkins in 1976, and are also known as Box–Jenkins models. ARIMA models are a common technique for performing nonstationary time series analyses. According to this technique, the predicted time series is generated by some random process, and although there exists uncertainty in some values in the series, the whole process still shows certain rules that can be presented. In the ARIMA model, predictions of future values in the series can be represented as a linear function of their lagged terms and lagged terms of random terms. Concerning a non-stationary time series $\{y_t\}$, we can first process it with dth-order differencing. If the differenced series $\{\Delta^d y_t\}$ is stationary, we can model it by performing ARMA(p,q) with the specification as follows:

$$\Delta^d y_t = a_1 \Delta^d y_{t-1} + \cdots + a_p \Delta^d y_{t-p} + e_t + b_1 e_{t-1} + \cdots + b_q e_{t-q} \quad (2.22)$$

In Equation 2.22, $\Delta^d y_t$ indicates the present value of the series that becomes stationary after taking differencing. $\Delta^d y_{t-1}$, ..., $\Delta^d y_{t-p}$ indicate the lagged values for the past p time periods in the differenced series. a_1, ..., a_p indicate the coefficients of autoregressions. e_{t-1} and e_{t-q} are the lag -1 and lag $-q$ random error terms. b_1 and b_q are the coefficients of moving averages. p and q are the numbers of order for autoregressions and moving averages, respectively.

2.2.4 Forecast combination

For the same time series, the different forecasting methods will produce different forecasted values. Combining these forecasted values together by certain weights, we can obtain the results of the forecast combination (or combination of forecasts). A forecast combination can effectively reduce the impact of random factors in the single forecasting model and thus improve the accuracy of forecasts. The most important issue for forecast combination is how to reasonably determine the weights of separate forecasts. The method proposed by Bates and Granger (1969) based on out-of-sample forecast variances is most often utilized. The basic process of applying this method is of two steps: First, calculate the sum-of-squares of the out-of-sample forecast errors for each forecast (namely, the forecast variance). Second, obtain the weight for each forecast model by minimizing the sum of all forecast variances (i.e., giving larger weights to the forecast with smaller variance and smaller weights to the forecast with larger variance). The formula for calculating the weights can be written as

$$W_j = \sigma_j^{-2} \Big/ \sum_{j=1}^m \sigma_j^{-2} \quad \text{and} \quad \sum_{j=1}^m W_j = 1, j = 1, 2, \cdots m \quad (2.23)$$

In the vector $W = (W_1, \ldots, W_m)^T$, the element W_j is the weight for each forecast, and σ_j^2 is the corresponding forecast variance.

Given the aforementioned weights, we can further obtain the result of the forecast combination by weighting all the forecasted values ($\hat{x}_j$):

$$X = \sum_{j=1}^m W_j \hat{x}_j \quad (2.24)$$

2.3 Summary

This chapter gives brief introduction to some frequently used methods in the studies of forecasting higher education finance. Among the forecasting methods based on the panel data approach, the fixed effect model and the random effect model are the most popular, and both of them estimate the effects of the independent variables on the dependent variables according to the average trend of historical data, and so predict the future trend of dependent variables. The question of whether the fixed or random effect model is more appropriate to certain data can be answered by implementing the Hausman test. For cross-national data, due to the existence of a strong heterogeneity, an important method called the panel times series model with heterogeneous slopes was developed. Among the forecasting methods based on the time series data approach, exponential smoothing and ARMA models are the most popular ones. Exponential smoothing mainly performs the forecasting by using the trend of change in the univariate time series, while the ARMA models are used in forecasting the relationships between multiple variables.

The aforementioned methods have been applied in the empirical research related to the forecasting of higher education finance in China. As shown in Table 2.1, the methods most used by earlier studies of Chinese scholars are multivariate linear regressions based on cross-sectional data. In recent years, important progress has been made in the use of panel data and time series methods for forecasting in higher education finance research. For example, Tang and Hu (2015) used panel data from 12 countries in 2001–2011 to forecast the structure and scale of China's financial investment in higher education during the 13th Five-Year Plan period with the method of panel times series model with heterogeneous slopes. Moreover, Zhao and Hu (2017) used time series data in 2006–2015 to forecast the proportion of financial investment between ordinary undergraduate and higher vocational colleges in China during the 13th Five-Year Plan period with methods such as trend analysis, H–W nonseasonal smoothing, exponential smoothing, and ARIMA models.

Table 2.1 Literature of higher education financial forecasting and main methods used

Reference	Data	Method
Mi and Guo (2005)	1991–2002 time series data of China	Multivariate linear regression
Liu and Yuan (2006)	Cross-sectional data in 2001 of 57 countries	Multivariate linear regression
Zhang (2015)	China 1992–2013 cross-sectional data	Multivariate linear regression
Tang and Hu (2015)	2001–2011 panel data of 12 countries	Panel times series model with heterogeneous slopes
Zhao and Hu (2017)	2006–2015 time series data of China	Trend analysis, Holt–Winters nonseasonal model, exponential smoothing, ARIMA, combination model

Appendix

Table A2.1 Summary of Stata commands for forecasting method

Forecasting method	Stata command	Notes
Panel data methods		
Fixed effect model	xtreg y x, fe	1. xtreg is the panel data command. 2. y indicates the dependent variable. 3. x indicates the independent variable. 4. fe indicates a fixed effect model.
Random effect model	xtreg, re/mle	1. re indicates a random effect model using the FGLS technique. 2. mle indicates a random effect model using maximum likelihood estimator.
Hausman test	hausman fe re	1. Performing Hausman's specification test for fixed and random effects.
Panel time series model with heterogeneous slopes	xtmg y x, cce/aug trend full	1. xtmg indicates estimating panel time series models with heterogeneous slopes. 2. cce indicates implementing mean group estimator. 3. aug indicates implementing augmented mean group estimator. 4. Trend specifies that a group-specific linear trend is to be included. 5. full provides the underlying group-specific regression results.
Time-series methods		
Single-exponential smoothing	tssmooth exponential d=x, p(a) f(s)	1. tssmooth indicates univariate time series smoothing and forecasting. 2. exponential indicates implementing single-exponential smoothing. 3. d indicates the new variable created through smoothing. 4. x indicates the original variable. 5. p(a) indicates the smoothing parameter (a$\in$[0,1]). 6. f(s) indicates the periods for the out-of-sample forecast.
Double-exponential smoothing method	tssmooth dexponential d=x, p(a) f(s)	1. dexponential indicates double-exponential smoothing. 2. d indicates the new variable created through smoothing. 3. x indicates the original variable. 4. p(a) indicates the smoothing parameter ((a$\in$[0,1]). 5. f(s) indicates the periods for the out-of-sample forecast.

(*Continued*)

Table A2.1 Continued

Forecasting method	Stata command	Notes
Holt–Winters seasonal smoothing	tssmooth shwinters d=x, f(s)	1. shwinters indicates the H–W seasonal smoothing. 2. d indicates the new variable created through smoothing. 3. x indicates the original variable. 4. f(s) indicates the periods for the out-of-sample forecast.
Holt–Winters nonseasonal smoothing	tssmooth hwinters d=x, p(a b) f(s)	1. hwinters indicates H-W nonseasonal smoothing. 2. d indicates the new variable created through smoothing. 3. x indicates the original variable. 4. p(a,b) indicates the smoothing parameter ((a,b$\in$[0,1]). 5. f(s) indicates the periods for the out-of-sample forecast.
Autoregressive model	arima y, ar(1/n)	1. arima indicates performing a dynamic regression model. 2. y indicates the dependent variable. 3. ar(1/n) indicates the autoregressive terms from the first order to the nth order.
Moving average model	arima y, ma(1/n)	1. arima indicates performing a dynamic regression model. 2. y indicates the dependent variable. 3. ma(1/n) indicates the moving average terms from the first order to the nth order.
Autoregressive moving average model (ARMA)	arima y, ar(1/n) ma(1/n)	1. This command includes both autoregressions and moving averages.
Autoregressive integrated moving average model (ARIMA)	arima y, arima(#p,#d,#q)	1. The command performs autoregressive integrated moving-average model l. 2. #p indicates 1 through p lags of autoregressions. 3. #q indicates 1 through q lags of moving averages. 4. #d indicates that the original sequence needs to go through several differentials before the sequence is stationary.

Notes

1 Cross-section dependent refers to the correlations between the cross-section units. These correlations stem from spatial patterns or some unobserved common factors. The discussion on this issue mainly comes from macroeconomics, as swift-moving globalization enhanced the interdependence of different countries in economics and social development. See a review from Vasilis Sarafidis and Tom Wansbeek titled "Cross-Sectional Dependence in Panel Data Analysis."
2 How to perform the test of stationarity for time series data is not the theme of this chapter. Readers can refer to textbooks in econometrics.

References

Bates, J., & Granger, C. W. J. (1969). The combination of forecasts. *Operational Research Society, 20*(4), 451–468.

Chatfield, C. (2001). *Time-series forecasting*. London: Chapman & Hall/CRC.

Eberhardt, M., & Teal, F. (2010). *Productivity Analysis in Global Manufacturing Production*. Discussion Paper 515, Oxford: Department of Economics, University of Oxford.

Feng, W. Q. (2008). *Economic Forecasting and Decision*. Wuhan: Wuhan University Press.

Gardner Jr., E. S. (1985). Exponential smoothing: The state of the art. *Journal of Forecasting, 4*, 1–28.

Greene, W. (2005). Reconsidering heterogeneity in panel data estimators of the stochastic frontier model. *Journal of Econometrics, 126*(2), 269–303.

Green, W. (2011). *Econometric Analysis* (7th edition). Hoboken, NJ: Prentice Hall.

Hill, R. C., Griffiths, W. E., & Lim, G. C. (2018). *Principles of Econometrics* (5th edition). New York: John Wiley and Sons, Inc.

Hu, R. W., & Wang, H. (2010). Forecast and implementing conception of Chinese educational funds investment intensified demand in 2020, *Research in Educational Development, 30*(1), 1–7.

Jin, Y. H., & Jin, S. N. (2011). *Advanced Econometrics*. Beijing: Peking University.

Liu, Z. Y., & Yuan, L. S. (2006). Study on the public ratio of investment in education of China. *Journal of Higher Education, 2*, 62–66.

Luo, L. Q. (2004). The systematic analysis of elementary educational expenditure of China: Structural analysis and gap forecasting. *Statistical Research, 12*, 13–17.

Mi, H., & Guo, S. J. (2005). Theoretical analysis & research demonstration of China's higher education financial input in the future ten years. *Education & Economy, 1*, 30–34.

Pesaran, M. H. (2006). Estimation and inference in large heterogeneous panels with a multifactor error structure. *Econometrica, 74*, 967–1012.

Pesaran, M. H., & Smith, R. P. (1995). Estimating long-run relationships from dynamic heterogeneous panels. *Journal of Econometrics, 68*, 79–113.

Tang, Y. P., & Hu, Y. M. (2015). Forecasting of government investment scale on the higher education during the thirteenth "five-year plan" in the economic new normal. *Chongqing Higher Education Research, 3*(6), 3–15.

Wang, S. M., Liu, Z. Y., & Sun, Z. J. (2003). The demand and supply of education expenditure in 2008 Beijing. *Educational Science Research, Z1*, 5–9.

Wang, S. Y. (2018). *Macroeconomic Forecasting Method Applications and System*. Beijing: Science Press.

Woodbridge, J. M. (2001). *Econometric Analysis of Cross Section and Panel Data* (1st edition). Cambridge, MA: The MIT Press.

Yue, C. J. (2008). The supply and demand of public education expenditure in China: An empirical prediction. *Peking University Education Review, 6*(2), 152–166.

Zhang, H. W. (2015). Research forecast of China's education financial input in the future ten years. *Journal of Chengdu Normal University, 31*(11), 19–24.

Zhao, R., & Hu, Y. M. (2017). Forecasting on the structure of financial investment in higher education during the "13th five-year": Based on the data of the ordinary and vocational universities. *China Higher Education Research, 9*, 24–29.

3 The adequacy and equity of the financial resources of higher education

Forecasting studies are quantitative estimates of future trends based on historical data. For the prediction of government funding for higher education, on the one hand, it is necessary to rely on scientific forecasting methods; on the other hand, we also need to make an in-depth analysis of the historical data of government funding for higher education. The past 20 years have been a flourishing period of time for higher education development in China. Benefiting from the expansion policy of higher education access at the national level, China's gross enrollment rate in higher education has climbed from 9.8% in 1998 to 42.7% in 2016, which is ahead of the target set out in the "Outline of the National Medium- and Long-Term Development Plan for China Education". The number of enrolled students at all levels of higher education increased more than seven times, from 3.6 million in 1998 to 28.93 million in 2016, making China a truly worldwide powerhouse for higher education. Over the past 20 years, public financial support for higher education has also grown, with total government funding for higher education increasing nearly ten times, from 53.5 billion US dollars in 2001 to 584.1 billion US dollars in 2015.

The analysis of historical data on China's government funding for higher education has long been the focus of scholarly attention. Many scholars have conducted in-depth studies on this topic and paid special attention to the changing trend of public expenditure on higher education and the adequacy of public expenditure (Li, 2008; Sun, 2009; Yue, 2011; Fang & Liu, 2018). Moreover, there are also studies discussing the equity of Chinese higher education finance (Hu, 2012; Ye, 2015). Based on international time series data and provincial panel data, this chapter tries to research the current status of public funding for higher education in China from the perspective of adequacy and equity, and lays the foundation for the following research on forecasting the public funding for higher education.

3.1 The adequacy of government funding for higher education

Public institutions are the main body of higher education in China, and public funds are the most important source of funds for the operation of public universities and colleges. Data from the China Education Finance Statistics Yearbook

DOI: 10.4324/9781003250524-3

show that more than 50% of the total revenue of public higher education institutions comes from government grants, while tuition fees account for only about 30%.[1] It can be seen that public finance plays a very important role in maintaining the adequacy of higher education funds in China, and the adequacy of higher education funds plays an important role in providing the financial guarantee for the entire higher education system. The adequacy of government funding for higher education is a common concern of scholars internationally, and even in the United States, where private universities and colleges are the main body of the higher education system, the state governments' funding mechanism and financial support for public institutions are also of great concern (Yue, 2011). The adequacy of higher education finance refers to the adequacy of government expenditure on higher education and reflects public finance's efforts to invest in higher education from one aspect. Referring to the research design of Yue (2011), this study is mainly based on the perspective of international comparison to examine the adequacy of China's higher education finance with the following three indicators: (1) government expenditure per tertiary student, (2) government expenditure in tertiary institutions as a percentage of gross domestic product (GDP), and (3) government expenditure in tertiary institutions as a percentage of total government expenditure.

3.1.1 International comparison of the government expenditure per tertiary student

Based on the level of economic development and population size, combined with data from the UNESCO Institute for Statistics (UIS), this study selected a total of 12 countries (except China) in three categories for international comparison. The first category is the Western developed countries of the United States, United Kingdom, France, Italy, Poland, Spain, and Australia; the second category is the developed countries in Asia of Japan and Korea; and the third category is the developing countries of India, Brazil, and Thailand.

Table 3.1 shows the government expenditure per tertiary student in 13 developed and developing countries (using international dollars). As can be seen from the table, the government expenditure per tertiary student in Western developed countries is generally higher, with the mean values increasing from 6385 international dollars in 2001 to 9316 international dollars in 2011, a growth rate of 45.9%. France, in particular, had the figure of 7917 international dollars for government expenditure per tertiary student in 2001, which was 2941 international dollars lower than the United States during the same period. However, by 2011 the government expenditure per tertiary student in France had reached 13,564 international dollars, ranking first among the sample countries, with an increase of 71.3%. For developed Asian countries (Japan and South Korea), their performance on government expenditure per tertiary student varies. Japan had a high starting point and fast growth rate. In 2011, the Japanese government expenditure per tertiary student was 4455 international dollars, far below the mean value for Western developed countries over the same period. And in 2011, this figure

Table 3.1 Government expenditure per tertiary student in 2001–2011 (international dollars)

	2001	2002	2003	2004	2005	2006	2007	2008	2009	2010	2011	Change rate
Western developed countries	6385	6656	6904	6927	7429	7825	7916	8346	8523	8897	931	45.9%
Australia	–	–	–	–	7067	7110	7370	7417	8189	836	8335	–
France	7917	831	9557	9904	10,182	10,878	11,930	12,632	13,580	13,362	13,564	71.3%
Italy	6783	7063	6368	6211	6249	7065	7047	8289	8346	8481	8687	28.1%
Poland	1977	2441	2365	2787	2954	2579	2775	3312	3604	4266	4544	129.8%
Spain	4850	5267	5612	5854	6211	7110	8072	9041	9422	9057	8872	82.9%
United Kingdom	5924	7776	7872	7984	10,041	9415	8520	7918	7375	8932	11,498	94.1%
United States	10,858	9079	9653	8823	9300	10,616	9700	9817	9144	9814	9713	–10.5%
Asian developed countries	4455	2743	3556	3767	3782	4046	4390	4876	3467	8080	5843	31.2%
Japan	4455	4543	533	5714	5586	5779	6415	7026	–	8080	8194	83.9%
Korea	–	943	1781	1820	1978	2314	2365	2726	3467	–	3491	–
Developing countries	3320	4100	1535	2298	2572	2335	3577	304	2999	2962	2690	–19.0%
Thailand	2399	–	–	2132	2476	303	–	254	2523	2132	2731	13.8%
Brazil	4241	4100	–	3275	3697	–	3577	3549	3631	3917	–	–
India	–	–	1535	1487	1542	1631	–	–	2844	2838	2650	–
China	2844	2586	2388	2189	2076	2219	2305	2580	2868	3057	4120	44.9%

Note: –, missing values.

reached 8194 international dollars, an increase of 83.9% from 2001, which was close to the mean value for Western developed countries over the same period. South Korea, by contrast, had a low starting point but a very high growth rate. In 2002, the government expenditure per tertiary student in South Korea was less than 1000 international dollars, but reached 3491 international dollars by 2011. However, compared with Japan, the figure of South Korea was substantially lower, and even lower than the figures of a few developing countries in certain years. For the selected developing countries, their government expenditure per tertiary student increased during 2001–2011. For example in China, the government expenditure per tertiary student was 2844 international dollars in 2001, then declined for several years, and began to recover in 2006, and returned to the level of 2001 in 2009 with rapid growth in the following two years (2010 and 2011). Overall, since 2010, China's government expenditure per tertiary student has substantially exceeded that of the main developing countries, and even that of South Korea, but still far away from that of Japan or Western developed countries.

In order to visually present the changing trend of government expenditure per tertiary student in the selected countries between 2001 and 2011, we made a line chart of three categories of countries (Western developed countries, Asian developed countries, and developing countries) as well as China (Figure 3.1). As can be seen from Figure 3.1, the government expenditure per tertiary student in Western developed countries was substantially higher than those in the other two categories and China, and the government expenditure per tertiary student increased continuously, with an even larger growth rate after the global financial crisis in 2008. Second, the government expenditure per tertiary student in Asian developed countries was also substantially higher than that in developing countries (i.e., India or Brazil) and China, and the average student expenditure increased

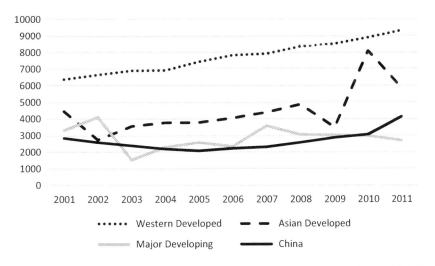

Figure 3.1 Government expenditure per tertiary student (international dollars) 2001–2011.

52 *Adequacy and equity of financial resources*

rapidly from 2003 to 2008, but declined substantially in 2009 largely due to the impact of the global financial crisis, then approached the level of Western developed countries with a rapid increase in 2010. Finally, China's government expenditure per tertiary student from 2001 to 2010 was closer to the mean value of the developing countries, and the gap began to increase from 2011, but still far from the mean value of the Asian developed countries or Western developed countries. In addition, the chart also shows that the government expenditure per tertiary student is positively correlated with the level of economic development, that is, the higher the level of economic development of the country, the higher the government expenditure per tertiary student.

3.1.2 International comparison of the proportion of financial investment in higher education

The government expenditure per tertiary student only measures the amount of government investment in higher education and does not take into account the actual financial resources of the government. The two indicators of "government expenditure on tertiary education as a percentage of GDP" and "government expenditure on tertiary education as a percentage of total government expenditure" are better to measure a government's efforts to invest in higher education. Here, the sample countries are still divided into three categories (except for China), with their averages plotted in line charts (Figures 3.2 and 3.3).

As can be seen from Figure 3.2, the government expenditure on higher education as a percentage of GDP in the Western developed countries was

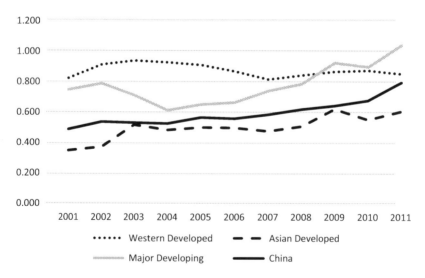

Figure 3.2 Fiscal expenditure on higher education in various countries as a percentage of GDP 2001–2011.

Adequacy and equity of financial resources 53

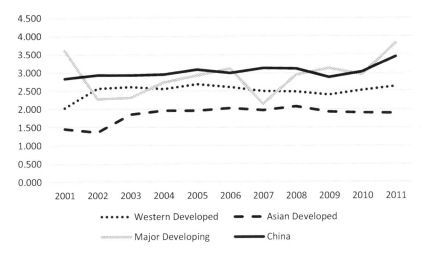

Figure 3.3 Fiscal expenditure (%) for all types of national higher education, 2001–2011.

significantly higher than the number in the Asian developed countries and China, and higher than the number in major developing countries before 2008. Second, the government expenditure on higher education as a percentage of GPD in Asian developed countries was on a volatile upward trend, but its average was lower than the percentage in China, with 2003 and 2009 being the closest. Moreover, the government expenditure on higher education as a percentage of GDP in Asian developed countries was significantly lower than the average in major developing countries. We speculate that this is related to the fact that major developing countries emphasized developing higher education and enlarging the scale of higher education in the context of their high-speed economic development in the past decade.[2] While the economic status of Japan or South Korea was relatively stable and even stagnant in the past decade, their demands on enlarging the scale of higher education were weaker than those of developing countries,[3] resulting in less investment in terms of percentage of GDP. However, the government expenditure per tertiary student in Japan and South Korea remained growing and was higher than the average for major developing countries. The major developing countries had a larger growth rate of higher education expansion, and their total investment in higher education could not increase proportionally, therefore, the average level of their government expenditure per tertiary student between 2001 and 2011 was still with negative growth. Finally, the government expenditure as a percentage of GDP in China was on the rise from 2001 to 2011; especially, its number in 2011 was close to 0.8%.[4] Figure 3.2 shows that the government expenditure on higher education has a weakly positive relationship with the level of economic development in a country.

54 *Adequacy and equity of financial resources*

As can be seen from Figure 3.3, government expenditure on higher education as a percentage of total public expenditure in the Western developed countries was no longer substantially higher than the percentages in other country categories and was basically in the middle, even lower than the average percentage in major developing countries with the exception of certain years. Second, the government expenditure on higher education as a percentage of total public expenditure in Asian developed countries was substantially lower than the percentages in other categories of countries and lower than the percentage in China, which did not exceed 2% between 2001 and 2011 and declined slightly after 2008. Third, the government expenditure on higher education as a percentage of total public expenditure in major developing countries fluctuated,[5] but its average was higher than the percentage in the Western developed countries for many years. Finally, China's government expenditure on higher education as a percentage of total public expenditure from 2001 to 2010 basically varied around 3%, but in 2011 there was a substantial rise, reaching 3.44%. Among the developed countries, their government expenditure on higher education as a percentage of total public expenditure was lower than the percentage in developing countries and changed little with a stable trend between 2001 and 2011. We speculate that this results from the difference in the investment system of higher education between developed and developing countries, as well as the relative stability of the scale and financial system of higher education in developed countries. Higher education in developed countries was already in the stage of massification before the 21st century, and many of them had achieved universal access to higher education. Higher education on such a large scale was never possible with relying only on government investment, therefore most developed countries gradually chose a diversified investment system since the 1990s. For countries like the United States and Japan where private higher education is the main body, the share of government expenditure on higher education is not very large (usually less than 50%), and the funds for higher education mainly come from tuition fees, social services, donations, and financial investment. However, for countries in Western Europe, like Germany, France, and Italy, their percentages remain high (usually larger than 60%),[6] mainly due to the dominant place taken by public higher education institutions. Higher education investment in developing countries, such as India and China, still relies on government expenditure, and government expenditure accounts for a relatively high proportion of total higher education investment, approaching or surpassing 50%.[7] This phenomenon reflects the relatively high level of emphasis and government efforts by major developing countries, including China, to invest in higher education between 2001 and 2011.

In order to further examine the correlations between the government expenditure on higher education as a percentage of GDP (i.e., the proportion of public investment in higher education), this study calculated the correlation coefficients on three indicators in all sample countries, and calculated the correlation coefficients on three indicators in each of the three categories of countries. The results are presented in Table 3.2. From this table, it can be found that for the full sample, there are significant positive correlations between the proportion of public

Table 3.2 The correlation coefficients between the proportion of public investment in higher education, GDP, and total public expenditure

	Proportion of public investment in higher education			
	Full sample	Western developed countries	Asian developed countries	Major developing countries
GDP	0.197**	0.217*	0.123	−0.015
Total public expenditure	0.201**	0.214*	0.124	−0.024

Note: *, **, *** statistically significant at the 0.1, 0.05, and 0.01 level, respectively.

investment in higher education and GDP or total public expenditure in most countries, which are significant at the level of 0.05. From the perspective of country categories, the Western developed countries' proportion of public investment in higher education is also positively related to their GDP or total public expenditure, which are significant at the level of 0.1. Although there are positive correlations between Asian developed countries' proportion of public investment in higher education and GDP or total public expenditure, the relations are not statistically significant. The major developing countries are more special, and their proportions of public investment in higher education investment are negatively correlated with GDP or total public expenditure, but they are not statistically significant. However, overall speaking, the sample countries' proportions of public investment in higher education are significantly related to GDP and total public expenditure, and there are some differences in the degree of correlations between different country categories.

3.2 Equity of government expenditure on higher education

The fairness of educational financial funds means that the allocation of educational financial funds is based on the principle of "equal opportunities", which ensures that every individual participating in the allocation of educational financial funds has equal opportunities to occupy educational funds. In other words, the way of resource allocation should ensure that all schools or educatees have the opportunity to obtain the same amount of resources under the same conditions. At present, there are several generally accepted principles for the fairness of educational financial funds: first, the principle of equal distribution; second, the principle of fiscal neutrality; third is to adjust the principle of special needs; fourth, the principle of cost compensation; and fifth, the principle of public resources flowing from affluence to poverty. From the view of public finance, fiscal balance refers to the balanced status of governments' revenue and expenditure at all levels (Public Finance Balance Project Team, 2006). For the higher education sector, fiscal balance can be understood both internally and externally. The internal balance refers to the status that public finance is distributed evenly across different sectors; the direct indicator is

56 *Adequacy and equity of financial resources*

the degree to which local higher education's financial dependence is on the local economies. If the degree of dependence is high, it demonstrates that higher education lacks financial independence and stability, and the financial resources of higher education are easily crowded out by other sectors. This can be measured by fiscal neutrality. The external balance refers to the status that difference exists in the distribution of government expenditure on higher education between different regions (generally in terms of the province). If there is a greater difference between the government expenditure on higher education across regions, the more unbalanced the distribution of higher education resources is, affecting whether to follow the principle of equal distribution of financial funds. This section will examine the balance of China's government expenditure on higher education from both internal and external perspectives, so as to reflect the fairness of the allocation of the financial funds of higher education. Unlike the method used in the analysis of adequacy in the previous section, this section does not use an international comparative approach, but uses the relevant data of 31 provinces and municipalities in China to examine the equity of Chinese higher education finance from the three aspects of neutrality, difference, and convergence.

3.2.1 Neutrality of higher education finance

3.2.1.1 The correlation coefficient between the government expenditure per tertiary student and GDP per capita

In this section, the correlation coefficient between the government expenditure per tertiary student and GDP per capita is simply termed "correlation coefficient". This indicator is mainly used to investigate the correlation between the government expenditure per tertiary student and GDP per capita in provinces and municipalities, which is one of the key indicators to measure the neutrality of higher education finance. According to studies on education finance (Du & Sun, 2009), the threshold of this indicator is generally set at 0.5, which means that if the correlation coefficient between the government expenditure per tertiary student and GDP per capita is less than 0.5, it demonstrates that the government expenditure on higher education is not highly dependent on the local economy, so that the internal balance is relatively strong.

Here, this study used data on the government expenditure per tertiary student and GDP per capita for the years 2006–2016 from 31 provinces and municipalities to calculate correlation coefficients, and the results are presented in Figure 3.4. Observing the graph, it can be seen that the correlation coefficient has been showing a relatively stable downward trend, from 0.76 in 2006 to 0.51 in 2012, and then slightly climbed to 0.58 in 2013 and 2014, and then declined again. Nevertheless, for most years during 2006–2016, the correlation coefficient between the government expenditure per tertiary student and GDP per capita was all above 0.5, leaving 2015 alone to be 0.49. This shows that China's higher education finance is still moderately dependent on the local economy and lacks the necessary financial independence, which implies moderate internal balance.

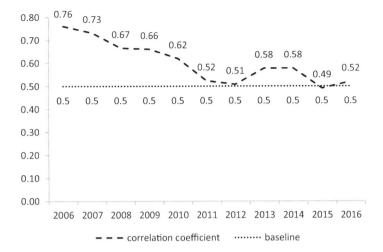

Figure 3.4 Correlation coefficient between the government expenditure per tertiary student and GDP per capita.

3.2.1.2 *The elasticity coefficient of the government expenditure per tertiary student to GDP per capita*

This study terms the elasticity coefficient of the government expenditure per tertiary student to the local GDP per capita simply as the "elasticity coefficient". This indicator is also one of the key indicators to examine the financial neutrality of higher education. The elasticity coefficient refers to the degree to which the unit change of the government expenditure per tertiary student is caused by the unit change of local GDP per capita. From the view of educational finance, the elasticity coefficient is the regression coefficient of the local GDP per capita on government expenditure per tertiary student,[8] which means the degree of sensitivity of higher education finance to the change of the local economy. If the elasticity coefficient is smaller, the higher education finance is less sensitive to the changes of the local economy, thus the degree of internal balance is higher. In contrast, if the elasticity coefficient becomes larger, the higher education finance is more sensitive to the changes of the local economy, thus the degree of internal balance is lower. Similar to the correlation coefficient, the elasticity coefficient also has a certain threshold. Generally speaking, if the elasticity coefficient is less than 0.1, it is considered that higher education finance is less dependent on the local economy, which means that the internal balance of higher education finance is higher.

The study conducted an econometric analysis of data from 31 provinces and municipalities from 2006 to 2016, collected the elasticity coefficients for each year, and plotted the results in Figure 3.5 (baseline 0.1). As can be seen from the figure, similar to the correlation coefficient, the elasticity coefficient is also

58 *Adequacy and equity of financial resources*

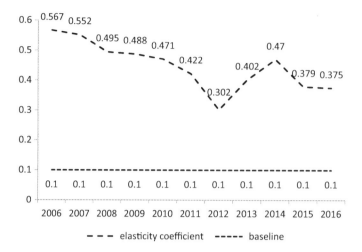

Figure 3.5 The elasticity coefficient of the government expenditure per tertiary students to GDP per capita.

basically in the downward channel. In 2006, the elasticity coefficient of the government expenditure per tertiary student to local GDP per capita was 0.57, and fell to a low level of 0.30 in 2012, then increased again, and stayed around 0.38 in 2015 and 2016. Nevertheless, the elasticity coefficient of higher education finance in China has almost been higher than the baseline 0.1, which shows that the government expenditure on higher education is too sensitive to the local economy, resulting in the weak independence of higher education finance, as well as the moderate degree of internal balance.

3.2.2 *Differences in the allocation of government expenditure per tertiary student*

There are many indicators to measure external balance (or regional imbalance) in educational finance, such as the Gini coefficient and the Theil coefficient. The Atkinson index, chosen in this study, has the advantage of adjusting the degree of preference (or aversion) to imbalances by setting the parameter *e* to better reflect the actual status of the economy (Liu, 2003). This index can be calculated as follows:

$$A_e = 1 - \left[(1/n) \sum_{i=1}^{n} [y_i / u]^{1-e} \right]^{1/(1-e)} \tag{3.1}$$

In the equation, A_e indicates the Atkinson index under given preference *e*; y_i indicates the government expenditure per tertiary student in province *i*; and *u* indicates the sensitivity-equivalent average expenditure. The Atkinson index is valued between 0 and 1, where 0 represents a fully balanced state and 1 represents a completely unbalanced state. Therefore, the closer the Atkinson index is to 0, the more balanced the financial allocation of higher education.

The study calculated the Atkinson index of China and its six regions[9] for the period 2006–2016, and the results are shown in Table 3.3, while Figure 3.6 uses a line chart to show the trends in different regions in a more intuitive way. From the view of the Atkinson index of the whole country, there was a relatively stable downward trend, from 0.122 in 2006 to 0.063 in 2016, indicating that the balance of higher education finance in China is increasing year by year. However, from the view of different regions, there was a quite different picture, which can be broadly divided into two groups: the first group, represented by North China, is of a decrease after an increase; the second group, represented by East China, is of an increase after the decrease. For the first group, in 2006, the Atkinson index in North China was almost twice the national level, mainly due to the imbalance in higher education finance between Beijing, Tianjin, and Hebei. However, after 2011, owing to the progress under national strategies such as Beijing–Tianjin–Hebei collaborative development, the Atkinson index in North China maintained a steady downward trend and was much lower than in other regions. For the second group, the Atkinson index in East China was only 0.056 in 2006, well below the national level, but suddenly rose to 0.169 after 2014, much higher than in other regions over the same period. This is mainly due to the imbalance of economic development within the region, resulting in the increasing imbalance of higher education finance. In East China, the difference in government expenditure per tertiary student was widening between the advanced provinces represented by Shanghai, Jiangsu, and Zhejiang, and the developing provinces of Anhui, Jiangxi, and Fujian.

Through this analysis of the fiscal balance of higher education, it can be seen that the degree of fiscal balance of higher education in China is still moderate, which is reflected in the moderate internal balance measured by indicators such as the correlation coefficient and elasticity coefficient, and the moderate external balance measured by the Atkinson index. Nevertheless, it can be found from the analysis of external balance by calculating the Atkinson index between 2006 and 2016 that the fiscal balance of the country as a whole was steadily increasing, which seemingly implies a tendency toward equalization. In studies related to public finance, this trend is referred to as the "convergence" of regional differences. This will be further analyzed in the next section.

3.2.3 The convergence of government expenditure on higher education

The concept of convergence stems from economics and is used to describe the economic phenomenon that "the levels of economic development in different countries are gradually getting closer over time". This concept was first proposed by American economists Barro and Sala-i-Martin (1992) and empirically tested with econometric models, and then widely used in researching regional differences

60 *Adequacy and equity of financial resources*

Table 3.3 Atkinson index of government expenditure per tertiary student

	2006	2007	2008	2009	2010	2011	2012	2013	2014	2015	2016
National	0.122	0.113	0.102	0.107	0.110	0.100	0.061	0.067	0.070	0.074	0.063
North	0.268	0.242	0.200	0.259	0.215	0.098	0.062	0.101	0.060	0.055	0.008
Northeast	0.016	0.004	0.006	0.000	0.026	0.239	0.175	0.173	0.003	0.084	0.079
East	0.056	0.069	0.062	0.047	0.040	0.085	0.007	0.006	0.169	0.175	0.135
Central South	0.058	0.029	0.012	0.031	0.025	0.029	0.030	0.035	0.014	0.035	0.032
Southwest	0.022	0.023	0.018	0.015	0.051	0.022	0.034	0.004	0.011	0.006	0.008
Northwest	0.121	0.161	0.168	0.130	0.145	0.002	0.008	0.003	0.003	0.007	0.006

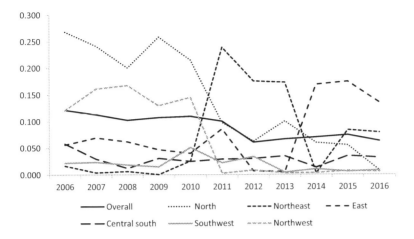

Figure 3.6 Atkinson index of government expenditure per tertiary student.

in economics and public finance. In the studies of educational finance in China, there were also some in-depth investigations on convergence, but most of them concentrated on basic education (Gu, 2008). Drawing on the methods used in the relevant research, this study used panel data from 31 provinces and municipalities in 2006–2016 to analyze the convergence of government expenditure on higher education in China. The model specification was set as follows:

$$\ln(exp_{i,t}) = e^{-\beta} \cdot \ln(exp_{i,t-1}) + aX_{it} + u_{it} \qquad (3.2)$$

In the equation, $exp_{i,t}$ and $exp_{i,t-1}$ indicate the *i*th province's government expenditure per tertiary student in year *t* and *t*–1, respectively. X indicates those control variables. The most important variable in the model is $e^{-\beta}$, which indicates the regression coefficient of the government expenditure per tertiary student in year *t*–1 on government expenditure per tertiary student in year *t*. If $e^{-\beta} > 1$ (equivalent as $\beta < 0$), it demonstrates that government expenditure per tertiary student in year *t* is always greater than that in year *t*–1, implying no convergence. Contrarily, if $e^{-\beta} < 1$ (equivalent as $\beta > 0$), it implies the existence of convergence. In addition, if no control variable X is added to the model, the model is an absolute convergence model (i.e., no other condition exists); and if some control variable X is added to the model, the model is called a conditional convergence model (i.e., a convergence conditional on the control variable X).

In order to further calculate the rate of convergence, Equation 3.2 can be transformed equivalently as follows:

$$\ln\left(\frac{exp_{i,t}}{exp_{i,t-1}}\right) = b \cdot \ln(exp_{i,t-1}) + aX_{it} + u_{it} \qquad (3.3)$$

where $b = -(1-e^{-\beta})$ becomes a key variable in determining whether the series is convergent or not. If $b < 0$, it indicates that the government expenditure per tertiary student is convergent, and β indicates the rate of convergence. If $b > 0$, then there exists no convergence.

Based on the preceding econometric model, this study used the population-averaged (PA) method in the panel data method to estimate the absolute convergence of government expenditure on higher education in the whole country as well as the six regions (North, Northeast, East, Central South, Southwest, and Northwest), and the results are shown in Table 3.4. According to the results of Table 3.4, the regression coefficient of the national model for the period 2006–2016 was $b = -0.062$, and it was statistically significant, indicating that there existed absolute convergence for government expenditure per tertiary in the country, and the rate of convergence was $\beta = 6.40\%$. Judging from the results of the six regions, the government expenditures per tertiary student in these regions were mostly of a certain degree of convergence (b valued between -0.079 and -0.159), of which the rate of converging in Central/Western China was faster, with the rates in Central South, Southwest, and Northwest China being 17.23%, 14.22%, and 15.37%, respectively. In comparison, those eastern regions were convergent at a slower pace, and the rates of convergence in North, Northeast, and East China were 9.64%, 8.55%, and 8.22%, respectively. It can be seen that for both the whole country and its regions, the difference in government expenditure per tertiary student was narrowing gradually, and the rate of the central or western region was faster than that of the eastern.

In the next step, on the basis of the absolute convergence model, this study added two control variables, the log of GDP per capita and the student–teacher ratio, to investigate whether the government expenditure per tertiary student of the whole country and its regions were conditionally convergent. Here, the log of GDP per capita is mainly used to control for differences in the levels of economic development in the provinces, while the student–teacher ratio is used to control for differences in the higher education quality in the provinces. The test results are presented in Table 3.5.

According to the results of Table 3.5, when controlling for the log of GDP per capita and the student–teacher ratio, the results changed substantially. First, the regression coefficient of the national model was smaller ($b = -0.051$), indicating that although convergence exists, the rate of convergence slowed ($\beta = 5.23\%$). Second, although the regression coefficients of the northeastern and north regions were negative, they were no longer statistically significant, indicating that after adding control variables, there were no significant conditional convergences in these two regions. Third, the regression coefficients of the central-south and the northwestern regions became larger, indicating that after controlling the level of economic development and the quality of higher education, these two regions converged faster, with rates of convergence reaching 29.18% and 20.56%, respectively. On the whole, there were still great differences in the government expenditure per tertiary student in the eastern and northeastern regions, which show no trend of conditional convergence, while the internal differences within the north,

Table 3.4 Absolute convergence of government expenditure on higher education

	National	North	Northeast	East	Central South	Southwest	Northwest
b	−0.062***	−0.092***	−0.082**	−0.079**	−0.159***	−0.133***	−0.143***
	(0.011)	(0.026)	(0.035)	(0.039)	(0.024)	(0.042)	(0.034)
Constant	0.701***	0.990***	0.897***	0.859**	1.597***	1.348***	1.443***
	(0.099)	(0.242)	(0.325)	(0.360)	(0.224)	(0.381)	(0.309)
β	6.40%	9.64%	8.55%	8.22%	17.23%	14.22%	15.37%
N	310	50	30	70	60	50	50

Table 3.5 Conditional convergence for government expenditure on higher education

	National	North	Northeast	East	Central South	Southwest	Northwest
b	−0.051***	−0.082**	−0.077	−0.064	−0.256***	−0.127*	−0.187***
	(0.013)	(0.034)	(0.066)	(0.053)	(0.041)	(0.068)	(0.036)
Log of GDP per capita	−0.012	−0.018	−0.000	−0.015	0.103***	−0.008	0.081**
	(0.011)	(0.041)	(0.080)	(0.056)	(0.035)	(0.065)	(0.038)
Student–teacher ratio	0.000	−0.005	0.025	−0.013	0.018	−0.018	0.041***
	(0.007)	(0.027)	(0.067)	(0.025)	(0.033)	(0.041)	(0.015)
Constant	0.723***	1.168*	0.429	1.109**	1.082	1.700*	0.340
	(0.166)	(0.617)	(1.378)	(0.536)	(0.682)	(0.875)	(0.419)
β	5.23%	8.55%	8.00%	6.61%	29.18%	13.54%	20.56%
N	310	50	30	70	60	50	50

central, and western regions were narrowing gradually, especially in Central South and Southwest China with an accelerating rate of convergence.

3.3 Summary

From the perspective of adequacy and equity, this chapter examines the allocation of government expenditure on higher education in China. Analysis based on international time series data shows that between 2001 and 2011, the government expenditure per tertiary student in China was considerably lower than that in Western developed countries and Asian developed countries, but gradually approached the average level of major developing countries and exceeded that level in 2010. The government expenditure on higher education as a percentage of GDP in China is lower than the average of Western developed countries and major developing countries, but considerably higher than the average of Asian developed countries, and China's government expenditure on higher education as a percentage of GDP was on the rise between 2001 and 2011. The government expenditure on higher education as a percentage of total public expenditure in China had surpassed Western developed countries and Asian developed countries, however, there was still a gap with the major developing countries in some years. The statistical results of these international comparisons reflect the high degree of emphasis and government efforts on investing in higher education in China, and the adequacy of government expenditure on higher education was gradually increasing. Analysis based on provincial panel data shows that China's higher education finance was not performing well on the internal balance indicators as measured by the correlation coefficient and elasticity coefficient, as well as the external balance indicators as measured by the Atkinson index. Nevertheless, by using the Atkinson index to analyze the external balance between 2006 and 2016, it shows that the external balance of financial allocation for higher education was steadily increasing at the national level. In addition, the PA model shows that there was absolute convergence of government expenditure on higher education in China and its six regions. And in both the whole country and its regions, the difference in government expenditure per tertiary student was narrowing gradually, and the rate of the central and western region was faster than that of the eastern. Meanwhile, the results of the conditional convergence model, which, including the level of economic development and quality of higher education, show that there were still great differences in the government expenditure per tertiary student in the eastern and northeastern regions, which show no trend of conditional convergence. Whereas the internal differences within the north, central, and western regions were narrowing gradually, especially in Central South and Southwest China with an accelerating rate of convergence.

Notes

1 According to the data from China Education Finance Statistics Yearbook (2012), in 2011 the total revenue of Chinese higher education institutions was 668 billion yuan, of which 376.3 billion yuan were from government funds and 181.2 billion yuan were from tuition fees, making up 54.7% and 26.3% of total revenue, respectively.

2 The gross enrollment rates of higher education in India, China, and Thailand were 9.78%, 9.83%, and 39.23%, respectively in 2001, and these numbers increased to 18.23%, 23.32%, and 50.03% in 2010.
3 The gross enrollment rates of higher education in Japan and South Korea were 49.3% and 83.3%, respectively, in 2001, and these numbers changed to 56.8% and 79% in 2010. South Korea's gross enrollment rate has been negative in recent years.
4 This is related to the policies proposed by the China National Medium- and Long-Term Outlines on Educational Reform and Development (2010–2020), such as "prioritize education development", "increase investment in education", and "raise the government expenditure on education as a percentage of GDP".
5 Another reason is because there are some missing values.
6 Countries in Western Europe have a larger share of government expenditure in total higher education expenditure, the GDPs in these countries are ranked top in the world, and their overall scales of higher education are smaller than developing countries due to their smaller population size, therefore, their government expenditure on higher education as a percentage of total public expenditure is less than developing countries.
7 For example in 2005, the government expenditure as a percentage of total higher education expenditure in the United States, Japan, India, and China were 34.7%, 33.7%, 80.9%, and 45%, respectively. Data of the United States, Japan, and India was obtained from UNESCO Education Data and Indicators, 2009; China's data was obtained from the China Education Finance Statistics Yearbook.
8 This can be expressed with the equation $\ln exp_i = \beta \ln(pgdp_i)$, where $\ln exp_i$ indicates the log of government expenditure per tertiary student in each province, $\ln pgdp_i$ indicates the log of GDP per capita in each province, and β is the elasticity coefficient.
9 According to the categories of regions made by the China National Statistical Bureau, North China includes Beijing Tianjin, Hebei, Shanxi, and Inner Mongolia; Northeast China includes Liaoning, Jilin, and Heilongjiang; East China includes Shanghai, Jiangsu, Zhejiang, Anhui, Fujian, Jiangxi, and Shandong; Central South China includes Henan, Hubei, Hunan, Guangdong, Guangxi, and Hainan; Southwest China includes Chongqing, Sichuan, Guizhou, Yunnan, and Tibet; and Northwest China includes Shan'xi, Gansu, Qinghai, Ningxia, and Xinjiang.

References

Barro, R. J., & Sala-I-Martin, X. (1992). Public finance in models of economic growth. *Review of Economic Studies*, *4*, 645–661.

Du, Y. H., & Sun, Z. J. (2009). *Research on China Compulsory Education Finance*. Beijing: Beijing Normal University Press.

Fang, F., & Liu, Z. Y. (2018). Change and revelation of state funding for higher education in China from 2005 to 2015. *China Higher Education Research*, *4*, 78–85.

Gu, J. F. (2008). An empirical research on China basic education finance convergence: On spatial econometrics view. *Education & Economy*, *4*, 48–53.

Hu, Y. Z. (2012). An empirical analysis on provincial regionally higher educational financial differences. *Research in Educational Development*, *32*(1), 36–40.

Li, W. L. (2008). *From Scarcity to Adequacy: Research on Higher Education Demand and Supply*. Beijing: Education Science Press.

Liu, Z. W. (2003). Review on methods measuring income inequality. *Journal of Statistics and Information*, *5*, 28–32.

Public Finance Balance Project Team (PFBPT). (2006). Practice and experience of public finance balance worldwide. *Review of Economic Research*, *10*, 14–41.

Sun, Z. J. (2009). Changes in university income in a decade of expansion in China: An interpretation. *Tsinghua Journal of Education, 4*, 72–80.

Ye, J. (2015). Trends and factors decomposition: The higher education across equity issue of expenditure of Chinese provinces based on the Gini coefficient and its decomposition and structural decomposition technique. *China Higher Education Research, 10*, 36–43.

Yue, C. J. (2011). The supply and demand of public tertiary expenditure: An international comparative study. *Peking University Education Review, 3*, 92–104+191.

4 Forecasting the scale of public investment in higher education

4.1 Research background

The 1993 "Outline of China's Education Reform and Development" (henceforth "The Outline") clearly sets out the goal of fiscal spending on higher education as a percentage of gross domestic product (GDP) reaching 4%. This indicator was also the baseline for measuring the level of fiscal input to education in major countries worldwide at that time. But it was not until 20 years later that China's national fiscal spending on education exceeded 4% of the GDP for the first time. However, the belated 4% involved China's fiscal policy on public education in a new predicament as some Chinese scholars began to use the "post-4% era" as the theme to discuss the future directions of China's fiscal spending on public education, as well as the issue of establishment of a long-term assurance mechanism for educational investment (Bao, 2012; Zhang & Lan, 2014; Hu & Tang, 2014). However, the studies of forecasting the scale of public investment in higher education are very limited.

For the past 20 years, China's higher education has been in a period of rapid development. After the implementation of higher education projects like the "211 Project", "985 Project", "2011 Collaborative Innovation Plan", and "double first-class" construction, China has invested enormous financial funds to support the development of universities, which has made the reputation and influence of Chinese universities in the world also rise rapidly. On the 2018 Global University Rankings released by *U.S. News & World Report*, there are 136 Chinese universities on the list (including Hong Kong and Macao), ranking second in the world, which fully demonstrates the remarkable outcomes achieved in the development of higher education in China. President Xi Jinping pointed out in the report of the 19th National Congress of the Communist Party of China that the intensified development and double first-class construction would be the top priorities of China's higher education development in the future. However, the GDP growth rate in China was less than 8% in 2012 and since then it has been falling to a "new normal" of economic development. Meanwhile, the government's financial support for higher education declined relative to that of other educational levels. According to the 2016 National Statistical Bulletin on the Implementation of Education Funds, among the indicators of budgetary educational expenditure and

DOI: 10.4324/9781003250524-4

operational expenditure per student at various educational levels, the growth rate of budgetary educational expenditure per student for higher education was the smallest (only 3.33%), and operational expenditure per student for higher education even had a negative growth rate, which would undoubtedly affect the steady development of higher education in China in the future. Therefore, whether the Chinese government can continue to provide adequate financial support for higher education has become an urgent question to be studied.

The practice of public investment in higher education and the course of economic development in developed countries, such as the United States, United Kingdom, and Japan, show that the scale of public investment in higher education is positively related to the speed of economic development (Barro, 1995; Krueger & Lindahl, 2001). Generally speaking, in a period of economic take-off, the scale of government-appropriated funds for higher education will grow faster, whereas in an economic downturn, the scale of government-appropriated funds for higher education will slow down and sometimes even be negative. In times of rapid economic growth, the increase in demand for higher education will increase the government investment in higher education. For example, in the mid-1960s and mid-1970s, when the U.S. economy was growing at a high rate, higher education grew at a rapid pace, whereas after the 1980s, as a result of the economic downturn, government-appropriated funds for higher education were relatively smaller. The development history of the United Kingdom, Japan, Australia, and other countries has similar characteristics (Zhu, 2004). This phenomenon also provides a practical basis for this study to build a forecasting model of the proportion of public investment in higher education by using the data of China's economic growth and higher education development scale in the past 20 years. Therefore, the central issue of this study is how to use data on economic growth and the scale of higher education development to scientifically predict the scale of China's public investment in higher education between the years 2021 and 2025.

4.2 Literature review

According to the internationally conventional method of linking the total scale of education investment with the level of economic development, Jin (1990) provided a flexible idea for forecasting the scale of public investment in higher education, by setting the upper limit as the total amount of public investment that the national economic strength could possibly afford and by setting the lower limit according to the minimum supply of graduates required by a country's economic growth. Based on the historical data of the number of enrolled students, Li (1988) constructed an econometric model to predict the scale of public investment in higher education. Based on China's data of government expenditure on higher education and gross national product during 1990–1999, Lang (2002) used various specifications of regression models to determine the adaptivity between the scale of public investment in higher education and the scale of national economic

70 *Forecasting the scale of public investment*

development and to forecast the scale of public investment in higher education in China in 2010. Jin (1990) summarized three kinds of methods to project the scale of public investment in higher education: (1) projecting by using the demand of social and economic development; (2) projecting by using the number of enrolled students at all educational levels and types, and the supply of talent needed to meet the goal of socioeconomic development; and (3) projecting by referencing to the national education cost standards. This study is intended to draw on the first two methods to predict the scale of public investment in higher education in China in the post-4% era.

The projection of the scale of public investment in education is closely related to the proportion of public investment in education, which reflects the government's emphasis and efforts on public education. Once the proportion of public investment in education is given, the scale of the government's public investment in education is determined, and the share that the government should allocate to education from the "cake" of public expenditure is clear.[1] In order to achieve the government's strategic goal that education should run ahead of the current economic development, it is necessary to ensure that the proportion of investment in education is higher than the international average level benchmarking on China's economic development level (Yue & Ding, 2003). Chinese scholars, including Yue and Ding (2003) and Liu and Yuan (2007), used the method of economic modeling based on cross-national data to forecast the proportion of China's public investment in education for 2010 and 2020, and their predicted values were about 4–4.5%.[2] The international studies on forecasting education finance focus more on the scale of investment (Rossi & Gilmartin, 1982; Tang & Yin, 2012), while there are relatively more Chinese studies focusing on the proportion of public investment in education (Yao & Ma, 2016), and some Chinese scholars have conducted research on the proportion of public investment in higher education (Li, 1988; Yue, 2011; Tang & Hu, 2015; Zhao & Hu, 2017). And this issue needs to be continuously studied, because it is not only related to the sustainable development of higher education but also related to the support and guarantee of government-appropriated funds that universities need to reform the talent-training system so as to respond to the changes of talent demand driven by economic and social development in the new normal.[3] In fact, despite the increasing scale of public investment in higher education, facing the vast expansion of higher education enrollment after 1999, the government expenditure per tertiary student declined year by year, and the government expenditure per local tertiary student fell even faster (Sun, 2009). Another noteworthy fact is that since 2004, private higher education institutions in China have experienced rapid development, with the undergraduate enrollment exceeding 1 million, reaching more than 5.5 million by 2013, around 18.43% of the total undergraduate enrollment in Chinese higher education.[4] As a result, the share of the private sector in total investment in higher education was increasing year by year. Taking the indicator of the proportion of tuition fees to total higher education revenue as an example, this indicator had climbed since the vast expansion in 1999, from 21.30% to a peak of 33.68% in 2008, then declined moderately, but remained above the level of 25%.

The study by Yue (2011) found that China's public investment in higher education did not reach the desired level of supply with response to the level of economic development, nor did it meet the basic needs for the development of higher education. From the perspective of supply capacity, the proportion of China's public investment in higher education could reach 0.81% and 0.90% in 2012 and 2020, respectively. From the perspective of essential demand, the index of public expenditure per tertiary student should exceed 70.0 and 53.6 in 2012 and 2020, respectively. Moreover, the proportion of public investment in higher education should fluctuate between 2000 and 2007. Yue's study is valuable in its forecasting methods, but considering the period of sampled data in the econometric model is 2000–2007, its forecasts are difficult to compare with the trend of global economic slowdown after 2008 caused by the financial crisis. Particularly for China, its GDP growth has slowed substantially since 2012, moving from a high growth rate for the 30-year period of "reform and opening up" to the new normal with a medium to high growth rate, while Yue's study (2011) performed the forecasting by setting the average growth rate of GDP per capita for the period 2008–2020 at 9%, which is almost impossible to achieve. Therefore, it is necessary to re-estimate the coefficients of models by using new time series data, so as to perform more reasonable forecasts of the proportion of China's public investment in higher education in 2021–2025.[5] The scientific forecasts of the scale and proportion of public investment in higher education in China in 2021–2025 will be the central issue to be solved in this study, which is also the main contribution of this study.[6]

4.3 Data and method

The study on the scale of public investment in higher education is find how big is the portion of the government's public investment in higher education. This study constructs a forecasting model of the proportion of public investment in higher education, and scientifically estimates the scale and proportion of public investment in higher education in China in the future.

4.3.1 Data and sample

The purpose of this study is to use historical data on higher education and economic development in China from 1995 to 2014,[7] to forecast enrollment in higher education, and the proportion and scale of public investment in higher education between 2021 and 2025. The variables in this study mainly include the government funding for higher education as a percentage of GDP, GDP growth rate, the proportion of tuition fees to total higher education revenue, and the enrollment size. These variables are related to indicators such as GDP, GDP growth rate, total higher education revenue, government funding for high education, income from higher education tuition fees, enrollment size, and the gross enrollment rate in higher education. Among them, the data of GDP and GDP growth rate are from the China Statistical Yearbook; the data of total higher education revenue, government funding for higher education, and income from higher education

72 Forecasting the scale of public investment

Table 4.1 Descriptive statistics on the main variables

Variable	Description of the variable	N	Mean	Standard deviation	Average annual increase
Y	Government funding for higher education as a percentage of GDP (%)	20	0.54	0.16	5.05%
dGDP	GDP growth rate (%)	20	9.61	1.77	9.61%
REDUR	Gross enrollment rate (%)	20	19.53	8.87	9.17%
TSHARE	The proportion of tuition fees to the total higher education revenue (%)	20	25.06	6.99	3.52%
STUSIZE	Number of enrolled students (10,000)	20	1469.57	904.06	12.64%

Notes: The average annual increase, i.e., the mean value of the annual increase, is calculated as $\left(\frac{\text{this year} - \text{last year}}{\text{this year}}\right) \times 100\% \Big/ 19$. Since dGDP itself is already a rate variable, its average annual increase is the same as its mean.

tuition fees are from the data of regular higher education institutions in the China Educational Finance Statistical Yearbook [including higher education institutions (HEIs) offering degree programs and higher vocational colleges but not those adult HEIs]; data on the enrollment size are from the China Statistical Yearbook, including undergraduates in regular HEIs, master students, and doctoral students; and the data of gross enrollment rates in higher education are from statistics on the access to higher education for the 18- to 22-year-old population in the Chinese Yearbook of Education Statistics. The descriptive statistics for the main variables are presented in Table 4.1.

As can be found in Table 4.1, over the 20 years from 1995 to 2014, government funding for higher education as a percentage of GDP had a mean value of 0.54 and a standard deviation of 0.16, with an average annual increase of 5.05%. The GDP growth rate had a mean value of 9.61 and a standard deviation of 1.77. The gross enrollment in higher education increased steadily, from 7.2% in 1995 to 37.5% in 2014, with an average annual increase of 9.17%. The share of higher education tuition fees to total revenue also remained a growing trend, from 13.57% in 1995 to 23.27% in 2014, with an average annual increase of 3.52%. Finally, the size of higher education enrollment maintained a high growth rate, with an average annual increase of 12.64%.

4.3.2 Specification of the forecasting model

To build the forecasting model, we mainly draw on the idea of Li's (1988) forecasting of the scale of public investment in higher education in China and use the time series methods for modeling. Based on the historical data from 1995 to 2014 with the rapid development of higher education scale and economy in China, the forecasting model of the proportion of public investment in higher education is constructed from the perspective that higher education development should meet the demand of the economic development, and its specification can be given as

$$Y_t = b_0 + b_1 STUSIZE_t + b_2 dGDP_t + b_3 TSHARE_t + U_t \quad (4.1)$$

$$STUSIZE_t = c_0 + c_1 REDUR_t + c_2 dGDP_t + c_3 TSHARE_t + V_t \quad (4.2)$$

In the equations, Y_t is the dependent variable, which indicates the proportion of China's public investment in higher education in year t. $STUSIZE_t$ indicates the full-time equivalent (FTE) enrollment in higher education institutions in year t (in millions).[8] $dGDP_t$ or $dGDP_{t-1}$ indicates the GDP growth rate in period t or $t-1$, respectively. $TSHARE_t$ indicates the proportion of tuition fees to total higher education revenue. U_t and V_t are the random error terms in the two equations.

STUSIZE is included in the model because the current size of higher education development will affect the scale of public investment in higher education. Therefore, the model includes the FTE enrollment in higher education as an independent variable. Practice in many countries shows that the growth rate of GDP is positively related to the growth rate of public investment in higher education. During the accelerating period of economic development, the growth rate of public investment in higher education will generally be relatively high, and during the stable and decelerating period of economic development, the government will reduce or slow down public investment in higher education. Therefore, the GDP growth variable (dGDP) is added to the model to reflect the adaptation of the proportion of public investment in higher education to the change of the economic development pace. Under ordinary circumstances, the size of higher education is affected by the growth rate of economic development and gross enrollment rate, so we use two simultaneous equations to build a model to forecast the proportion of public investment in higher education. $REDUR_t$ is the gross enrollment ratio for higher education in year t. China's plan for higher education enrollment is formulated by the Ministry of Education according to the existing capacity of higher education institutions and the needs of economic development. Because the annual change in the size of higher education enrollment is affected by the admission rate set by the Ministry of Education, the admission rate differs among provinces, and the data are not included in the China Education Statistics Yearbook, this study substitutes it with the gross enrollment rate variable. In addition, as the previous analysis points out, the number of students in private higher education institutions has been close to one-fifth of total enrollment, and for institutional reasons, the funds for running Chinese private higher education institutions mainly rely on tuition fees, with very limited financial support received from the government. To control for the impact of the scale of students in private higher education institutions, the number of enrolled private students should be included in the model as a control variable, but considering that there is no data on enrollment in private higher education institutions before 2002 in the relevant statistical yearbook, we intend to use the proportion of tuition fees to the total revenue in higher education (TSHARE) as a proxy variable to control for the impact of student size in private higher education institutions.

4.4 Empirical results

4.4.1 Results of econometric modeling

Drawing on Li's (1988) forecasting perspective that higher education development adapts to the needs of economic development, based on the historical data of 20 years (1995–2014) with high-speed development of both higher education and economy, this study uses the two-stage least squares (2SLS) method to estimate the results, which can be found in Table 4.2. The main difference between model A and model B is that the former uses current GDP growth (namely $dGDP_t$) in the

Table 4.2 Estimates of the structural equation model

	Model A	Model B
Stage 2: Y_t		
$STUSIZE_t$	0.016***	0.017***
	(0.002)	(0.002)
$dGDP_t$	−0.018***	
	(0.004)	
$dGDP_{t-1}$		−0.017***
		(0.004)
$TSHARE_t$	0.004	0.002
	(0.002)	(0.002)
Constant	0.394***	0.413***
	(0.031)	(0.036)
N	20	19
R^2	0.944	0.939
Stage 1: $lnSTUSIZE_t$		
$dGDP_t$	0.398*	
	(0.203)	
$dGDP_{t-1}$		0.633***
		(0.169)
$TSHARE_t$	0.163*	0.165*
	(0.091)	(0.070)
$REDUR_t$	0.921***	0.926***
	(0.076)	(0.061)
Constant	−11.205***	−13.782***
	(1.454)	(1.376)
N	20	19
R^2	0.970	0.977

Notes: *, **, and *** indicate significant levels of 0.1, 0.05, and 0.01, respectively. Numbers in brackets are the robust standard errors.

first-stage regression, while the latter uses lagged GDP growth (namely $dGDP_{t-1}$) in the first-stage regression. The results of the regressions show that the estimated coefficients of the two models are relatively close, especially at the second stage. It is not difficult to find by comparing the R^2 of the two regressions, that the goodness of fit for both A and B does not differ substantially at two stages of regressions, with the former having a higher R^2 at the first forecasting stage, and the latter having a higher R^2 at the second forecasting stage. Taking into account the characteristics of a planned economy in China (the budget of the current year is mainly based on the final accounts of the previous year), the results of model B are used here for forecasting.

4.4.2 In-sample forecast accuracy

Forecast accuracy is an important guarantee for the scientificity of forecasting. Therefore, based on the results of the forecasting model, we calculate the in-sample (1996–2014) forecast accuracy, including two indicators: the deviation and the root-mean-square error (RMSE). The deviation refers to the degree to which the forecast value (E_i) deviates from the real value (R_i), which can be expressed as a percentage and calculated as $\dfrac{E_i - R_i}{R_i} \times 100\%$. RMSE can be a more accurate measure of the degree to which the forecasted value deviated from the real value, and its computing formula is $\sqrt[2]{\left(\sum E_i - R_i\right)^2 / n}$, where n indicates the sample size.

The left of Figure 4.1 presents the forecasted and real values of the enrollment size and provides statistical indicators of the forecast accuracy. From the results of the first-stage forecast of the enrollment size, the forecast values in 1996–2008 are generally accurate, and the deviations are more obvious in 2009–2014, and the magnitude of deviation changes from negative to positive. This is mainly due to the impact of the global financial crisis in 2009, and the issue of undergraduate students' job-searching became more critical in China. The Chinese government carried out the policy of expansion of postgraduate enrollment to reduce the

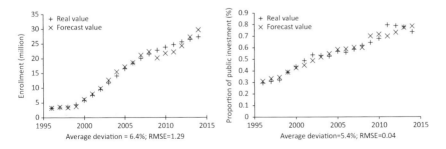

Figure 4.1 Predictive accuracy of the student size and investment ratio in higher education.

76 *Forecasting the scale of public investment*

pressure on employment. In that year, it was beginning to promote professional education programs for postgraduate students, bringing about the opportunity to expand the enrollment of postgraduate students. The number of postgraduate entrants in 2009 reached as many as 510,900, an increase of 14.4% over 2008. Overall, the average forecast deviation for all years was 6.4%, with the RMSE equal to 1.29. These statistics show that the first stage has high accuracy in predicting higher education enrollment.

Similarly, on the right of Figure 4.1, the forecast value and real value of the proportion of public investment in higher education are presented. As can be seen from the figure, at the second stage the results of the forecast value of the proportion of public investment in higher education are not substantially deviated in most years, but some obvious estimate biases can be found around 2010, the most prominent being in 2011. For this situation, we speculate that there are two reasons. On the one hand, the higher education enrollment size was underestimated in 2011; on the other hand, as the result of the public opinion and academia's concern about the issue that 4% had not been achieved, in 2011 the public investment in education increased substantially, the government expenditure on education as a percentage of GDP reached 3.93%, the national investment in education increased by 22.02% over 2010, and the public investment in higher education increased even more, with a 44.71% increase in the government expenditure per tertiary student, which was the largest increase among the per-student expenditure at all educational levels. Overall, the average forecast deviation of the proportion of public investment in higher education in all years was 5.4%, and the RMSE was only 0.04, both of which were better than the forecast values of enrollment size at the first stage. Therefore, it can be assumed that all the forecast deviations are within the acceptable range, the forecasting model is appropriate to the trend of China's economic and educational development, and the results of forecasting have relatively high accuracy.[9]

4.4.3 Forecast of higher education student size

Based on the results of the first-stage regression, we have forecasted the higher education student size in China between 2021 and 2025, and the results are shown in Table 4.3. In addition, Table 4.3 presents forecasted values of two key variables in the first stage of regression: the gross enrollment ratio and the proportion of tuition fees to total higher education revenue. Considering that the two variables themselves have some inherent trends, we use the time series recursive smoothing method for estimation. A recursive smoother is a kind of method that forecasts future development trends based on the changing pattern over time of the historical variable, and it occupies an important position in forecasting univariate time series data, which can make a dynamic out-of-sample prediction based on the historical trend of data. In this section, we mainly adopt the Holt–Winters (hwinters) method, which has the advantage of optimizing the forecast accuracy by adjusting the two parameters.

Table 4.3 Forecasted results of the higher education student size in China from 2021 to 2025

Year	Gross enrollment ratio (%)	Proportion of tuition fees to total revenue (%)	Student size (in millions) Upper-middle growth rate (6.5%)	Student size (in millions) Lower-middle growth rate (5.5%)
2021	51.15	24.41	41.74	41.11
2022	53.41	24.54	43.85	43.22
2023	55.67	24.67	45.97	45.33
2024	57.93	24.80	48.08	47.45
2025	60.19	24.93	50.20	49.56

The gross enrollment ratio of higher education has always been an important index of higher education development in China. "The Outline of the National Education Medium- and Long-Term Reform and Development Plan (2010–2020)" clearly states that China's gross enrollment ratio in higher education should reach 40% by 2020. However, the actual data show that after 2010, China's higher education has entered a period of leapfrog development: the gross enrollment ratio has successfully grown from 30% (2012) to 40% (2015). According to the latest data from the China Education Statistics Yearbook, China's gross enrollment rate in higher education reached 42.7% in 2016, ahead of the goal set by "The Outline". In line with this rapid development trend, we used hwinters (0.4, 0.6) to forecast the gross enrollment ratio in higher education, and found that between 2021 and 2025, China's higher education will continue to show a leapfrog trend, with a gross enrollment ratio of 60.19% by 2025.

To forecast the proportion of tuition fees to total higher education revenue, we need to consider the impacts of higher education expansion (starting from 1999) and private education (starting from 2004). We tried different combinations of parameters and compared their forecast accuracies, and finally decided to choose the results of hwinters (0.9, 0.1), not only because it conformed most to the existing changes of data, but also the average of forecasted values most approached the historical trend of 2004–2014. According to the forecasted results, from 2021 to 2025, China's proportion of tuition fees to total higher education revenue will remain at a relatively stable level, around 24%.

Finally, let us examine the growth situation of the student size. We set economic growth rates at two levels: upper-middle growth rate (6.5%) and lower-middle growth rate (5.5%). The forecasted results show that if China's economy maintains a high growth rate, then the higher education student size at all levels will maintain a rapid growth rate, from 41.74 million in 2021 to 50.2 million in 2025, an increase of 43.30% and 73.47% relative to 2016, with an average annual growth rate of 4.7%. If China's economy maintains a moderate and low growth rate, the growth of higher education student size at all levels will also be relatively moderate, from 41.11 million in 2021 to 49.56 million in 2025, an increase of

78 *Forecasting the scale of public investment*

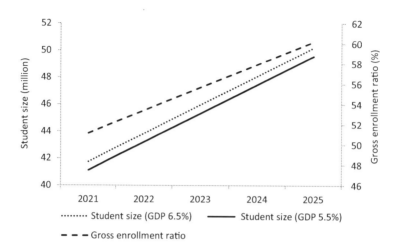

Figure 4.2 Forecasted values of gross enrollment ratio and student size for 2021–2025.

42.06% and 71.26% relative to 2016, with an average annual growth rate of 4.5%. It can be seen that as long as China's economy remains stable, under the circumstance of an increasing gross enrollment ratio year by year, the higher education student size will maintain a rapid growth trend during the 14th Five-Year Plan (see Figure 4.2).

4.4.4 Forecast of the proportion and scale of public investment in higher education

In the previous section, the forecasts of several key variables were performed according to the regression results of the first stage. Next, we will forecast the proportion and scale of public investment in higher education based on the forecasted results at the first stage and the regression results at the second stage. The results are shown in Table 4.4. Consistent with the assumption of economic growth rate in the first-stage forecast, we considered the upper-middle growth rate (6.5%) and lower-middle growth rate (5.5%), and reported the forecasted value of the proportion and scale of China's higher education public investment. As can be found in Table 4.4, if China's economic development maintains an upper-middle growth rate in the future, its public investment in higher education as a percentage of GDP will reach 1.046% in 2021 and steadily climb to 1.187% in the following years. If China's economic development remains at a lower-middle growth rate, the public investment in higher education as a percentage of GDP will also rise steadily between 2021 and 2025, and the percentage will be slightly higher than that of the upper-middle growth rate. Similarly, if China maintains an economic growth rate of 6.5%, the total public investment in higher education will increase from 1069.6 billion yuan to 1561.4 billion yuan during 2021–2025, an increase of

Forecasting the scale of public investment 79

Table 4.4 Forecast of the proportion and scale of public investment in higher education in China for 2021–2025

	Scenario 1: Upper-middle growth rate (6.5%)		Scenario 2: Lower-middle growth rate (5.5%)	
	Proportion (%)	Scale (in billion)	Proportion (%)	Scale (in billion)
2021	1.046	10,696	1.053	10,366
2022	1.081	11,775	1.088	11,302
2023	1.116	12,949	1.123	12,310
2024	1.152	14,226	1.158	13,394
2025	1.187	15,614	1.194	14,560

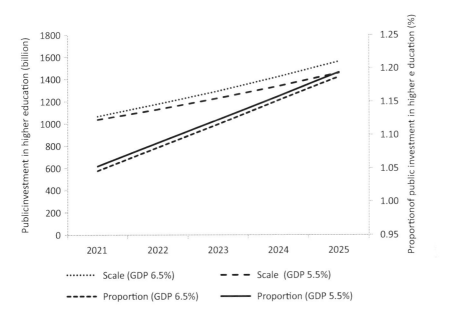

Figure 4.3 Forecasted values of the proportion and scale of public investment in higher education for 2021–2025.

45.98%. Surely, if China's economic growth rate falls to 5.5%, the scale of public investment in higher education will also decline by 2025, to about 1456 billion yuan, which is still 40.47% higher than in 2021.

It is not difficult to find from the aforementioned forecasts (see Figure 4.3) that low economic growth in China will inevitably lead to a relative reduction in the scale of public investment in higher education, but the public investment in higher education as a percentage of GDP will also increase. This is mainly because of the rigidity of government expenditure in higher education, and the fact that the student size of higher education will not change substantially in an economic slowdown. Therefore, even in the situation of an economic downturn, the government might reduce its expenditure on higher education, but the proportion of higher education expenditure in total government spending may be higher.

4.5 Conclusion

After China enters the "new normal" of economic development, the country's demand for all kinds of talent, especially high-level innovative talent, will grow, and the support and guarantee of governmental funds are even more important, which are needed for reform of the talent-training system driven by colleges' and universities' response to the change of the specifications of talent demand in economic and social development in the new age. Based on the empirical analysis of data of China's economic growth rate and higher education development scale in the past 20 years, this study presents the forecast results, including student size and the proportion and scale of public investment in higher education, during the upcoming 14th Five-Year period (2021–2025), and obtains the following main conclusions.

First, by 2025, China's gross enrollment rate in higher education is expected to reach 60%. Since the beginning of the 21st century, China's higher education has been in a flourishing phase, becoming the world's largest higher education system. Relevant statistics show that, based on the school-age population aged 18–22 years, China's gross enrollment rate in higher education reached 40% in 2015, and the goals set out in "The Outline" were achieved five years ahead of schedule, laying a solid foundation for China to move toward the massification of higher education. By forecasting the time series of higher education gross enrollment ratio, it is revealed that the gross enrollment ratio will exceed 50% and 60%, respectively, in 2021 and 2025, which requires advance allocation and overall consideration by relevant administrative departments in the future planning.

Second, in the 14th Five-Year, China's higher education will continue to be in an expanding period; the size of all types of students at all levels is expected to increase to about 50 million. According to the latest data from the China Education Statistics Yearbook, there were 28.94 million students at all levels of higher education (excluding adult education) in China in 2016. The forecast results of this study indicate that after 10 years (i.e., 2025), the number of higher education students in China will reach about 50 million. The rapid expansion of the student size will inevitably pose a challenge to the financial input of higher education, and the relevant administrative departments need to build more active fiscal policies to ensure the stability of government funding per student.

Third, in the 14th Five-Year period, if China's economy maintains steady growth, then China's public investment scale in higher education can also persist with stable growth. According to the forecast results in this study, if China's economic growth rate remains at 6.5%, the change range of the proportion of public investment in higher education in 2021–2025 will be from 1.046% to 1.187%, and the change range of scale of public investment in higher education will be from 1069.6 billion yuan and 1561.4 billion yuan. Similarly, if China's economic growth rate remains at 5.5%, the change range of the proportion of public investment in higher education in 2021–2025 will be from 1.053% to 1.194%, and the change range of the scale of public investment in higher education will be from 1036.6 billion yuan to 1456 billion yuan. Therefore, as long as China's economy maintains a relatively stable development trend, it can provide more adequate financial security for higher education.

According to the aforementioned research conclusions, in order to better guarantee the sustainable development of China's higher education, to provide high-quality talent reserves for the construction of an innovative nation, and to provide adequate financial support for the construction of a powerful higher education country, this study puts forward the following three policy recommendations.

First, appropriately control for student size during the 14th Five-Year Plan period, to promote the orderly and benign expansion of higher education under the premise of ensuring the quality of higher education. According to Martin Trow's theory, China's higher education has entered the stage of mass higher education and will gradually enter to the stage of universal higher education. The forecast results of this chapter show that if the current growth rate persists, the student size in China will witness the massification of higher education during the 14th Five-Year Plan period (i.e., the gross enrollment rate of higher education exceeds 50%). On the one hand, the higher education massification can enable more college-aged people to enjoy the benefits of the higher education expansion, but, on the other hand, it may also lead to a series of problems such as the decline in the higher education quality and depreciation of diplomas, due to excessive expansion. In fact, the higher education expansion in our country is not only an old problem but is facing a new situation. The undergraduate expansion began in 1998, followed by postgraduate expansion. In 2018, the China Ministry of Education issued new files to request for "a modest expansion of doctoral student size". It can be said that the higher education expansion has become the new normal for the development of higher education in China. However, how to provide adequate financial support for the expansion to ensure the adequacy of hardware facilities, teaching staff, and teaching conditions is a more serious problem. As the data quoted in the introduction of this chapter show that in recent years, the average student funding of higher education in China has been facing great pressure, so the government should appropriately control the expansion of student size, so as to provide a strong guarantee for the quality of higher education.

Second, scientifically estimate the average student cost, and appropriately design the per-student comprehensive quota and the tuition standards of universities with different types and quality based on the principle of higher education cost-sharing. Because China's universities have not established an internal cost accounting system, there are weak motivations for colleges and universities to improve their efficiency of using government funds and reducing operating cost, resulting in, for example, overestimation of the annual budget, too much fund balance by the end of the year, unused funds, and waste of funds near the end of the year. "The National Development and Reform Commission's Notice on Announcing the Tuition Standards of Universities under Central Government Administration" (No. 1434),[10] which was issued in 2007, has already passed its five-year frozen period for tuition fees, but the university tuition policies in many provinces have not been adjusted and remained unchanged at the level of 3000–5000 yuan per academic year. While the consumer price, and faculty and staff wages grow steadily at the same pace as GDP, the per-student cost is bound to grow rapidly. Moreover, China's current tuition system does not reflect the necessary differences between universities at different levels and with different qualities. This situation is not good for both education equity and education efficiency.[11] At present, there is an urgent need to scientifically estimate the operating cost and per-student comprehensive quota, so as to provide reliable data for the financial allocation of higher education. In addition, according to the principle of cost-sharing in higher education, it is also necessary to set separate tuition standards for colleges and universities of different types and quality, to ensure a stable source of revenue for higher education institutions.

Third, to improve the financial adequacy of higher education, gradually establish a long-term mechanism for the growth of the average student funding for higher education. The forecasted results for higher education from 2021 to 2025 show that as long as China's economic development maintains a steady growth trend, the Chinese government will be able to guarantee the annual growth of the scale of public investment in higher education. However, if the use of incremental funds is not well-planned, there will still be an embarrassing situation of negative growth in public funds for higher education. Therefore, the government should consider establishing and improving a long-term mechanism for increasing the appropriated funds per student in higher education year by year. More importantly, the objective requirements of creating an innovative country and world-class universities will inevitably direct China's public funding for higher education to a number of key universities and key disciplines in the future. Therefore, the Chinese government should scientifically plan the use of incremental funds to improve the efficiency of the use of these funds on the basis of ensuring equity.[12]

The healthy and stable development of higher education cannot be separated from the scientific planning and policy guidance of the government, and the scientific forecasting of the development index of higher education is an important basis for the government to formulate development plans and public investment policies. At present, in the field of higher education, researchers do not pay enough attention to forecast research, resulting in research limitations in terms of data, methods, results, etc., which cannot provide accurate information for higher education administrations, and government planners still rely on the historical data and empirical judgment, bringing invisible constraints on the development of higher education. Looking to the future, the use of new technologies such as big data and cloud computing are rising, and Chinese higher education scholars should keep up with the pace of the times, constantly explore and innovate, and make full use of new technologies to conduct forecast research, in order to

Forecasting the scale of public investment 83

better support and promote the scientificity and perspectives of the planning of the development of China's higher education.

Appendix: Forecasting the higher education student size and its scale of public investment during the 13th Five-Year Plan period

This appendix uses the lower limit model and the upper limit model to forecast the proportion of public investment in higher education between 2016 and 2020.

A4.1 Specification of the lower limit model

To build the forecasting model, this study is carried out on the basis of cross-national data and partly draws on Yue's (2011) modeling idea of forecasting the proportion of public investment in higher education, taking GDP as the major explanatory variable. Unlike Yue's study, we do not adopt the method of by-year regressions, but make full use of the panel data characteristics, taking into account the differences in the higher education funding system of various countries, and adopt the panel time series model with heterogeneous slopes. This model is generally in the following form:

$$y_{it} = \beta_i x_{it} + u_{it} \quad (A4.1)$$

$$u_{it} = \alpha_{1i} + \lambda_i f_t + \varepsilon_{it} \quad (A4.2)$$

$$x_{it} = \alpha_{2i} + \lambda_i f_t + \gamma_i g_t + e_{it} \quad (A4.3)$$

In Equations A4.1 to A4.3, i indicates the country, and t indicates the time. In Equation A4.1, y_{it} and x_{it} are observable dependent variables and independent variables in year t of country i, respectively. β is the country slope of an observable independent variable, and u_{it} contains the nonobservable variable and error term. In Equation A4.2, the nonobservable variable consists of two parts: the group fixed effect α_{1i} and the unobservable common factor f_t. The group fixed effect is primarily used to control for cross-group heterogeneity that does not change over time, while f_t is primarily used to control for time-varying heterogeneity and cross-sectional dependence.[13] In Equation A4.3, α_{1i} and f_t are still used to indicate the group fixed effect and unobservable common factors. In addition, g_t is also inserted into the equation to control for other factors that f_t does not contain. u_{it}, ε_{it}, and e_{it} are all white noise terms.

Specifically, this study uses the following models to forecast the proportion of China's public investment in higher education between 2016 and 2020:

$$Y_{it} = a_i Y_{i,t-1} + b_i \ln\text{GDP}_{i,t-1} + c_i \ln\text{FIN}_{i,t-1} + u_{it} \qquad (A4.4)$$

$$u_{it} = \alpha_{1i} + \lambda_i f_t + \varepsilon_{it} \qquad (A4.5)$$

$$Y_{i,t-1} = \alpha_{2i} + \lambda_i f_t + \gamma_i g_t + e_{it} \qquad (A4.6)$$

$$\ln\text{GDP}_{i,t-1} = \alpha_{3i} + \lambda_i f_t + \gamma_i g_t + d_{it} \qquad (A4.7)$$

$$\ln\text{FIN}_{i,t-1} = \alpha_{4i} + \lambda_i f_t + \gamma_i g_t + d_{it} \qquad (A4.8)$$

where Y_{it} is the proportion of public investment in higher education of country i in year t, Y_{it-1} is the first-lagged variable of the proportion of public investment in higher education, $\ln\text{GDP}_{it-1}$ is the GDP (in the natural log form[14]) of country i in year $t-1$, and $\ln\text{FIN}_{it-1}$ is the total public expenditure of country i in year $t-1$ (in the natural log form). Other variables are interpreted as previously mentioned.

For panel time series models with heterogeneous slopes, there are generally three types of estimators, i.e., the mean group (MG) estimator proposed by Pesaran and Smith (1995), the common correlated effects mean group (CCEMG) estimator by Pesaran (2006), and augmented mean group (AMG) estimator proposed by Eberhardt and Teal (2010). Since CCEMG and AMG estimators include cross-sectional averages in the current time and other variables that reflect the common macroeconomic dynamics of different countries in the current time, so they cannot be used to forecast the future periods of the proportion of public investment in higher education in China. This study will only use four estimators – MG, MG-trend, AMG-impose, and AMG-impose-trend[15] – to perform the estimations and select the suitable model based on the RMSE of the forecasted results.

A4.2 Specification of the upper limit model

To build the forecasting model, we mainly draw on the idea of Li's (1988) forecasting the scale of public investment in higher education in China and use the time series methods for modeling. Based on the historical data from 1995 to 2014 with the rapid development of the higher education scale and economy in China, the forecasting model of the proportion of public investment in higher education is constructed from the perspective that the higher education development should meet the demand of the economic development, and its specification can be given as follows:[16]

$$Y_t = b_0 + b_1 \ln\text{STUSIZE}_t + b_2 d\text{GDP}_t + b_3 \text{TSHARE}_t + U_t \qquad (A4.9)$$

$$\ln\text{STUSIZE}_t = c_0 + c_1\text{REDUR}_t + c_2\text{dGDP}_t + c_3\text{TSHARE}_t + V_t \quad (A4.10)$$

In the preceding equations, Y_t is the dependent variable, which indicates the proportion of China's public investment in higher education in year t. $\ln\text{STUSIZE}_t$ indicates the FTE enrollment in higher education institutions in year t (in log form). dGDP_t or dGDP_{t-1} indicates the GDP growth rate in period t or $t-1$, respectively. TSHARE_t indicates the proportion of tuition fees to total higher education revenue. U_t and V_t are the random error terms in the two equations.

lnSTUSIZE is included in the model because the current student size of higher education will affect the scale of public investment in higher education. Therefore, the model includes the FTE enrollment in higher education as an independent variable. As previously mentioned, practice in many countries shows that the growth rate of GDP is positively related to the growth rate of public investment in higher education. During the accelerating period of economic development, the growth rate of public investment in higher education will generally be relatively high, and during the stable and decelerating periods of economic development, the government will reduce or slow the public investment in higher education. Therefore, the GDP growth variable (dGDP) is added to the model to reflect the adaptation of the proportion of public investment in higher education to the change of the economic development pace. Under the ordinary circumstances, the size of higher education is affected by the growth rate of economic development and gross enrollment rate (Wu, 2010; Kharas & Kohli, 2011; Khor, 2015), so we use two simultaneous equations to build a model to forecast the proportion of public investment in higher education. REDUR_t is the gross enrollment ratio for higher education in year t.[17] China's plan for higher education enrollment is formulated by the Ministry of Education according to the existing capacity of higher education institutions and the economic development needs. Because the annual change in the size of higher education enrollment is affected by the admission rate set by the Ministry of Education, the admission rate differs among provinces, and the data are not included in the China Education Statistics Yearbook, so this study substitutes it with the gross enrollment rate variable. In addition, as the previous analysis points out, the student size in private higher education institutions has been close to one-fifth of the total enrollment, and for institutional reasons, the funds for running Chinese private higher education institutions mainly rely on tuition fees, with very limited financial support received from the government. To control for the impact of student size in private higher education institutions, the number of enrolled private students should be included in the model as a control variable, but considering that there is no data on enrollment of private higher education institutions before 2002 in the relevant statistical yearbook before 2002, we intend to use the proportion of tuition fees to the total revenue in higher education (TSHARE) as a proxy variable to control for the impact of student size in private higher education institutions.

A4.3 Results of the lower limit forecast model of the proportion of public investment in higher education

Based on data on the proportion of public investment in higher education, the economic development level, and the capacity of government expenditure in developed countries and countries with similar economic levels to China between 2001 and 2011, this study uses a panel time series model with heterogeneous slopes. When using the panel time series method, it is necessary to examine whether the dependent variable is a stationary time series in advance. Therefore, the unit root test is required. Considering that the model uses the data of proportion of public investment and GDP in different countries, there may be high heterogeneity and cross-sectional dependence. This study uses the Cointegrated Augmented Dickey-Fuller (CADF) test proposed by Pesaran, and the test results show that the dependent variable is a nonstationary time series ($Z = 4.848$), applicable to the panel time series model with heterogeneous intercepts.

In the model shown in Equations A4.4–A4.8, we use logged GDP rather than per capita GDP for two main reasons. First, the difficulty of forecasting the per capita GDP growth rate. It should consider not only the historical trend of GDP per capita itself but also the adjustment of the complex factors of population change; otherwise it is difficult to ensure the scientificity. Second, we found that studies such as Liu and Yuan (2006) and Yue (2011), which used per capita GDP to forecast the proportion of public investment in education or higher education, generally had a moderate model fit in terms of R^2 (roughly 0.1–0.3), so we used GDP instead of per capita GDP in our forecast (See Table A4.6).[18]

As mentioned earlier, there are three types of estimation methods for panel time series models with heterogeneous slopes. Considering the need for forecasting, this study uses four models: MG, MG-trend, AMG-impose, and AMG-impose-trend. Results for the full sample are presented in Table A4.1. Model A is estimated using the MG method, and the estimated coefficient of the independent variable Y_{it-1} is significant at the 0.01 level, which means that the proportion of public investment in higher education in year t is affected by the proportion in year $t–1$. In contrast, the independent variable $\ln GDP_{it-1}$ has a positive effect but is not significant. Model B adds the trend variable to model A to control for the impact of the time trend, but the results show that the trend variable is not significant. In addition, the results of the subsample for each country (the last row of Table A4.1) also show that there is no country's trend variable significant at the 0.05 level. Model C is estimated using the AMG-impose method, and the results show that Y_{it-1} has no significant impact, while $\ln GDP_{it-1}$ has a significantly positive effect. This shows that from the overall situation of different countries, the total GDP in the previous year is closely related to the proportion of public investment in higher education in the current year. In fact, the faster the total economic growth, the greater the demand for high-quality talent in one country, so it is needed to increase public investment in higher education. Model D added the time trend to model C, resulting in no statistically significant impact on all independent variables, and only 15.4% of countries (or two countries) among all subsamples have

Table A4.1 Results of lower limit models (full sample)

	Model A MG	Model B MG-trend	Model C AMG-impose	Model D AMG-impose-trend	Model E MG	Model F MG-trend	Model G AMG-impose	Model H AMG-impose-trend
Y_{it-1}	0.3626*** (0.1153)	0.2883** (0.1328)	0.1062 (0.1203)	0.0225 (0.1268)	0.2354* (0.1214)	-0.0733 (0.2473)	-0.0002 (0.1169)	-0.2361 (0.1619)
$\ln GDP_{it-1}$	0.0163 (0.0694)	0.0205 (0.1532)	0.1650** (0.0654)	0.1094 (0.1344)	-0.2578 (0.2844)	-0.5010 (0.5645)	0.3130 (0.2685)	0.2157 (0.3614)
$\ln FIN_{it-1}$	—	—	—	—	0.2674 (0.2440)	0.2258 (0.6348)	-0.1606 (0.2665)	-0.4145 (0.4655)
trend	—	-0.0054 (0.0126)	—	0.0018 (0.0129)	—	0.0280 (0.0232)	—	0.0302 (0.0186)
Constant item	0.2140 (2.0033)	0.4147 (4.1949)	-3.8565** (1.8677)	-2.0126 (3.5530)	1.0026 (2.9273)	9.0188 (6.1978)	-3.6174* (2.0662)	5.9740 (6.1864)
N	109	109	109	109	109	99	109	99
Proportion of trend significant at 0.05 level	—	0	—	0.154	—	0	—	0
RMSE	0.0509	0.0466	0.0476	0.0420	0.0483	0.0440	0.0445	0.0403

Note: Standard errors of estimated coefficients in parentheses.

88 Forecasting the scale of public investment

significant time trends. Models E to H control for the total government expenditure lnFIN$_{it-1}$ in year $i-1$ on the basis of models A to D. The results show that not only does the variable itself have no significant effect on the dependent variable, but it also changes the direction of the impact of lnGDP$_{it-1}$ on Y_{it-1} and lowers its levels of significance. Our study suggests that this is because there exists high collinearity between lnGDP$_{it-1}$ and lnFIN$_{it-1}$ (the coefficient of correlation is 0.9845), so the results of models E to H could not be used for forecasting. Overall, models B and D, which add time trends, do not show significant time trends, so models A and C are more appropriate for forecasting. Compared with model A, model C has a substantially lower RMSE, indicating that model C has better statistical characteristics and thus is more suitable for forecasting. Notably, Table A4.1 shows only the results of the full sample, and our study also needs to consider the suitable model used for forecasting based on the results of the Chinese subsample. The results of the Chinese subsample are given in Table A4.2.

As can be seen from Table A4.2, the results of models E to H of the Chinese subsample have problems similar to those of the full sample in Table A4.1 and are therefore not suitable for forecasting. The time trends in models B and D are not significant, so models A and C are better. The coefficients of the independent variables in model A are not significant, and the coefficient of lnGDP$_{it-1}$ in model C is significant at the 0.01 level, showing the same pattern as the full sample. This suggests that for China the total GDP in the previous year and the proportion of public investment in higher education in the current year are changed proportionately, which is very similar to the international trend described earlier. Because of the rapid GDP growth and the large demand for all kinds of talent (especially highly skilled people with higher education), China needs to increase the scale and proportion of public investment in higher education to meet the needs of economic development.

In summary, models E to H in Tables A4.1 and A4.2 are not suitable for forecasting (although their RMSEs are low). And model C in Table A4.2 is also very consistent with international trends and Chinese reality. Therefore, based on the results of model C in Table A4.2, this study uses the following formula to forecast the proportion of China's public investment in higher education between 2016 and 2020:

$$Y_{it} = -6.1405 - 0.4473 Y_{it-1} + 0.2443 \ln \text{GDP}_{it-1} \qquad (A4.11)$$

In the next five years, China's economic growth will be in the new normal and the economic growth will slow. Therefore, by using the forecasting formula in Equation A4.11, this study considers both the upper-middle growth rate (7.5%) and lower-middle growth rate (6.5%). While forecasting the proportion of public investment in higher education in China, this study also forecasts the scale of public investment in higher education in the same period (in current U.S. dollars). All forecasted results are presented in Table A4.3. Also from Table A4.3, the proportion of China's public investment in higher education increased year by year between 2016 and 2020, from 0.8295% in 2016 to 0.8732% in 2020 (the GDP

Table A4.2 Results of lower limit models (the Chinese sample)

	Model A	Model B	Model C	Model D	Model E	Model F	Model G	Model H
	MG	MG-trend	AMG-impose	AMG-impose-trend	MG	MG-trend	AMG-impose	AMG-impose-trend
Y_{it}	0.9452	0.9692	-0.4473	-0.4520	0.6392	0.5892	-0.9420	-1.1803
	(0.7289)	(0.7673)	(0.7046)	(0.7613)	(0.7835)	(0.9342)	(0.7422)	(0.9013)
$\ln GDP_{it-1}$	0.0439	0.1603	0.2443***	0.2215	-0.3315	-0.4219	-0.1918	-0.9852
	(0.0792)	(0.2176)	(0.0766)	(0.2159)	(0.3718)	(0.7863)	(0.3522)	(0.7586)
$\ln FIN_{it-1}$	—	—	—	—	0.4587	0.5217	0.5139	1.0659
					(0.4440)	(0.6749)	(0.4206)	(0.6511)
trend	—	-0.0213	—	0.0042	—	0.0071	—	0.0570
		(0.0367)		(0.0364)		(0.0528)		(0.0509)
Constant	-1.1931	-4.4221	-6.1405***	-5.5064	-2.5039	-1.6063	-7.0497***	0.7548
	(1.8685)	(5.9088)	(1.8062)	(5.8629)	(2.2512)	(7.1202)	(2.1326)	(6.8689)
RMSE	0.0292	0.0284	0.0290	0.0256	0.0413	0.0413	0.0418	0.0378

90 *Forecasting the scale of public investment*

Table A4.3 Forecasted values of the proportion and scale of public investment in higher education in China (lower limit) for 2016–2020

	Scenario 1: Upper-middle growth rate (7.5%)		Scenario 2: Lower-middle growth rate (6.5%)	
	Percentage (%)	Scale (US$ billions)	Percentage (%)	Scale (US$ billions)
2016	0.8318	995.85	0.8295	974.73
2017	0.8454	1088.04	0.8418	1053.52
2018	0.8570	1185.68	0.8517	1135.15
2019	0.8695	1293.18	0.8627	1224.51
2020	0.8815	1409.49	0.8732	1319.95

Note: The data of China's GDP between 2011 and 2014 came from the World Bank, so the forecasted values are the same for both scenarios 1 and 2 during 2012–2014. The GDP data after 2015 were calculated by setting the annual growth rate at 7.5% and 6.5%, respectively, based on the GDP of 2014.

growth rate in 2016–2020 is set to be 6.5%), or from 0.8318% to 0.8815% (the GDP growth rate in 2016–2020 is set to be 7.5%), which is basically consistent not only with the proportion of public investment in the major Western developed countries, which maintain at the level of 0.8% in most years, but also very close to the proportion of public investment in major developing countries in recent years, such as India, Thailand, and Brazil. (The numbers of India and Thailand were 1.283% and 0.80% in 2011, and that of Brazil was 0.883% in 2010.) Therefore, even if China's economic growth might slow in the future, it is still necessary to maintain the intensity of investment, so as to keep the level of government expenditure on higher education close to the average level of Western developed countries and also to keep pace with the growth of public investment in major developing countries.

As can be found in Table A4.3, if China maintains its economic growth rate at 7.5%, the total scale of China's public investment in higher education will increase from 99.585 billion USD to 140.949 billion USD between 2016 and 2020, an increase of 41.54%. It is for sure that if China's economic growth slows to 6.5%, the scale of public investment in higher education will increase from 97.473 billion USD to 131.995 billion USD between 2016 and 2020, an increase of 35.41%. Therefore, in the next five years, under the condition that the economy remains basically stable, the Chinese government still has more room for higher education investment to further promote the all-round development of higher education.

A4.4 Results of upper limit forecast model on the proportion of public investment in higher education

Drawing on Li's (1998) forecasting perspective that higher education development adapts to the needs of economic development, based on the historical data of 17 years (1995–2011) with high-speed development of both higher education and the economy, this study uses the two-stage least squares (2SLS) method to estimate. The results can be found in Table A4.4. The main difference between model A and model B is that the former uses current GDP growth (namely $dGDP_t$) in the first-stage regression, while the latter uses lagged GDP growth (namely $dGDP_{t-1}$) in the first-stage regression. The results of regressions show that the estimated coefficients of the two models are relatively close, especially at the second stage, and the estimated coefficients are almost the same. It is not difficult to find by comparing the R^2 of the two regressions that the goodness of fit for both A and B does not differ substantially at the two regression stages. Taking into account the characteristics of a planned economy in China (the budget of the current year is mainly based on the final accounts of the previous year), the results of model B are used here for forecasting.

Table A4.5 presents the forecasted values based on the estimates of model B in Table A4.4. Similar to the lower limit model, this study takes into account

Table A4.4 Results of the upper limit model

	Model A	Model B
Stage 2: Y_t		
$lnSTUSIZE_t$	0.2576***	0.2648***
	(0.0382)	(0.0431)
$dGDP_t$	−0.0137***	
	(0.0044)	
$dGDP_{t-1}$		−0.0114***
		(0.0040)
$TSHARE_t$	−0.0079**	−0.0090**
	(0.0038)	(0.0042)
Constant	−3.3066***	−3.4170***
	(0.5112)	(0.5853)
N	17	16
R^2	0.9632	0.9516
Stage 1: $lnSTUSIZE_t$		
$dGDP_t$	−0.0047	
	(0.0107)	
$dGDP_{t-1}$		−0.0106
		(0.0084)
$TSHARE_t$	0.0340***	0.0343***
	(0.0043)	(0.0042)
$REDUR_t$	0.0832***	0.0844***
	(0.0054)	(0.0061)
Constant	13.8713***	13.8989***
	(0.0886)	(0.0706)
N	17	16
R^2	0.9953	0.9951

Notes: *, **, and *** indicate significance at the 0.1, 0.05, and 0.01 level, respectively. Robust standard errors are in the parentheses.

Table A4.5 Forecasted values of the proportion and scale of public investment in higher education in China for 2016–2020 (upper limit)

	Scenario 1: Upper-middle growth rate (7.5%)		Scenario 2: Lower-middle growth rate (6.5%)	
	Percentage (%)	Scale (US$ billions)	Percentage (%)	Scale (US$ billions)
2016	0.9808	117.424	0.9950	116.916
2017	0.9983	128.486	1.0125	126.709
2018	1.0162	140.597	1.0304	137.328
2019	1.0345	153.858	1.0486	148.847
2020	1.0532	168.388	1.0674	161.351

Table A4.6 Results of models with the per capita GDP (full sample)

	(1)	(2)	(4)	(5)
	MG	MG-trend	AMG-impose	AMG-impose-trend
Y_{it-1}	0.3692***	0.2821**	0.1203	0.0197
	(0.1146)	(0.1313)	(0.1202)	(0.1266)
$lnGDP_{it-1}$	0.0070	0.0173	0.1516**	0.1006
	(0.0795)	(0.1520)	(0.0719)	(0.1322)
trend		−0.0055		0.0016
		(0.0118)		(0.0123)
Constant	0.5890	0.8404	−0.6628	0.0844
	(0.8249)	(1.3574)	(0.7317)	(1.1138)
N	109	109	109	109
RMSE	0.0511	0.0466	0.0479	0.0421
Trend is a significant proportion at the 0.05 level	NA	0	NA	0

Note: lnPGDP is the natural log of per capita GDP.

the two scenarios of upper-middle growth rate (7.5%) and lower-middle growth rate (6.5%) and gives the forecasted values of the proportion and scale of public investment in higher education in China (See Table A4.7 for the results of the first-stage estimates).[19] As can be seen from Table A4.5, the proportion of China's public investment in higher education will increase rapidly to 1.0674% (GDP growth rate 6.5%) or 1.0532 % (GDP growth rate 7.5%) in 2020, which surpasses the average level of major Western developed countries between 2001 and 2011. Similarly, Table A4.5 shows that if China maintains an economic growth rate of 7.5%, the total scale of China's public investment in higher education will increase from 117.424 billion USD to 168.388 billion USD between

Table A4.7 Forecasted values of China's gross enrollment rate, student size, and proportion of tuition fees

	Gross enrollment rate (%)	Student size (in log form)		Proportion of tuition fees (%)
		Upper-middle growth rate (7.5%)	Lower-middle growth rate (6.5%)	
2012	30	17.27	17.27	27.44
2013	34.5	17.69	17.69	27.99
2014	35.24	17.77	17.77	28.53
2015	36	17.86	17.86	29.07
2016	36.77	17.94	17.95	29.62
2017	37.55	18.02	18.03	30.16
2018	38.35	18.11	18.12	30.70
2019	39.16	18.20	18.21	31.24
2020	40	18.29	18.30	31.79

Notes: The variable dGDP is in its actual values for 2012–2014. The variable REDUR is in its actual values in 2012 and 2013 and is estimated afterward according to the target values set by the Outline of National Medium- and Long-Term Education Reform and Development (2010–2020), namely, 36% in 2015 and 40% in 2020. Based on these numbers, we calculated the gross enrollment rate with the formula $REDUR_{2013}(1 + r)^2 = REDUR_{2015}$, and obtained r–0.02151, resulting in the gross enrollment rate of 35.242% in 2014. Similarly, by the formula $REDUR_{2015}(1 + r)^5 = REDUR_{2020}$, we obtained $r = 0.02129$, thus the gross enrollment rates for 2016–2020 were 36.766 %, 37.549%, 38.348%, 39.164%, and 40% accordingly. The proportion of tuition fees is estimated using the time series recursive smoothing method, in which double exponential smoothers and Holt–Winters smoothers are able to perform forecasting above one year with annual data. By comparing the results from different parameters, this study selected the results of hwinters(0.9, 0.1), because it best conforms to the existing changes, and its average forecasted value of 2012–2020 is closest to the average of 2004–2011. (The year 2004 is when the student size in private higher education institutions reached 1 million. After 2004, the number of students in private higher education institutions were growing steadily year by year except 2008.) We also used the double exponential method to try different combinations of parameters and found that the in-sample forecast accuracy was not as good as that of hwinters(0.9, 0.1). If we used the default setting, the out-of-sample forecasted values would continue to decline rapidly, even to a negative value, which is obviously far from the real situation. Although its RMSE is 2.6833, even lower than that of hwinters(0.9, 0.1), it is still not appropriate to be used.

2016 and 2020, an increase of 43.40%. If China's economic growth falls to 6.5%, the scale of public investment in higher education will also decline by 2020, to about 161.351 billion USD, yet still 38% higher than 2016. Therefore, if the financial support should be provided based on the principle of higher education development matching the growth rate of economic development, China's public investment in higher education should have a faster growth rate than its current level, which is also beneficial to catching up with the average level of Western developed countries. Compared with the forecasted results of the lower limit model (i.e., forecasting based on supply trends), it is possible that the upper limit model is of greater value to the Chinese government in formulating higher education funding policies.

94 *Forecasting the scale of public investment*

Notes

1 Here we assume that government spending as a percentage of GDP is fixed in the short term. Percentage of public education investment = Government spending as a percentage of GDP × Proportion of government expenditure on education to total government expenditure.
2 Zeyun Liu and colleagues used data of 23 middle-income countries to build the model, and the predicted values of the proportion of China's public investment in education are 3.7% and 4.54% in 2010 and 2020, respectively. Changjun Yue and colleagues set the GNP average annual growth rate at 7.18%, and the predicted values of Chinese public investment in education were 4.04% and 4.3% in 2010 and 2020, respectively. Based on the view that the growth rate of educational investment should run ahead, their study recommended that the range of proportion of public investment in education for China were 4.0–4.5% and 4.5–5.0% in 2010 and 2020, respectively.
3 For example, since 2010, the "Excellent Engineer Education and Training Project" has been implemented. There are 1257 programs and 514 disciplines at the postgraduate level in 208 higher education institutions that carried out the reform pilot in accordance with the "Excellent Engineer Education and Training Project", covering about 130,000 students. In November 2013, the Ministry of Education, in conjunction with the Ministry of Human Resources and Social Security, formulated and promulgated the "Opinions on Further Promoting the Reform of the Training Model for Postgraduate Students with Professional Degrees", which focuses on vocational needs, emphasizes training of practical capacity, and bridges the industry–university collaboration, so as to establish a training model for professional degrees with Chinese characteristics that is suitable for economic and social development. Since 2011, 6155 enterprises have signed up with universities to participate in the training of talent, of which 626 enterprises have become the first group of state-level engineering practice and education centers. The universities have invested a total of 2.2 billion yuan as special funds, and contracted enterprises have invested about 420 million yuan. ("What will be the measures to improve the quality of undergraduate education in an all-round way?" Daliang Zhang, Director of the Department of Higher Education in China Ministry of Education, "WeChat Education" platform of the Information Office of the China Ministry of Education, November 17, 2014.)
4 Here we only include the data of undergraduate enrollment, because the admission of postgraduate students in private higher education institutions started very late and the number was very limited. According to the Chinese Yearbook of Education Statistics, the enrolled master students in 2012 and 2013 were 155 and 355, respectively.
5 Concerning the selection of the forecasting period of 2021–2025, there are two considerations. On the one hand, China is used to set a five-year cycle development plan, and 2020 is the last year of the targeting year set by "The Outline" and 2021–2025 are the five years for the 14th Five-Year Plan. On the other hand, the time period of forecast based on the time series model should not be too long, because forecasting for more than 10 years faces many uncontrolled intervention factors, making it difficult to ensure the out-of-sample accuracy for forecasts.
6 Please refer to the Appendix for the forecasts of scale of public investment in higher education during China's 13th Five-Year Plan (2016–2020).
7 As the proportion of financial investment in higher education data can only be found at present 2014 statistics for the year, this study uses 1995–2014 for the time series data for the year.
8 The current population size may also be one of the factors affecting the proportion of public investment in higher education, but its correlation coefficient with the current higher education enrollment is too high ($r = 0.9733$), which will result in a serious issue of collinearity if putting them together in the model at the same time. In addition, the

forecasting of higher education enrollment is also one of the main research goals of this study, so the current population size is not included in the forecasting model.
9 This study does not provide the out-of-sample forecast accuracy, which is mainly because the sample size used in this study is very small ($T = 19$) and is not suitable to divide the sample into two parts: one for coefficient estimates of the forecasting model and the other for performing out-of-sample forecast accuracy. Inferring from the acceptable results of the in-sample forecast accuracy computed in the text, it is reasonable to assume that the model will also have high out-of-sample forecast accuracy.
10 The notice requires that in the next five years (2007–2011), the standard of tuition fees and accommodation fees for all types of universities at all levels should not be higher than the relevant standards set in the autumn of 2006.
11 There are studies showing that among the students enrolled in high-level universities, the percentage of urban students are disproportionally higher than the percentage of rural ones, and the gap continues to rise. This suggests that a higher proportion of students with high socioeconomic status are receiving both a high level of higher education and a relatively low tuition fee. From the view of the whole society, this is not fair. Moreover, the long-term low-level tuition fees cannot compensate for the operating cost of the universities, but also absorb other teaching and scientific research funds, which is not good for improving higher education efficiency.
12 For example, increasing government expenditure on universities in the central and western regions, to reduce these universities' high reliance on revenue from tuition fees.
13 Cross-section dependent refers to the correlations between the cross-section units. These correlations stem from spatial patterns or some unobserved common factors. The discussion on this issue mainly comes from macro-economics, as speeding globalization enhances the interdependence of different countries in economics and social development. See a recent review from Vasilis Sarafidis and Tom Wansbeek titled "Cross-Sectional Dependence in Panel Data Analysis".
14 In order to ensure cross-national comparability, the GDP data of China was extracted from the world bank database, instead of the China Statistical Yearbook.
15 For AMG model, there are three estimation methods. The first is to add the aforementioned observed variables, i.e., the cross-sectional average of each variable. The second is to add a unit coefficient for each group by subtracting c.d.p. from the dependent variable in each group. The third is to add a set of time trend variables for each group in the first method. The last two methods remove the common dynamic process (c.d.p.) in the current time, so it can be used to forecast values in future times.
16 This is a recursive model and can therefore obtain consistent estimates by using 2SLS.
17 The data of gross enrollment ratio were extracted from the China Education Statistical Yearbook.
18 Model 1 in Table A4.6 presents the estimation results by using per capita GDP.
19 The forecasted values of student size and the proportion of tuition fees at the first stage of regression can be found in Table A4.7.

References

Bao, C. (2012). Post-4% era: The guarantee and usage of China's education funds. *Journal of the Chinese Society of Education*, 9, 9–12.

Barro, R. J. (1995). Education and economic growth. *Annals of Economics and Finance*, 14(2), 301–328.

Eberhardt, M., & Teal, F. (2010). *Productivity Analysis in Global Manufacturing Production*. Discussion Paper 515, Oxford: Department of Economics, University of Oxford.

Hu, Y. M., & Tang, Y. P. (2014). Apportion of education budget in the post-4% era: An empirical study based on transnational data. *Journal of Beijing Normal University (Social Sciences)*, *5*, 13–24.

Jin, X. B. (1990). Some issues in determining the ratio of educational investment. *Journal of Beijing Normal University (Social Sciences)*, *4*, 5–12.

Kharas, H., & Kohli, H. (2011). What is the middle income trap, why do countries fall into it, and how can it be avoided? *Global Journal of Emerging Market Economies*, *3*, 281–289.

Khor, N. (2015). *China's Looming Human Capital Crisis: Upper Secondary Educational Attainment Rates and the Middle Income Trap*. Rural Education Action Program (REAP) Working paper 280. Stanford: Stanford University.

Krueger, A. B., & Lindahl, M. (2001). Education for growth: Why and for whom? *Journal of Economic Literature*, *39*(4), 1101–1136.

Lang, Y. F. (2002). *Study on the Mode of Investment in Higher Education in China*, Doctoral Dissertation, Harbin Engineering University.

Li, Y. N. (1988). *Research on Educational Economics*. Shanghai: Shanghai People's Press.

Liu, Z. Y., & Yuan, L. S. (2006). Study on the public ratio of investment in education of China. *Higher Education Research*, *2*, 62–66.

Liu, Z. Y., & Yuan, L. S. (2007). An international comparative study on the public ratio of investment in education. *International and Comparative Education*, *2*: 32–36.

Pesaran, M. H. (2006). Estimation and inference in large heterogeneous panels with a multifactor error structure. *Econometrica*, *74*, 967–1012.

Pesaran, M. H., & Smith, R. P. (1995). Estimating long-run relationships from dynamic heterogeneous panels. *Journal of Econometrics*, *68*, 79–113.

Rossi, R. J., & Gilmartin, K. J. (1982). *Models and Forecasts of Federal Spending for Elementary and Secondary Education*. New York: Human Sciences Press.

Sun, Z. J. (2009). Changes in university income in a decade of expansion in China: An interpretation. *Tsinghua Journal of Education*, *4*, 72–80.

Tang, H. W. V., & Yin, M. S. (2012). Forecasting performance of grey prediction for education expenditure and school enrollment. *Economics of Education Review*, *31*, 452–462.

Tang, Y. P., & Hu, Y. P. (2015). Forecasting of government investment scale on the higher education during the thirteenth "five-year plan" in the economic new normal. *Chongqing Higher Education Research*, *3*(6), 3–15.

Wu, X. (2010). Economic transition, school expansion and educational inequality in China, 1990–2000. *Research in Social Stratification and Mobility*, *28*(1), 91–108.

Yao, J. J., & Ma, L. L. (2016). An analysis on the amount and structure of educational finance investment in "Post 4% Age". *Research in Educational Development*, *36*(5), 17–21.

Yue, C. J. (2011). International comparative study on the supply and demand of higher education funds. *Peking University Education Review*, *9*(3), 92–104.

Yue, C. J., & Ding, X. H. (2003). International comparison on the percentage of educational expenditure. *Educational Research*, *5*, 58–63.

Zhang, X. M., & Lan, Z. Y. (2014). Post-4% era-a research on public financial system for education in China. *Journal of National Academy of Education Administration*, *4*, 19–26.

Zhao, R., & Hu, Y. (2017). Forecasting on the structure of financial investment in higher education during the "13th five-year": Based on the data of the ordinary and vocational universities. *China Higher Education Research*, *9*, 24–29.

Zhu, C. F. (2004). International comparative research on higher education funding systems. *Review of Economic Research*, *60*, 8–20.

5 Forecasting the allocation structure and proportion of public investment for different types of higher education institutions

In 2014, General Secretary Xi Jinping proposed at a meeting of the Asia-Pacific Economic Cooperation (APEC) that one of the "new normal" characteristics of China's economy is that "China's economic growth rate has changed from high speed to upper-middle speed", and under the new normal, China's economic structure will face optimization and upgrading, where high-tech industries and tertiary industries will rapidly grow and innovation will become the main driving force of China's economic growth. This new dynamic of economic development also poses new challenges to the development of higher education in China. How to strengthen the talent cultivation that is needed for economic and social development and how to improve the quality and relevance of talent cultivation in universities have become the most important tasks in the development and reform of higher education. Since 2010, higher education has implemented the "Excellent Engineer Education and Cultivation Program", and in August 2012 the Ministry of Education promulgated the "Basic Requirements for Entrepreneurship Education for Undergraduate Students (Trial)" to comprehensively promote the scientific, institutionalized, and standardized construction of entrepreneurship education in colleges and universities. In January 2017, the State Council issued the 13th Five-Year Plan for the national education development, which pointed out that China should continue to promote the experiment program for the cultivation of top undergraduate students in basic disciplines and encourage universities to improve professional training programs and build a scientific curriculum system and learning support system by targeting characteristics of student cultivation at different levels and types. The reform of the undergraduate cultivation system shows the universities' compliance with the change of economic and social demand for talent as well as their beneficial explorations. Under the background of the new economic normal of the "post-4% era" in China, and in the new period of the 13th Five-Year Plan, the reform of the public investment system of higher education is imperative, and how to optimize the allocation of financial resources in the higher education system is an important issue related to whether the reform of higher education can be smoothly carried forward (Hu & Tang, 2014).

Based on the data of government expenditure on higher education institutions offering degree programs (henceforth HEIs) and higher vocational colleges (HVCs) in China from 2005 to 2014, this chapter uses a model combining trend analysis, autoregressive integrated moving average (ARIMA), double-exponential smoothing, and the Holt–Winters nonseasonal model to forecast the proportion of public investment allocation between HEIs and HVCs in China from 2015 to 2020 and uses provincial panel data to forecast the ratio of public investment between local HEIs and HVCs. Finally, some suggestions are put forward to optimize the allocation structure of higher education funding in China.

5.1 Current allocation structure of public investment in higher education in China

5.1.1 Current allocation structure of public investment in higher education institutions under different administrations in different regions

The imbalance of the external allocation of public investment in higher education is mainly reflected in the imbalance of higher education investment between institutions under different administrations and in different provinces. Among the institutions under different administrations, the gap in government funding is closely related to the preferential investment policy in China's higher education funding, and the government invests limited educational resources in an extremely few number of core higher education institutions, that is, it provides key universities represented by centrally administrated universities with tremendous funds. The "985 Project" starting in 1999 and the "Action Plan for the Revitalization of Education for the 21st Century" directed the flow of funds mainly concentrated in centrally administered institutions, while locally administered institutions mainly relied on collecting funds by themselves. Luo and Ma (2013) reviewed the progress of fundraising, allocation, and use of funds in regular HEIs in China for the past 20 years; and described and analyzed the revenue and expenditure structure of higher education funds. They found that the gap between the average funding revenue of centrally and locally administered HEIs showed an enlarging trend. In 1994, the average revenue of locally administered HEIs was only 45% of the average revenue of centrally administered HEIs and continued to decline after 2000, when the average revenue of locally administered HEIs was only about 13% of the average revenue of centrally administered HEIs. These different revenue structures are very closely related to the preferential policy of higher education funding, making the situation of inadequate funding for locally administered HEIs even more serious. A study by Liu and Chen (2013) found that in 1997 the government expenditure per tertiary student in the nation was 6523 yuan, while the government expenditure per tertiary student in H province was 5493 yuan. By 2006, the government expenditure per tertiary student in the nation was 5552.5 yuan, while the government expenditure per tertiary student in H province was reduced to 2728 yuan. Compared with 1997, the government expenditure per tertiary student in the nation fell by 15%, while the government expenditure per tertiary student in H province decreased by 50%. With the expansion of the public higher education, the gap between the government expenditure per tertiary

Forecasting the allocation structure 99

student in some provinces and the government expenditure per tertiary student in the nation was enlarging, and the availability of local government finance also decreased substantially, showing signs of overburdening (Liu & Chen, 2013).

Figure 5.1 shows the change in the proportion of government expenditure on higher education of centrally administered HEIs (CHEIs) and locally administered HEIs (LHEIs) in China between 1995 and 2014. The revenue of government funding for CHEIs was on the rise, from 11.9 billion yuan in 1995 to 136.3 billion yuan in 2014, with an average annual growth rate of 13.7%.[1] After 1999, the share of CHEIs to the total government expenditure on higher education decreased year by year and was surpassed by LHEIs. Although the total amount of government funds received by LHEIs substantially exceeds that of CHEIs, the share of LHEIs' revenue from government funds to the total government expenditure on higher education for all HEIs increased from 51.2% in 1999 to 70.9% in 2014, with an average annual growth rate of 20.2%. Although LHEIs surpass CHEIs in terms of total government funding and average annual growth rate, it is necessary to mention the following facts: According to the statistics from the Ministry of Education, the number of regular HEIs in China rose from 1022 in 1998 to 2263 in 2008, an increase of more than 120%. Among them, the number of LHEIs increased from 759 in 1998 to 2152 in 2008, and the proportion of LHEIs in the total number of all HEIs increased from 74% in 1998 to 95% in 2008. The enrollment of LHEIs increased from 2.258 million in 1998 to 18.505 million in 2008, accounting for 93.2% of the total higher education enrollment in China (NETEASE, 2019). Therefore, we need to pay more attention to the government funding gap between the two types of HEIs and their changes.

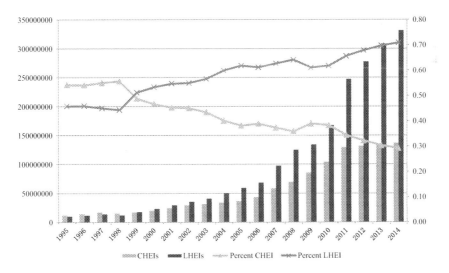

Figure 5.1 The changes in the proportion of government funding for CHEIs and LHEIs in 1995–2014.

100 *Forecasting the allocation structure*

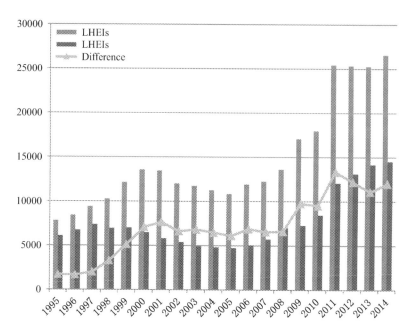

Figure 5.2 The changes in the average student budgetary expenditure for CHEIs and LHEIs in 1995–2014.

Figure 5.2 shows the changes in the financial gaps between CHEIs and LHEIs in 1995–2014 from the perspective of average student budgetary expenditure. Looking into the average student budgetary expenditure of HEIs under different administrations, the average level of CHEIs is substantially higher than that of LHEIs. In 1995–2014, the average student budgetary expenditure of CHEIs maintained at the level of 7.8–26.6 thousand yuan, but the average student budgetary expenditure of LHEIs only lay between 6.1 thousand and 14.6 thousand yuan, and the gap between the two was very clear. More specifically, in 1995–1997, the gap in average student budgetary expenditure between CHEIs and LHEIs was not obvious, but with the reform of the higher education administration system and the structural adjustment of central and local HEIs in 1998, the gap gradually widened. In 2001–2008, the gap in the average student budgetary expenditure between CHEIs and LHEIs showed a stagnation tendency, the change of the gap was not obvious. But in 2009, the gap between CHEIs and LHEIs gradually widened again. In 2009, the average student budgetary expenditure in CHEIs was 17,055.44 yuan, while the average student budgetary expenditure of LHEIs was 7298.36 yuan, with a difference of 9757.08 yuan between them. By 2014, the difference between the two increased to 12,033.04 yuan. It can be seen that current higher education funding has a great impact on higher education resource allocation, and the relative weakness of the lack of government funds in local institutions increasingly emerged.

5.1.2 Current allocation structure of public investment in higher education institutions of different types

Not only is the allocation of higher education financial resources between different administrations and regions imbalanced, but also the funding scale and average expenditure between HEIs offering degree programs and HVCs are also quite large. Zhang and Wang (2013) found that the structure of revenue source in China's HVCs had certain limitations, compared with the revenue source of HEIs, and the share of government funds received by HVCs in their total revenue was much lower, while the share of tuition fees in total revenue was high. In 2010, tuition fees accounted for HVCs' 41.5% total revenue, reflecting the oversharing of higher education costs in families. Moreover, the disparity in the structure of funding sources for HVCs between different provinces was very substantial, and the range of HVCs' revenue among different provinces was as high as 8 billion yuan in 2008. According to data from the China Education Statistics Yearbook and the China Education Finance Statistics Yearbook, the educational expenditure per HVC student was 3000 yuan in 2005, and rose to 14,209 yuan in 2014, with an increase of about 3.7 times. During the same period, the average educational expenditure per HEI student was 16,207 yuan (in 2005) and 29,508 yuan (in 2014), respectively, an increase of around 0.8 times. However, in absolute terms, the average educational expenditure of HVC students in 2014 still did not reach the level of HEIs in 2005 and was less than half of the HEIs' average educational expenditure level in 2014 (only 48.15%). It is precisely because the current investment in higher vocational education still has a few prominent problems to some degree, such as the incomplete mechanism for multichannel financing and stable public investment, so the overall level of investment in higher vocational colleges is still low, and the regional gaps are still substantial. In November 2014, the Ministry of Finance issued an announcement to request that the average government expenditure on higher vocational colleges should not be lower than 12,000 yuan by 2017 (CMOE, 2014). However, it remains a question deserving further study whether this requirement confirms the actual needs.

Figure 5.3 shows the change of enrollment in two types of higher education institutions as well as the change of proportion of HEIs' enrollment to the total between 2005 and 2014. From the view of the total amount, in 2005, the enrollment of HEIs nationwide reached 8.4882 million, which grew continuously over the next nine years, with an average annual growth rate of 6.85%. While the enrollment of HVCs during the same period was 7.1297 million, with a difference of nearly 1.36 million, and the average annual growth rate was merely 3.91%. In 2014, the enrollment of HEIs increased to 15.4107 million, and the enrollment of HVCs was 10.0663 million, resulting in a difference of about 5.344 million. Looking into the proportion of HEIs' enrollment to the total higher education student size (GSTUR), there is an increasing trend year by year, from 0.543 in 2005 to 0.605 in 2014. The widening gap between the student size in HEIs and that in HVCs puts forward new demands for the allocation of public investment in higher education.

102 *Forecasting the allocation structure*

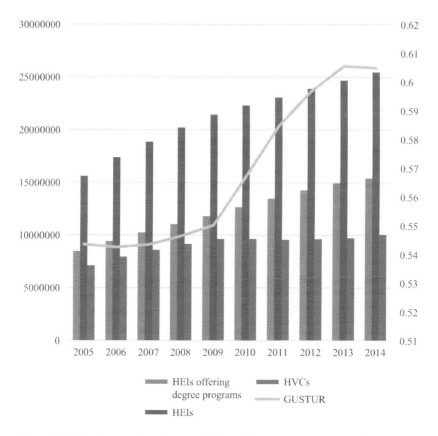

Figure 5.3 The change of enrollment of HEIs offering degree programs and HVCs, and the proportion of HEIs' enrollment to the total in 2005–2014.

Figure 5.4 shows the change of average student budgetary expenditure in centrally administered HEIs offering degree programs and local HVCs, as well as the ratio of HEIs' average student budgetary expenditure to HVCs' average student budgetary expenditure in 2005–2014. From the view of average student expenditure, in 2005–2014, the average student budgetary expenditure of centrally administered HEIs increased year by year. It went from 10,851.34 yuan in 2005 to 25,421.92 yuan in 2011, and decreased to 25,269.69 yuan in 2013, then rebounded to 26,585.24 yuan in 2014. The average annual growth rate over the nine years was 10.47%. During the same period, the average student budgetary expenditure of HVCs increased year by year, with an average annual growth rate of 14.7%, which is about 4% points higher than the average growth rate of average student budgetary expenditure for HEIs. Looking into the changing trend of the average student budgetary expenditure ratio of the two types of institutions (GVEXPP), in 2005–2014, the ratio of average student budgetary expenditure of centrally administered HEIs to that of HVCs shows a hump-shaped trend, which

Forecasting the allocation structure 103

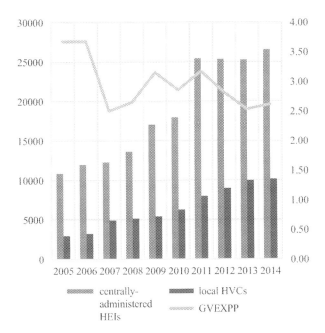

Figure 5.4 The change of average student budgetary expenditure of centrally administered HEIs offering degree programs and local HVCs and their ratio in 2005–2014.

changes in the range between 2.50 and 3.68 with a downward trend on the whole. However, by 2014 the average student budgetary expenditure of centrally administered HEIs was still about 2.5 times of local HVCs, so the gap between the average student budgetary expenditure of HVCs and the average student budgetary expenditure of HEIs should not be underestimated.

5.2 Forecast of the allocation structure of public investment in higher education in China

Due to the limitation of methods and data availability, the existing research mainly focuses on the differences of higher education finance between different administrations and provinces, while the research on the allocative structure of higher education finance in different types of universities is relatively rare, and systematic studies are still lacking. Based on the econometric model analysis of time series data and panel data in a certain period of time, this study will forecast the proportion of public investment in HEIs offering degree programs and HVCs in China. The current funding model shows substantial differences in average student funding between HEIs and HVCs. The important question in the research of allocation of higher education finance is to scientifically derive the standard of the ratio of average student funding between the two different types of institutions

104 *Forecasting the allocation structure*

(Song et al., 2015). Therefore, a study is needed to carry out systematic and in-depth research on how to allocate the higher education funding resources between institutions of different economic levels and different types (HEIs and HVCs[2]) according to the economic development level and economic structure in current China. This study will not only provide a decision-making reference for the government to further improve and perfect the macro-control policy on higher education finance but also be of great practical significance to ensure the sustainable development of higher education in China.

5.2.1 Forecast models and methods

This study focuses on the external structure of the financial investment allocation of higher education in China in the post-4% era and aims to solve the problem of how to slice the financial "cake" of higher education according to different types of colleges and universities (general undergraduate institutions/higher vocational education). Different types of colleges and universities in the direction of personnel training and teaching, research models, and other aspects of great differences, such as higher vocational colleges for practical teaching, have higher requirements and not only need practice equipment, venues, etc. but also need the configuration of dual-teacher teachers, as well as joint training with enterprises special programs. Therefore, it is necessary to distinguish between the financial investment allocation of these two different types of colleges and universities (HEIs and HVCs); construct an econometric model based on historical data such as the ratio of the scale of ordinary undergraduate colleges and higher vocational education, and the proportion of the average financial budget expenditure of students; and reasonably predict the allocation ratio of the future financial funds of these two types of colleges and universities.

5.2.1.1 Data source and model setting

This study refers to the classification in the relevant statistical yearbook, divides regular higher education institutions into those offering degree programs and those higher vocational colleges, and focuses on the allocation of public investment in higher education in these two types of institutions. This study uses historical data, such as the enrollment ratio of HEIs to HVCs and the ratio of average student budgetary expenditure of HEIs to HVCs, to build the econometric models to forecast the allocative proportion of public investment in higher education. Specifically, the data on the budgetary educational expenditure of HEIs and HVCs and average student budgetary expenditure was derived from the China Education Finance Statistical Yearbook (2006–2015), and the data on student size was derived from the China Statistical Yearbook (2006–2015). A preliminary time series model for forecasting the allocative proportion of public investment in different types of higher education institutions is as follows:

$$Y_t = b_0 + b_1 \text{GSTUR}_t + b_2 \text{GVEXPP}_t + U_t \tag{5.1}$$

$$Y_t = b_0 + b_1 \text{GSTUR}_t + b_2 \text{GVEXPP}_t + b_3 Y_{t-1} + U_t \qquad (5.2)$$

$$Y_t = b_0 + b_1 \text{GSTUR}_t + b_2 \text{GVEXPP}_{t-1} + U_t \qquad (5.3)$$

where Y_t is the proportion of public investment in HEIs to the total public investment in higher education in year t; Y_{t-1} is the proportion in year $t-1$; GSTUR_t is the proportion of the student size in HEIs to the total higher education student size in year t; GVEXPP_t is the ratio of the average student budgetary expenditure of HEIs to that of HVCs, and U_t is the stochastic error term in the model. Some scholars found (Sun, 2009), after the higher education expansion, the average student funding for locally administered HEIs tended to decline, and its difference with the average student funding of centrally administered HEIs gradually widened. Therefore, as a forecasting model, this study intends to use average student budgetary expenditure of centrally administered HEIs as the numerator of this ratio variable (GVEXPP_t), which better reflects the financial needs of higher education development, and use the average student budgetary expenditure of local HVCs as the denominator.

Based on the data in 2005–2014 on the ratio of HEIs' enrollment to the total higher education enrollment, average student budgetary expenditure of centrally administered HEIs and locally administered HVCs, and so on, we make use of the aforementioned models (5.1 to 5.3) to conduct estimates of the proportion of allocative proportion of budgetary expenditure.

5.2.1.2 Forecasting method

5.2.1.2.1 TIME SERIES MODEL

The trend analysis of time series is a traditional modeling method that chooses an appropriate trend model to conduct analysis based on the basic rule of the development and change of the time series itself, or the trend of change. The variable y_t indicates a time series, and we can typically do the forecasting by using a model in the following polynomial form:

$$y_t = \alpha_0 + \alpha_1 t + \alpha_2 t^2 + \cdots + \alpha_k t^k + u_t \qquad (5.4)$$

The traditional trend analysis of time series uses models to forecast the long-term trend in y_t, and the error term u_t reflects variations other than the long-term trend of y_t.

5.2.1.2.2 ARIMA MODEL

The autoregressive integrated moving average model, or ARIMA model, was proposed by Box and Jenkins in 1976 and is also known as the Box–Jenkins model. The ARIMA model has been widely applied in all kinds of time series analyses (Box et al., 2007). Different from the trend analysis of time series, the ARIMA

106 *Forecasting the allocation structure*

model recognizes that the forecasted time series is generated by a certain stochastic process, and although there exists uncertainty in some values in the series, the whole process still contains certain rules that can be accurately characterized. In the ARIMA model, the forecasted values in the series can be represented as a linear function of the lagged terms and the current values or lagged values of the stochastic terms. The general form of the model is as follows:

$$y_t = a_0 + a_1 y_{t-1} + \cdots + a_p y_{t-p} + \varepsilon_t + b_1 \varepsilon_{t-1} + \cdots + b_q \varepsilon_{t-p} \tag{5.5}$$

If the series y_t becomes a stationary series after d times of differencing, i.e., y_t is distributed $I(d)$, then in the d-differencing ARMA(p, q) model, p is the number of orders for the autoregressive model AR(p), q is the number of orders for the moving average model MA(q), and ε_t is the white noise.

5.2.1.2.3 EXPONENTIAL SMOOTHING MODEL

Exponential smoothing is a special form of weighted moving average filter. Its basic idea is that the value of any period is the weighted average of the actual observation value in the current time period and the smoothed value in the previous period. The feature of weighting is to give greater weight to the values near the forecast periods, and smaller weights to the values far from the forecast periods. The weights decline geometrically, so this method is called exponential smoothing. According to the order of exponentials, this model can be mainly divided into single-exponential smoothing, double-exponential smoothing, and triple-exponential smoothing. Considering the total periods that this study has, we intend to use double-exponential smoothing.

Given a time series as $x_1, x_2, \ldots, x_t$, and t as the total periods of the time series, the basic formula for double-exponential smoothing is

$$S_t^{(1)} = \alpha x_t + (1-\alpha) S_{t-1}^{(1)} \tag{5.6}$$

$$S_t^{(2)} = \alpha S_t^{(1)} + (1-\alpha) S_{t-1}^{(2)} \tag{5.7}$$

where S_t indicates the smoothed value in period t, x_t indicates the actual value in period t, S_{t-1} is the smoothed value in period $t-1$, and α is the smoothing parameter with a range of [0, 1].

5.2.1.2.4 HOLT–WINTERS NONSEASONAL MODEL

The Holt–Winters nonseasonal model is a multiparameter exponential smoothing model, and the results of exponential smoothing depend on the smoothing parameters. Different from general single-exponential smoothing, this model has two smoothing parameters α and β ($0 \leq \alpha, \beta \leq 1$) (Gardner & Joaquin, 2008). Using EViews packages, we can compute the optimal smoothing parameters, and further estimate the intercept and slope, so as to estimate the model and conduct forecasting on the time series data using the model. a_t is the intercept and b_t is the slope, and the expression of the forecast model expression is

$$X_{t+T} = a_t + b_t T \tag{5.8}$$

$$a_t = \alpha x_t + (1-\alpha)(a_{t-1} + b_{t-1}) \tag{5.9}$$

$$b_t = \beta(a_t - a_{t-1}) + (1-\beta)b_{t-1} \tag{5.10}$$

5.2.1.2.5 FORECAST COMBINATION

For the same time series, the different forecasting methods will produce different forecasted values. Combining these forecasted values with certain weights, we can obtain the results of a forecast combination (or combination of forecasts). A forecast combination can effectively reduce the impact of random factors in the single forecasting model and thus improve the accuracy of forecasts. The most important issue for a forecast combination is how to reasonably determine the weights of separate forecasts. The method based on out-of-sample forecast variances is utilized most often. The basic process of applying this method is of two steps: First is to calculate the sum-of-square of the out-of-sample forecast errors for each forecast (namely, the forecast variance). Second is to obtain the weight for each forecast model by minimizing the sum of all forecast variances, i.e., giving larger weights to the forecast with smaller variance, and smaller weights to the forecast with larger variance (Tang et al., 2003). The formula for calculating the weights can be written as

$$W_j = \sigma_j^{-2} \bigg/ \sum_{j=1}^{m} \sigma_j^{-2} \quad \text{and} \quad \sum_{j=1}^{m} W_j = 1, \ j = 1, 2, \cdots m \tag{5.11}$$

In the vector $W = (W_1, \ldots, W_m)^T$, the element W_j is the weight for each forecast, and σ_j^2 is the corresponding forecast variance.

Given the aforementioned weights, we can further obtain the result of the forecast combination by weighting all the forecasted values ($\hat{x}_j$):

$$X = \sum_{j=1}^{m} W_j \hat{x}_j \tag{5.12}$$

5.2.2 Forecasted results

5.2.2.1 Results of model estimation

The two independent variables in model 1 are regressed with their current values, and both of them pass the significance test at a 10% level, with an adjusted coefficient of determination $\overline{R}^2$ of 0.65 (Table 5.1). Model 2 adds an independent variable

Table 5.1 Forecast model result of the proportion of public investment in HEIs offering degree programs

Variable	Model 1	Model 2	Model 3
Y_{t-1}	NA	0.7043***	NA
		(4.9128)	
$GSTUR_t$	−0.4731*	0.0028	−0.3693**
	(−2.3217)	(0.0227)	(−3.1099)
$GVEXPP_t$	0.0261*	0.0092	
$GVEXPP_{t-1}$	(2.0900)	(1.5961)	0.0236**
			(3.3044)
Constant	1.0384***	0.2146	0.9813***
	(7.5598)	(11975)	(12.4318)
R^2	0.7255	0.9417	0.8507
$\overline{R}^2$	0.6471	0.9067	0.8010
F-Statistic	9.2509	26.9205	17.0981
DW stat	1.2920	1.9731	2.5079
RMSE	0.0121	0.0039	0.0068

Notes: Standard errors are in the parentheses. *, **, and *** indicate the estimated coefficients are significant at the 10%, 5%, and 1% levels, respectively. The RMSE is the square root of the square of the difference between observed values and predicted values divided by the total periods n, and its calculation formula is $RMSE_t = \sqrt{\dfrac{\sum_{t=1}^{n}(\hat{y}_t - y_t)^2}{n}}$.

Y_{t-1}, and Y_{t-1} is significant at the 1% level, while $GVEXPP_t$ and $GSTUR_t$ become insignificant after adding the lag 1 variable Y_{t-1}. According to the possible time lag of the funding impact, model 3 substitutes $GVEXPP_t$ with its lag 1 variable $GVEXPP_{t-1}$, i.e., the ratio of centrally administered HEIs' average student budgetary expenditure to locally administered HVCs' average student budgetary expenditure is affected by the ratio variable in period $t-1$. All variables in model 3 pass the significance tests. Considering that in model 2, in which Y_{t-1} is added, the variables $GSTUR_t$ and $GVEXPP_t$ are not statistically significant, so model 1 and model 3 are more appropriate. Compared with model 1, the goodness of fit and adjusted $\overline{R}^2$ of model 3 are better, and the root-mean-square error (RMSE) of model 1 is nearly two times that of model 3. Taken together, the statistical characteristics of model 3 are better, and its Durbin–Watson (DW) statistic is around 2.5, indicating that the model does not have autocorrelations, which is suitable for forecasting.

Comparing the results of the aforementioned models, we use model 3 to forecast the allocated proportion of China's higher education investment in different types of institutions between 2015 and 2020. The expression of the forecast model is

$$Y_t = 0.9813 - 0.3693 GSTUR_t + 0.0236 GVEXPP_{t-1} \quad (5.13)$$

5.2.2.2 Results of national and provincial forecasts

Through previous analysis of the changing trends of GSTUR and GVEXPP in 2005–2014, GSTUR showed an increasing trend year by year over time, so the trend model, the double-exponential smoothing model, the Holt–Winters nonseasonal model, and the combination model were selected for forecasting the series GSTUR. However, GVEXPP does not have a clear up or down trend between 2000 and 2014, so the ARIMA model, double-exponential smoothing model, and the Holt–Winters nonseasonal model were selected for forecasting the series GVEXPP.

5.2.2.2.1 FORECAST OF THE SERIES GSTUR

Trend analysis is to discover the pattern in data that shows the future movement of a series based on its historical values. As can be seen from Figure 5.1, the ratio of student size is on a rising trend on the whole. According to the model, we first constructed the trend variable t and then fitted all kinds of trend models on the annual data of student size ratio. We finally found that the degree of fit was highest in the cubic polynomial form, which had an adjusted coefficient of determination R^2 as high as 0.9848, and had each regression coefficient pass the t-test at the 1% level. The trend forecast equation for student size (GSTUR) is

$$GSTUR_t = 0.5634 - 0.0223T + 0.0057T^2 - 0.0003T^3 \tag{5.14}$$

Using EViews 7.0 packages to perform double-exponential smoothing to the series GSTUR, we obtained the optimal parameter α = 0.9998, and the RMSE of this model was 0.0057, lower than 1%, which was a highly accurate forecast. The Holt–Winters nonseasonal model was further used to predict the series GSTUR and obtained the optimal parameters α = 0.9997 and β = 1. The RMSE of the model was 0.0058, which provides justification for using this model to do the forecasting. Here we obtained the forecasted values and relative errors of each model, as shown in Table 5.2.

The results show that the combination forecast model, which combines the trend model, exponential smoothing model, and Holt–Winters nonseasonal model, is superior to these three forecast models alone in terms of forecast accuracy. By taking the reciprocal of the variance, we obtained the optimal weights of the trend model, the exponential smoothing model, and the Holt–Winters nonseasonal model $W = (0.6269, 0.1866, 0.1865)^T$. Therefore, we finally used the combination forecast model to forecast the proportion of student size variable GSTUR in 2015–2020,[3] and the forecasted results are shown in Table 5.3.

5.2.2.2.2 FORECAST OF THE SERIES GVEXPP

Observing the changing trend of GVEXPP in Figure 5.2, it is found that the ratio of centrally administered HEIs' average student budgetary expenditure to local HVCs' average student budgetary expenditure fluctuated between 2005 and 2014,

110 Forecasting the allocation structure

Table 5.2 Forecast results of the trend model, exponential smoothing, Holt–Winters nonseasonal smoothing, and combination model

Year	Original series	Trend analysis	Relative error	Single-exponential smoothing	Relative error	Holt–Winters smoothing	Relative error	Forecast combination	Relative error
2005	0.5435	0.5465	0.559	0.5418	−0.319	0.5418	−0.319	0.5418	0.231
2006	0.5425	0.5392	−0.610	0.5469	0.818	0.5469	0.817	0.5469	−0.078
2007	0.5434	0.5396	−0.699	0.5415	−0.350	0.5415	−0.350	0.5415	−0.569
2008	0.5464	0.5460	−0.067	0.5443	−0.370	0.5443	−0.371	0.5443	−0.180
2009	0.5501	0.5565	1.157	0.5493	−0.151	0.5493	−0.151	0.5493	0.669
2010	0.5671	0.5693	0.391	0.5530	−2.324	0.5530	−2.324	0.5539	−0.622
2011	0.5846	0.5826	−0.351	0.5840	−0.106	0.5840	−0.106	0.5840	−0.260
2012	0.5968	0.5945	−0.374	0.6022	0.909	0.6022	0.910	0.6022	0.105
2013	0.6055	0.6033	−0.356	0.6089	0.563	0.6089	0.563	0.6089	−0.013
2014	0.6049	0.6072	0.379	0.6142	1.546	0.6142	1.546	0.6142	0.815

Table 5.3 Forecast results for the proportion of student size variable GSTUR in 2015–2020 with combination model

Year	2015	2016	2017	2018	2019	2020
Combination forecast	0.6042	0.5968	0.5827	0.5610	0.5305	0.4900

Table 5.4 Results for ADF unit root test

	t-Statistic	p-Value
ADF test	–4.6785	0.0089
1% significant	–4.5826	
5% significant	–3.3209	
10% significant	–2.8013	

Autocorrelation	Partial Correlation		AC	PAC	Q-Stat	Prob
		1	0.232	0.232	0.7149	0.398
		2	–0.338	–0.414	2.4329	0.296
		3	–0.092	0.147	2.5773	0.461
		4	–0.021	–0.230	2.5865	0.629
		5	0.122	0.292	2.9446	0.709
		6	0.202	–0.032	4.1740	0.653
		7	–0.144	–0.120	5.0072	0.659
		8	–0.319	–0.179	11.096	0.196
		9	–0.142	–0.135	13.503	0.141

Figure 5.5 Autocorrelation and partial autocorrelation functions.

with no clear trend characteristics, so to forecast this series, this study will not use the traditional fit of trend but the autoregressive moving average (ARMA) model. The ARMA model requires that the series data be stationary. By performing the augmented Dickey–Fuller (ADF) unit root test on the original values of the series GVEXPP, the results of the test, as shown in Table 5.4, reveal that the value of ADF statistics are smaller than the critical value, indicating that the series GVEXPP is a stationary time series, which can be directly used in the ARMA model. By performing autocorrelation analysis of the stationary series GVEXPP, we can obtain its autocorrelation function and the partial correlation function diagram (see Figure 5.5). The area between the lines is formed by the positive and negative double standard deviation of the autocorrelation and the partial autocorrelation. Observing Figure 5.5 we can find that the partial autocorrelation function begins to attenuate with smaller fluctuations from the lag 2 period, from which emerges a trend of rapid convergence. The autocorrelation function also suddenly decreased and maintained inside the range of two times the standard error, with truncations. According to the principle of model fitting, the series can be modeled using AR(2) or MA(2). After comparison and calculation, we obtained the results of the model parameter estimation and statistical tests. Under the same conditions, the Akaike information criterion (AIC) and Bayesian information criterion (BIC) of AR(2) model are small, meanwhile the reciprocals of eigenvalues of the AR(2) model are all in the unit circle, indicating that the model is stationary. Considering the actual situation of economic variables, and the acceptability of goodness of fit, AR(2) is initially determined as a stationary and ideal forecast model.

The corresponding model expression is

$$\text{GVEXPP}_t = 2.8572 - 0.3324(\text{GVEXPP}_{t-2} - 2.8572) + v_t \qquad (5.15)$$

By conducting a white noise test on the residuals of the model, it is found that the Q value of the residual series is less than the critical value of the chi-square distribution at the 0.05 level, so the random error term of the model is a white noise series. At the same time, the mean absolute percentage error (MAPE) of the model is 6.18, less than 10, which can be considered a highly accurate forecast model. Therefore, we can use the AR(2) model to conduct forecasts.

In a similar manner, by applying the reciprocal of the variance to the series GVEXPP, we obtained the optimal weights of the ARMA model, the double-exponential smoothing model, and the Holt–Winters nonseasonal model $W = (0.6269, 0.1866, 0.1865)^T$. In the same way, we obtained the combination forecast results of the ratio of centrally administered HEIs' average student budgetary expenditure to local HVCs' average student budgetary expenditure (GVEXPP) as shown in Table 5.5.

5.2.2.2.3 FORECAST OF THE SERIES Y_T

Furthermore, we conducted forecasting Y_t based on formula 5.13 and obtained a series Y_f as shown in Table 5.6.

According to the aforementioned forecast values, we depicted in Figure 5.6 the proportion of public investment in HEIs to the total public investment in higher education (Y_f), the proportion of the student size in HEIs to the total higher education student size (GSTUR), and the ratio of HEIs' average student budgetary expenditure to that of HVCs (GVEXPP$_f$) in 2016–2020. It can be found that during the period of the 13th Five-Year Plan, the proportion of HEIs' student size and

Table 5.5 Forecast results of combination model for GVEXPP (the ratio of centrally administered HEIs' per student budgetary expenditure to local HVCs' per student budgetary expenditure) in 2015–2020

Year	2015	2016	2017	2018	2019	2020
Combination forecast	2.7154	2.6701	2.6280	2.5827	2.5363	2.4910

Table 5.6 Forecast values of Y_f in 2015–2020

Year	2015	2016	2017	2018	2019	2020
Y_f value	0.8201	0.8252	0.8293	0.8363	0.8465	0.8604

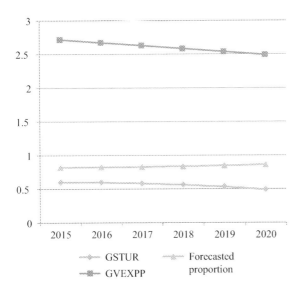

Figure 5.6 The feasible interval of the proportion of public investment in HEIs offering degree programs in 2016–2020.

the ratio of average student budgetary expenditure of HEIs to HVCs will go down considerably, and the proportion of HEIs' public investment will increase within the range of 0.82 to 0.86.

5.2.2.2.4 FORECAST OF THE PUBLIC INVESTMENT RATIO OF LOCAL HEIS TO HVCS

On June 15, 2016, the State Council officially issued "The General Office of State Council's Guidance on Speeding Up the Education Development in the Central and West China", which focuses on supporting the construction of one university in 13 provinces (Hebei, Henan, Inner Mongolia, Shanxi, Jiangxi, Guangxi, Hainan, Guizhou, Yunnan, Tibet, Qinghai, Ningxia, and Xinjiang) without higher education institutions under the administration of Ministry of Education (MOE) according to the principle of "one university for one province", so as to train senior engineering and management talent for "Belt and Road" construction.

There is no detailed data on the student size for MOE-administered universities and local HEIs at the provincial level in the statistical yearbook, and there are

114 *Forecasting the allocation structure*

no MOE-administered universities in those 13 provinces. Moreover, there are no missing data for the 13 provinces in 2005–2014. Based on these reasons, in order to maintain data consistency, this study takes the local HEIs and HVCs in the 13 provinces as the research objects and uses the provincial panel data to establish the following model for forecasting:

$$Y_{it} = a_i + b_1 GSTUR_{it} + b_2 GVEXPPA_{i,t-1} + u_{it}, \quad i = 1,\ldots,n, \quad t = 1,\ldots,T \quad (5.16)$$

where i indicates the ith province, t indicates the tth year, Y is the public investment in local HEIs offering degree programs as a percentage of total public investment in all local institutions, GSTUR is the student size in local HEIs offering degree programs as a percentage of the total student size in all local institutions, and $GVEXPPA_t$ is the ratio of local HEIs' (offering degree programs) average student budgetary expenditure to local HVCs' average student budgetary expenditure. Table 5.7 shows the descriptive statistics for each variable.

First, a mixed model was established for the sample. A characteristic of the mixed model is that for all individuals and sections, the model has the same regression coefficients and intercept terms. The estimated results after running the mixed model are as follows:

$$Y_t = 0.6248 + 0.2049 GSTUR_t + 0.00136 GVEXPPA_{t-1} \quad (5.17)$$

$$\begin{cases} \hat{Y}_{1t} = \hat{\gamma}_{Hebei} + \hat{b}_1 GSTUR_{1t} + \hat{b}_2 GVEXPPA_{1t-1} \\ \quad = (0.6045 + 0.0194) + 0.2514 GSTUR_{1t} + 0.0107 GVEXPPA_{1t-1} \\ \hat{Y}_{2t} = \hat{\gamma}_{Henan} + \hat{b}_1 GSTUR_{2t} + \hat{b}_2 GVEXPPA_{2t-1} \\ \quad = (0.6045 + 0.0182) + 0.2514 GSTUR_{2t} + 0.0107 GVEXPPA_{2t-1} \\ \cdots \\ \hat{Y}_{13t} = \hat{\gamma}_{Xinjiang} + \hat{b}_1 GSTUR_{13t} + \hat{b}_2 GVEXPPA_{13t-1} \\ \quad = (0.6045 - 0.0163) + 0.2514 GSTUR_{13t} + 0.0107 GVEXPPA_{13t-1} \end{cases} \quad (5.18)$$

Next, we built a model with individual fixed effects and found that Qinghai, Yunnan, and Hebei were the three regions with the largest intercepts. By applying

Table 5.7 Descriptive statistics for variables (2005–2014)

Variable	Mean	Median	Maximum	Minimum	Standard deviation
Y	0.768	0.767	0.9879	0.5751	0.0694
GSTUR	0.548	0.555	0.6730	0.3808	0.0683
GVEXPPA	1.794	1.653	4.2027	0.8736	0.6474

the F test, the results showed that the null hypothesis of the identical intercept for different individuals in the model was rejected, demonstrating that it is reasonable to establish a model with individual fixed effects rather than the mixed model. Based on the fixed effect model, we forecasted the public investment in HEIs offering degree programs as a percentage of total public investment in higher education for 13 provinces in 2015–2020.

According to the forecasted results (Table 5.8), we found that for most provinces in 2015–2020 (Hebei, Henan, Shanxi, Jiangxi, Hainan, Guizhou, Tibet, and Ningxia), the share of public investment in local HEIs offering degree programs was on a yearly rising trend, and the share of public investment in HVCs was on a yearly downward trend. Consistent with the national trend, for the provinces of Yunnan and Xinjiang, the shares of public investment in local HEIs were on a downward trend, and the shares of public investment in HVCs increased accordingly. Whereas for Inner Mongolia, Guangxi, and Qinghai, there existed some fluctuation in the shares of public investment in local HEIs, of which Guangxi and Qinghai fluctuated more. However, on the whole, Guangxi's share of public investment in HEIs was on the rise, and Qinghai showed a downward trend, while Inner Mongolia slightly fluctuated within a mean of about 0.690.

5.3 Main conclusions and policy implications

5.3.1 Main conclusions

In the new period of the 13th Five-Year Plan, how to rationally allocate the public investment proportion of higher education between higher education institutions

Table 5.8 Forecast results for the public investment in local higher education institutions offering degree programs (HEIs) as a percentage of total public investment in higher education, 2015–2020 by province (fixed effect model)

Province	2015	2016	2017	2018	2019	2020
Hebei	0.7967	0.8014	0.8079	0.8131	0.8191	0.8245
Henan	0.7946	0.7983	0.8020	0.8056	0.8093	0.8130
Inner Mongolia	0.6959	0.6960	0.6962	0.6962	0.6961	0.6960
Shanxi	0.7498	0.7529	0.7564	0.7603	0.7640	0.7675
Jiangxi	0.7815	0.7862	0.7908	0.7955	0.8001	0.8048
Guangxi	0.7732	0.7684	0.7776	0.7738	0.7875	0.7798
Hainan	0.7798	0.7811	0.7827	0.7844	0.7863	0.7883
Guizhou	0.7855	0.7856	0.7858	0.7859	0.7859	0.7860
Yunnan	0.7975	0.7942	0.7912	0.7898	0.7885	0.7861
Tibet	0.7721	0.7785	0.7845	0.7906	0.7965	0.8026
Qinghai	0.8387	0.8360	0.8332	0.8338	0.8345	0.8329
Ningxia	0.7406	0.7422	0.7439	0.7455	0.7472	0.7488
Xinjiang	0.7373	0.7356	0.7343	0.7327	0.7309	0.7293

(HEIs) offering degree programs and higher vocational colleges, to ensure the comprehensive development of higher education, narrow the gap between the education development level of underdeveloped provinces and the national level, and secure the supply of high-quality human capital, has become an important question that urgently needs to be solved. Based on the analysis of data, such as the student size ratio of HEIs offering degree programs to HVCs and the average student budgetary expenditure in China from 2005 to 2014, this study used a combination model of trend analysis, ARIMA, double-exponential smoothing, and a Holt–Winters nonseasonal model to predict the allocative proportion of public investment between HEIs and HVCs in 2015–2020, and used provincial panel data to research the ratio of public investment between local HEIs and HVCs. The main conclusions are as follows:

1. From the perspective of the scale of higher education development, the enrollment of HEIs and HVCs in China increased year by year between 2005 and 2014, but the average annual growth rate of HVCs' enrollment was only about half that of HEIs, and the gap on the scale between HEIs and HVCs continued to increase. In terms of average student expenditures, although the ratio of centrally administered HEIs to locally administered HVCs decreased between 2005 and 2014, as of 2014, the average student expenditure of centrally administered HEIs was still about 2.5 times that of locally administered HEIs, demonstrating the existence of allocation imbalance on public investment in higher education between different types of institutions.
2. As per the econometric model, which was based on national time series data, forecasted, during the 13th Five-Year Plan period (2016–2020), if the student size ratio of HEIs offering degree programs changed between 0.6 and 0.49, and the average student budgetary expenditure ratio of centrally administered HEIs to locally administered HVCs remained between 2.67 and 2.49, the feasible interval of the public investment in HEIs as a percentage of total public investment in higher education is 0.83–0.86, showing an upward trend. Accordingly, the feasible interval of the public investment in HVCs as a percentage of total public investment in higher education was 0.17–0.14, showing a downward trend.
3. Building the panel data model with individual fixed effects in 13 provinces that had no HEIs administered under the Ministry of Education, the results showed that during the 13th Five-Year Plan period, for the provinces of Hebei, Henan, Shanxi, Jiangxi, Hainan, Guizhou, Tibet, and Ningxia, the shares of public investment in HEIs offering degree programs were on a yearly increasing trend, and the shares of public investment in HVCs showed a downward trend, which was in line with the trend of national change. For Yunnan and Xinjiang provinces, the shares of public investment in HEIs were on a yearly decreasing trend, meanwhile, for Inner Mongolia, Guangxi, and Qinghai, the shares of public investment in HEIs fluctuated.

5.3.2 Policy implications

From the overall forecasted results, during the 13th Five-Year Plan period, China's public investment in HEIs offering degree programs as a percentage of total public investment in higher education will continue to increase, and the share of public investment in HVCs will decline. Meanwhile the ratio of HVCs' student size to the total higher education enrollment will continue to increase during the 13th Five-Year Plan period, so the government expenditure in higher vocational education will be far from the pace of higher vocational development, and the structural imbalance of higher education finance will continue to hinder the development of higher vocational colleges, which contradicts with the educational goals of developing new patterns of higher vocational education. To this end, the following policy recommendations are proposed:

1. **Appropriately adjust the allocation of total public investment in higher education between HEIs offering degree programs and HVCs, and narrow the gap on public investment between HVCs and HEIs.**

As pointed out by the "Guidance on Promoting the Coordinated Development of Secondary and Higher Vocational Education" issued by the Ministry of Education in 2011, the standard of average student budgetary funding for HVCs should gradually reach the funding standard of the same type of HEIs offering degree programs within the same area. As pointed out by the "Decision on Speeding Up the Development of Modern Vocational Education" issued by the State Council in 2014, it is necessary to raise the level of guarantee for the development of vocational education, and provincial governments should be urged to gradually raise the average student funding standard or government funding standard. Government funding should be dominant in higher vocational education investment, which is also the cornerstone of the development of higher vocational education (Zhou & Hou, 2014). Therefore, while appropriately adjusting the allocation of total public investment in higher education between HEIs and HVCs, we should pay more attention to the allocative ratio of average student funding, and take the narrowing of the public investment gap between HVCs and HEIs as the principle, to invest in HVCs and ensure the stable development of higher vocational education in accordance with the economic development requirements of different regions and the development of vocational education needs.

2. **Guide enterprises and society to increase investment and improve the funding mechanism for higher vocational education.**

Colleges and enterprises are the two main subjects of vocational education. And enterprises, as the main entities to be served by vocational education, should be fully motivated to provide higher vocational development with more technical and financial support. Relevant policies should be utilized to encourage enterprises and social funds to invest in vocational education and expand the sources of vocational education finance. In 2015, the Ministry of Education issued an announcement on the "Action Plan for the Improvement of the Management level of Vocational Colleges (2015–2018)", which again proposed the implementation of average student funding policy, the establishment of a multichannel funding mechanism, and improvement of the financial security level. In addition, local governments and educational administrations should establish a performance-oriented system of the average student funding to improve the efficiency of the utilization of funds.

3. **Strengthen vocational education cooperation with the countries of the One Belt One Road Initiative, and optimize the professional structure of higher vocational colleges to meet the demand for skilled talent in China's industrial transformation.**

In the context of "One Belt One Road" and the cultivation of innovative and entrepreneurial talents, the construction needs of an industrial transformation require further accelerating the adjustment of the disciplinary structure of higher vocational colleges, supporting the training model of innovative talent in higher vocational colleges, and striving to improve students' professional competencies in order to meet the needs of technically skilled talent for industrial transformation and upgrading, and economic and social development. The implementation of the One Belt One Road Initiative requires strengthening vocational education cooperation with One Belt One Road countries; building internationally advanced vocational colleges; and encouraging vocational colleges to hire outstanding teachers from abroad or subsidizing students from higher vocational colleges to conduct overseas internships, and training technically skilled talent with an international perspective and knowledge of international rules, as well as training the talent needed for the overseas production and operation of Chinese enterprises. Whether vocational colleges can successfully seize this opportunity, financial security is key. The optimization of the disciplinary structure of higher vocational colleges can be promoted by establishing a management mechanism of average student funding standard appraised by discipline. For example, those disciplines that are urgently needed for regional development planning and industrial transformation and upgrading can be appraised with a higher quotient, and those disciplines that do not meet the needs of economic and social development can be appraised with a lower quotient. The establishment of an appropriate disciplinary funding mechanism will provide adequate financial security for the training of professionally skilled talent.

Notes

1 The average annual growth rate in this chapter is the geometric growth rate. The growth rate during the 19 years is $1363/119 = 11.4538$, so the average growth rate is $11.4538^{\wedge}(1/19) - 1 = 13.7\%$. The same calculation applies to rates later in the chapter.
2 According to the International Standard Classification of Education (ISCED) promulgated by the United Nations Educational, Scientific, and Cultural Organization (UNESCO) in 1997, this study divides tertiary education (level 5) into academically based (5A) and vocationally based (5B). The ISCED describes academically based edu-

cation (5A) as "largely theoretically based and are intended to provide sufficient qualifications for gaining entry into advanced research programs and profession with high skills requirements". The ISCED describes vocationally based education (5B) as "practically oriented/occupationally specific and is mainly designed for participants to acquire the practical skills, and know-how needed for employment in a particular occupation or trade or class of occupations or trades – the successful completion of which usually provides the participants with a labor-market relevant qualification". From these definitions, it can be seen that in China, higher education institutions offering degree programs belong to the 5A level, and higher vocational colleges belong to the 5B level. At present, there is no postgraduate degree programs offered in China's higher vocational colleges, only vocational and bachelor degrees. Postgraduate degrees belong to level 6, which are offered in HEIs in China. Therefore, we divide institutions in China into two general categories: HEIs offering degree programs and higher vocational colleges.

3 Because the statistical data on educational funds for educational development in China are generally publish after the March of the following year, and the official publication of statistical yearbook will be delayed for one more year, this study used relevant data in 2000–2014 to forecast the student size as well as the ratio of centrally administered HEIs' per student budgetary expenditure to the local HVCs' per student budgetary expenditure in 2015.

References

Box, G. E. P., Jenkins, G. M., & Reinsel, G. C. (2007). *Time Series Analysis Forecasting and Control* (3rd edition). New Jersey: Prentice-Hall.

CMOE (China's Ministry of Education). (2014). *The Opinion on Constructing and Perfecting the Reform-Oriented and Performance-Oriented Per Student Funding System and Speeding up the Development of Modern Higher Vocational Education* (Jiao Cai [2014] No.352). Retrieved June 8, 2021, from http://www.moe.gov.cn/jyb_xxgk/moe_1777/moe_1779/201502/t20150209_185746.html

Gardner Jr., E. S., & Joaquin, D. S. (2008). Exponential smoothing in the telecommunications data. *International Journal of Forecasting*, 24(1), 170–174.

Hu, Y. M., & Tang, Y. P. (2014). Apportion of education budget in the post-4% era: An empirical study based on transnational data. *Journal of Beijing Normal University (Social Sciences)*, 5, 13–24.

Liu, T. Z., & Chen, X. D. (2013). On the phenomenon of formulated public higher education financial resource allocation pattern: evidence from H province. *Education and Economics*, 2013(2), 38–42.

Luo, J. P., & Ma, L. T. (2013). Analysis on the effectiveness of the allocation of funds in Colleges and universities in China. *Education Exploration*, 9, 22–24.

NETEASE. (2019). Education news. Retrieved from January 20, 2019, from http://edu.163.com/09/1110/08/5NODLJQF00293L7F.html

Song, F. J., Hu, W., & Liu, S. X. (2015). The analysis of financial input structure imbalance problem of China's higher education. *Education Science*, 31(6), 31–35.

Sun, Z. J. (2009). Changes in university income in a decade of expansion in China: An interpretation. *Tsinghua Journal of Education*, 4, 72–80.

Tang, X. W., Zhou, Z. F., & Shi, Y. (2003). The variable weighted functions of combined forecasting. *Computers & Mathematics with Applications*, 45(4–5), 723–730.

Zhou, J. W., & Hou, L. Z. (2014). The analysis on the regional differences of China's financial education funds to the contribution of economic development. *Inquiry into Economic Issues*, 8, 150–155.

6 Research on the standard for teaching funding and average student funding in higher education

6.1 History of the funding model of China's central universities

Central universities are at the center of Chinese higher education. Central universities are higher education institutions under the administration of central ministries and are also known as centrally administered universities. In order to adapt to and accelerate the development of central universities, the central government's investment in central universities has been continuously increasing, and the funding model has also experienced a four-stage development (Wang, 2012): "base plus growth" (1955–1985), "comprehensive quota plus special subsidies" (1986–2002), "basic expenditure plus project expenditure" (2002–2008), and "average student comprehensive quota" (2008–present).

6.1.1 Funding model of "base plus growth" (1955–1985) in central universities

Since 1955, Chinese government funding for the central universities had been relatively stable, until 1985 when central universities began to implement the allocation method based on a certain quota, during which time there has not been much change. The quota method is the basis of the "base plus growth" funding model. According to the "Joint Announcement on Strengthening the Establishment of Quotas for the Education, Culture and Health Services" issued in 1995, "the so-called quota is to reasonably determine the various staff registration, housing and equipment standards, administrative and operational expenses, and the reserves of equipment according to the size or the needs of the government-affiliated institutions" (Gu, 2012). On this basis, the follow-up approval of university grants is mainly achieved by means of "base plus growth". Under this funding model, the central government takes the allocation of funds in the previous year as the basis, considers the changes in the development of the current year, then determines the amount of the appropriated funds for the current year. If the student numbers, teacher numbers, and other aspects of that year did not change substantially, then the universities would receive about the same amount of funds as the previous year.

The operation of this kind of allocation mode is relatively simple, mainly taking into account the historical funding levels to determine the current funding levels. This model has certain reasonability, which simplifies the decision-making process, and needs much less information from the universities. In the initial period of higher education in China, the number of universities was relatively small, and the type of universities and the structure of disciplines were relatively simple, so the "base plus growth" funding model had certain applicability, and showed some positive results for ensuring the steady development of higher education institutions in accordance with the conventional pace. However, it is easy for this model to produce higher education stratification. Furthermore, this kind of funding model has more restrictions on university expenditures and is in favor of universities making their medium- and long-term strategic plans in accordance with their own development needs, so it is difficult to ensure the long-term development of universities on the need for government funds.

6.1.2 Funding model of "comprehensive quota plus special subsidies" in central universities (1986–2002)

From the mid-to-late 1980s to the beginning of the 21st century, with the rapid development of higher education, China's higher education institutions have changed greatly in both quantity and scale, and the drawbacks of the "base plus growth" funding model are becoming more prominent. In October 1986, after a joint investigation by the former Ministry of Finance and the National Education Commission, it was decided to promulgate the "Measures for the Implementation of the Financial Management Reform of Higher Education Institutions". This document stipulated that

> the budgets of annual education expenses of higher education institutions are approved by the method of comprehensive quota plus special subsidies in light of the national financial resource, which are managed by the administration departments in accordance with the needs of students at different levels and different subjects, the different circumstances in the area where the institution is located.

Therefore, beginning in 1986, China's higher education funding implemented the model of "comprehensive quota plus special subsidies". The principles of "self-response, no renewals for overspending, surplus saved, self-balancing" were also enacted.

The combination of comprehensive quota plus special subsidies is actually a combination funding model with simple formulas and estimations. Under this funding model, the financial allocation of higher education institutions is divided into two parts: the comprehensive quota and the special subsidies. Among them, the comprehensive quota follows the previous management method of fixed amount and number, by multiplying the number of students by the average student funds. It distinguishes between different quotas according to the students' level, subject, and major. Special subsidies are a supplement to the comprehensive quota, and in the course of implementation, the educational administrations and financial departments approve the allocation separately in accordance with the national policy orientation toward universities and the special needs of some colleges and universities, such as funds for the construction of new and key disciplines, major and laboratory construction, special project subsidies, and funds for retirees.

In the higher education funding model of "comprehensive quota plus special subsidies", the comprehensive quota is the main part, and the calculation process of the quota is divided into three steps. The first step is to determine the average student quota. The national undergraduate cultivation costs are classified according to different majors, and colleges and universities in different regions are selected as samples for accounting. The data obtained by accounting divided by the number of students is the calculation criteria for the average student quota at a point in time. The second step is to determine the full-time equivalent (FTE) number of students in colleges and universities. First, the university students are divided into three categories: doctoral students, master's students, and undergraduate students in normal courses and short-cycle courses. Then, the different conversion factor criteria for each type of student are determined. In the third step, according to the actual number of students and the conversion coefficient of various types of colleges and universities, the FTE of students can be calculated. According to the "General Higher Education Basic Conditions Indicators (Trial)" (Jiaofa [200] No.2) promulgated by the Ministry of Education, the FTE student numbers = (Doctoral student numbers × 2) + (Master's student numbers × 1.5) + (Undergraduate students in normal courses and short-cycle courses × 1).

Under this funding model, many colleges and universities obtain more government funds through the expansion of enrollment, in order to ensure that colleges and universities have sufficient financial funds to maintain their operation. Coupled with the higher education expansion policy formally implemented by the Ministry of Education in 1999, the vast majority of colleges and universities in China began to rapidly increase the student size and expand to new campuses to solve the serious shortage of teaching land with the support of local governments. At the same time, because the construction of new campuses requires huge capital funds, many colleges and universities began to borrow from banks to supplement construction funds, causing huge debt problems.

6.1.3 Funding model of "basic expenditure plus project expenditure" (2002–2008) in central universities

Beginning in 2002, the state ministries began to reform the budget system and implemented the model of "basic expenditure plus project expenditure". The budget of basic expenditure is still in accordance with the management principle of a fixed amount and fixed number. The basic expenditure can guarantee the normal operation and completion of daily work in governmental and government-affiliated units. Personnel expenditure and daily public expenditure constitute the basic expenditure budget. The project expenditure budget is an annual project expenditure plan prepared in addition to the basic expenditure for colleges and universities to complete their special development needs, including capital construction projects, administrative projects, and other projects.

In order to adapt to the reform of the national budget system, education departments have also adjusted the funding model to higher education institutions. For colleges and universities, the annual basic expenditure to ensure normal operation and complete daily tasks should be attributed to the basic expenditure budget in the mode of "basic expenditure and project expenditure". Unlike the previous model, which approved comprehensive quotas based only on the number of students, the personnel funds in the basic expenditure of the new model include salaries of faculty and staff, funds for retired personnel, and student financial support (scholarship, stipend, and student loan), but only the number of faculty and staff and the number of retired personnel were used to approve personnel expenditure, and the number of students was used to approve the amount of public expenditure (Gong, 2011). This kind of funding model made colleges and universities begin to give more emphasis to the ratio of students to teachers, and no longer blindly expand enrollment. However, because the project expenditure within each institution had different needs, the phenomenon of universities "competing for financial resources by lobbying administrators in Beijing" began to appear.

6.1.4 Funding model of "comprehensive quota for students" (2008–present) in central universities

In 2008, the Ministry of Finance and the Ministry of Education established a budget allocation system for central universities with the "average student comprehensive quota plus special funds" as the main body. The main policy measures were to refine the standard of the funding standard of the average student comprehensive quota, incorporate the basic scientific research funds for central universities, introduce the performance-based funding mechanism, and incorporate the compensation funds for social services.

In accordance with the regulations set by the "Ministry of Finance and the Ministry of Education's Announcement on Improving the Budget and Funding System of Central Universities" (Jiao Cai [2008], No. 232), the government set the principle of "basically equal on personnel funds and differences reflected in public funds", refined the standard of the average student comprehensive quota, and improved the funding methods for basic expenditure for colleges and universities. The specific measures are as follows. First, the composition and basic criteria of public funds and personnel funds were reasonably determined. According to the current financial situation, combined with the estimated proportion of personnel funds and public funds to average student expenditure, the basic standards for public funds and personnel funds were approved to be 3000 yuan per student and 4000 yuan per student, respectively. Second was to set the conversion coefficient of public funds according to the discipline. That is, the different levels of the disciplinary conversion coefficient were set according to the 11 major disciplines of undergraduate teaching in higher education. For different disciplines, there was a quota standard for public funds, reflecting the differences in operational costs of different disciplines. Third was the establishment of a dynamic adjustment mechanism. According to the development needs of central universities, combined with the financial situation, the level of price changes, the number of students changes, and other factors, the public funds and personnel funds base quota standards were allowed to be dynamically adjusted.

The basis of the disciplinary conversion coefficient of public funds was 3000 yuan, forming seven conversion coefficients (1, 1.25, 1.33, 1.5, 2, 2.5, 3), which further resulted in seven types of personnel and public funds accordingly (see Table 6.1). The standards of average student funding were refined to seven levels, corresponding to different disciplines or majors: for literature, history, philosophy, 7000 yuan per student per year; for law, economics, science, management, and education, 7750 yuan per student per year; for engineering, 7990 yuan per student per year; for medicine, 11,500 yuan per student per year; for literature (arts), 10,000 yuan per student per year; for art students in pure art institutions, 13,000 yuan art per student per year; for physical education, ethnology, archaeology, mineral oil and marine engineering, journalism, and agronomy, 8500 yuan per student per year.

Since then, the undergraduate comprehensive quota in universities directly under the administration of the central government were set according to the disciplinary conversion coefficient for public funds, but the standards were considerably improved. Currently, the standards of undergraduate comprehensive quota implemented by the Ministry of Education are personnel funds, 6000 yuan per student per year; and public funds, 6000 yuan per student per year (Sun et al., 2015). In addition, some special majors and special institutions of small scale are preferably funded. The average student comprehensive quota for postgraduates is a set unified funding standard according to master's programs (22,000 yuan per student per year) and doctoral programs (28,000 yuan per student per year), but no disciplinary and institutional differences are taken into account.

In 2015, in order to further reform the central university funding model, and at the same time be a model role for local universities, the Ministry of Education and the Ministry of Finance issued the "Announcement on Reform and Improvement of the Central University Budget and Funding System" (Jiao Cai [2015], No. 467), which clearly proposed to improve the basic expenditure system. On the basis of the current system of average student quota, a relatively stable mechanism for the total amount of average student quota funding for undergraduates in central universities would be gradually established: a two- to three-year cycle to maintain the basic stability of the total amount of average student quota funding for undergraduates in each central university during the cycle. After the end of each cycle comes approval of the next cycle of the total amount of average student quota funding for undergraduates in central universities. At the same time, the government would timely adjust the standard of average student quota funding for undergraduates and guide the central universities to reasonably adjust their enrollment scale and disciplinary structure, according to the central government's financial situation and other circumstances.

Standard for teaching funding 125

Table 6.1 Average student comprehensive quota standard of undergraduates in central universities after the 2008 reform

Discipline/student category	Average student comprehensive quota standard	Quota standard of personnel funds	Quota standard for public funds		
			Quota standard for public funds	Disciplinary coefficient of public funds	Basic standards for public funds
Philosophy	7000	4000	3000	1	3000
Economics	7750	4000	3750	1.25	3000
Law	7750	4000	3750	1.25	3000
Education	7750	4000	3750	1.25	3000
Of which: Physical education	8500	4000	4500	1.5	3000
Literature	7000	4000	3000	1	3000
Of which: Arts	10000	4000	6000	2	3000
Journalism	8500	4000	4500	1.5	3000
History	7000	4000	3000	1	3000
Of which: Ethnology, Archaeology	8500	4000	4500	1.5	3000
Science	7750	4000	3750	1.25	3000
Engineering	7990	4000	3990	1.33	3000
Of which: Mineral oil, Marine Engineering	8500	4000	4500	1.5	3000
Agronomy	8500	4000	4500	1.5	3000
Medicine	11500	4000	7500	2.5	3000
Management	7750	4000	3750	1.25	3000

6.2 Current status of average student funding in local higher education institutions

Local colleges and universities are mainly sponsored and run by provincial and municipal governments, so most of the funds allocated for local universities come from local governments. Compared with the relatively unified funding policy and clear funding model of central universities, the average student funding of local colleges and universities was in a loose state, and the funding level was relatively low for a long time. However, this would change in 2010 when the Ministry of Finance and Ministry of Education issued the "Opinion on Further Improving the Level of the Average Student Funding in Locally-Administered Higher Education Institutions Offering Degree Programs". This section first summarizes the general practice of local universities' appropriated funds and then introduces the current situation of the average student funding in some provinces.

6.2.1 Overview of local higher education institutions' appropriated funds

For local colleges and universities, budgeting plays a key role in the approval process of their appropriated funds, and the relevant data filled in the budget report are the main basis for the approved funds. Local colleges and universities submit their budgets to the local government's department of education and finance, which adopted an "up twice, down twice" process (Li, 2016). In the "first up" stage, colleges and universities summarize and organize basic information data, such as the number of students, discipline categories, number of faculty and staff, and assets, then submit them to the government's department of education and department of finance together with the application for special funds for the following year. In the "first down" stage, the government will approve the number of basic funds for the next year according to the basic information data submitted by colleges and universities. According to the application for special funds, the government conducts research and demonstrations and makes a preliminary determination of the amount of special funds arrangements for colleges and universities for the next year in light of the needs of social and economic development and the development needs of colleges and universities. In the "second up" stage, colleges and universities take into account the basic funds and special funds arrangements approved by the government to prepare their budgets for the next year, refine the expenditure items, and submit the budget to the government's department of education and department of finances for examination. In the "second down" stage, the government's department of education and department of finance summarize and review the budget data submitted by the colleges and universities, and submit the budget to the local people's congress for consideration. After passing the consideration of the local people's congress, the budgets of colleges and universities will be approved and the funds for next year will be appropriated.

In the accounting of basic appropriations, after 2008, local colleges and universities began to account their basic funds of the government appropriations in their provinces or cities in accordance with the Ministry of Education's "Announcement on Improving the Budget and Funding System of Central Universities" (Jiaocai [2008], No. 232). In terms of specific modalities for funding approval, there are two broad approaches. The first approach is the method of "average student comprehensive quota" plus "funds for retirees". This approach integrates all the public funds and the funds of personnel without the funds of retirees into the average student comprehensive quota and calculates the funds according to the number of students in different disciplines and the disciplinary conversion coefficient. Funds of retirees and medical expenses are accounted for separately. The second approach is that the public funds are accounted according to the average student quota, but the personnel funds are accounted separately. This approach calculates the public funds by colleges' and universities' average student quota only, which is based on the number of students in different disciplines and the disciplinary conversion coefficient. Personnel funds are divided into three categories, namely, on-job personnel funds, off-job personnel funds, and retiree funds, then calculated, respectively.

Considering that the level of average student funding in local colleges and universities has always been lower than that of central universities (Sun, 2009), the Ministry of Education and the Ministry of Finance issued the "Opinions on Further Improving the Level of Average Student Funding Level of Local Higher Education Institutions Offering Degree Programs" (Cai Jiao [2010], No. 567) in November 2010, proposing to further improve the level of average student funding for local college students. All localities should formulate the basic criteria for the allocation of funds to local college students in accordance with the reasonable needs of colleges and universities. On this basis, combined with the financial situation, price change level, changes in the number of college students, wage standard adjustment, and other factors, the dynamic adjustment mechanism of average student funding standards for local higher education institutions should be established, and the level of average student funding should be gradually improved. In principle, in 2012, the average student funding level of local colleges should be no less than 12,000 yuan.

From 2010, the central financial government established a mechanism of "replacing subsidy by award". For those provinces whose average student funding level reached 12,000 yuan, the central government would give a certain amount of bonus each year. For other provinces that had not yet reached the average student funding level of 12,000 yuan, the central government would provide a proportion of subsidies based on the funding requirements. The specific proportion of subsidies were determined by the basic proportions (eastern region 25%, the central and western regions 35%) as well as the number of students, provincial-level financial growth, and other factors, so as to help the average student funding level in these provinces to meet the standard.

6.2.2 Average student funding policies in some provinces

Although there are Ministry of Education documents as a reference, because of the different financial situations of provinces and cities, as well as different situations

128 *Standard for teaching funding*

of development of higher education, the process of reaching the standard for the average student funding varies from place to place. This section focuses on the provinces that have undertaken the reform of the average student funding in accordance with the Ministry of Education documents and introduces their latest funding policies and funding criteria.

At the end of 2011, the Department of Finance and the Department of Education in Henan province issued the "Opinions on The Implementation of Further Improving the Level of Average Student Funding in Higher Education Institutions Offering Degree Programs" (Yu Cai Jiao [2011], No. 339). The document proposed that the average student funding for colleges and universities in the province would not be less than 9000 yuan by the end of 2011 and 12,000 yuan by the end of 2012. The allocation of funds was mainly based on the number of students in the previous year (excluding those students with higher tuitions fees, such as Chinese–foreign cooperative institutions and software vocational colleges) and the determined institution types (conversion coefficient: comprehensive, 1.33; science and engineering 1.29; agriculture and forestry, 1.5; medicine, 2.5; normal education, 1.25; economics and finance, 1.25; politics and law, 1.25; sports, 1.5). At the same time, doctoral students, master's students, and undergraduate students in normal courses and short-cycle courses should be converted in accordance with the prescribed proportion, to reflect the difference in operational costs.

At the beginning of 2014, the Finance Bureau and the Education Commission in Tianjin Municipality issued a document "On Improving the System of Average Student Funding in Higher Education Institutions Offering Degree Programs in Tianjin" (Jin Cai Jiao [2014], No. 5), proposing to improve the standard of average student funding, and finally achieve the goal of not less than 12,000 yuan in 2014, and not less than 13,000 yuan in 2015 (CMOE, 2014). In accordance with the principle of "staff funds in accordance with the structure of students and teachers, public funds reflect the differences in operational costs", improve the approved method of the basic expenditure budget of colleges and universities, reasonably determine the standards for the allocation of funds for active personnel and public funds for students, and continue to be approved according to the actual number of retirees and relevant standards. The following is done: First, the basic criteria are established. Based on the current level of funding for college students, taking into account the scale of operational costs, the structure of students, and the maintenance of steady growth of funds, the basic criteria for the allocation of funds for active and public funds are determined. The second is to set the conversion coefficient. According to the actual level of staff funds currently in service, as well as the differences between different levels of operation and disciplinary categories, the conversion factor of the funds serving personnel shall be set according to the institution category,[1] and the conversion coefficient of public funds shall be set according to the level of operational costs and the disciplinary categories.[2] Third is the establishment of a dynamic adjustment mechanism. According to the development needs of colleges and universities, combined with the financial situation, price changes, school size, wage standards, and other factors, the average student funding standard should be dynamically adjusted. Colleges and universities should consider the development goals, institutional conditions, social needs, and so on, to reasonably target, plan scientifically, optimize the professional setting of disciplines, highlight the advantages of operations, and avoid blindly expanding the scale. For colleges and universities whose students exceed the reasonable scale of operation, the basic standard and conversion coefficient of the average student funding should be adjusted. For undergraduate students, master's students, and doctoral students, there are corresponding disciplinary conversion coefficients.

On April 1, 2014, the Department of Finance and Department of Education in Fujian province issued the "Announcement on Further Improving the Average Student Funding Level of Province-administered Public Higher Education Institutions Offering Degree Programs" (Min Cai Jiao [2014], No. 16). The announcement pointed out that at the end of 2012, the average student funding level for colleges and universities in Fujian had reached 12,000 yuan, but still needed to be improved. In 2014, the standard of average student comprehensive quota for undergraduates in province-administered colleges and universities was raised from 4900 yuan to 5500 yuan. The provincial government further subdivided the funding coefficients of the average student comprehensive quota, reflecting the orientation of differentiated support. Taking the differences of disciplines to further subdivide the coefficients of some disciplines can give full play to the guiding role of government funding and promote the development of colleges and universities according to their own characteristics. Regarding the student level, the quota for a doctoral student was 18,000 to 20,000 yuan per year per student (engineering and medicine were 20,000 yuan per year per student, and other disciplines were 18,000 yuan per year per student; these funds were separate from the doctoral student general scholarship); the quota for a master's student is 12,000 to 13,000 yuan per student per year (engineering and medicine were 13,000 yuan per year per student, and other disciplines were 12,000 yuan per year per student; all these funds were separate from the master's student general scholarship); the quota for an undergraduate student was 5500 yuan per student per year (the conversion factors of all disciplines were literature, 0.9; science, 1; engineering, 1.5; agriculture, forestry, and marine, 1.6; sports, 1.3; public security, 1.4; art, 1.5; general medicine, 1.6; clinical medicine, 2.0).

On May 26, 2015, the Department of Finance and Department of Education in Hebei province issued the announcement on "The Measures for the Management of the Average Student Funds in Hebei Province" (Ji Cai Jiao [2015], No. 102), which determined the average funding standard for undergraduate students in provincially administered universities to be 12,000 yuan per student a year, and by the end of 2016, those colleges and universities collaboratively built with the Ministry of Education should achieve average annual student funds of 16,000 yuan. Moreover, the average student funds of higher education institutions offering degree programs were allocated according to the level of students, student disciplinary conversion coefficients, and the results of a financial performance evaluation. There were four levels of students: undergraduate students in normal courses, undergraduate students in short-cycle courses, master's students, and doctoral students. With reference to the national statistical caliber, the conversion coefficient of undergraduate students in normal courses (including preparatory students) was 1, that of master's students was 1.5, that of doctoral students was 2, and that of undergraduate students in short-cycle courses was 0.7. Referring to the method of average student public funds documented in the Ministry of Finance and the Ministry of Education's "Notice on Perfecting the Budget and Funding System of Central Universities" (Jiaocai [2008], No. 232), and combined with the actual situation of the discipline structure of colleges and universities in Hebei province, the funding conversion coefficient was set according to the discipline, that is, the different levels of disciplinary conversion coefficient were set according to the 11 major disciplines of undergraduate teaching in higher education, to reflect the difference in the operation cost in different disciplines. The specific conversion coefficients were philosophy, 1; economics, 1.25; law, 1.25; education, 1.25 (of which physical education was 1.5), literature, 1 (of which art was 2, and journalism was 1.5); history , 1; science, 1.25; engineering, 1.5; agriculture, 1.5; medicine, 2.0; and management, 1.25.

From the preceding description, we can find that different provinces take different approaches in setting the standard of average student comprehensive quota, and most of them have met the requirement set by the document that claimed that the average student funding level of local higher education institutions should be no less than 12,000 yuan (Jiao Cai [2010], No. 567). The standards of the more economically developed provinces are slightly higher than those of medium-sized and underdeveloped economies. Moreover, different conversion coefficients have been formulated for college type or discipline type to reflect the difference in the operation cost. For example, Henan province set the conversion coefficient based on the type of institution, but Fujian and Hebei provinces set the conversion coefficient based on the discipline category, while Tianjin set a different conversion coefficient according to the institution level and discipline categories. In addition, different levels of students (undergraduate students, master's students, doctoral students) have also been given different standards of student quota. The comprehensive quota of master's students and doctoral students was set to be 1.5–1.6 times and 1.8–2.0 times of undergraduates, respectively, to reflect talent training cost differences at the different levels.

6.3 Teaching funding model for public universities in developed countries

The previous section made a brief analysis on the change of the higher education funding model in China and the current policies of average student funding to provincially administered colleges and universities in local governments. This section will explain the teaching funding model in public colleges and universities in developed countries, in order to provide some reference for the reform of higher education funding in China. The so-called funding model refers to the criteria, methods, and forms used by the government for education allocation (Zhou, 2012). Overviewing the developed countries of the world, the funding model can be divided into two categories: direct funding and indirect funding.

Direct funding means that the government or third-party organizations (such as a funding council) allocate funds directly to universities, and the universities decide for themselves the allocation and use of funds under the corresponding financial management regulations. Indirect funding is allocated to students in the form of student financial support, which is then paid to the universities. The approaches of developed countries to higher education funding vary widely; particularly the United States and the United Kingdom exemplify many of the characteristics. Public colleges and universities in the United States are managed by the states, so they show a variety of coexisting models, while in the United Kingdom, universities are all managed by the Higher Education Funding Council, so its funding model is relatively uniform.

6.3.1 Funding model for public universities in the United States

The United States has the world's most developed higher education system. Its public colleges and universities are organized and managed by the states, and the state government is the main funding body of public colleges and universities. Higher education in the United States operates through a market-regulating mechanism, and the state government guarantees more than half of the operating funds for state universities. A state's higher education funding is managed by a higher education management committee, and the appropriated funds for higher education include education recurrent funding, capital funding, and project funding. In the funding model, there are generally four kinds: incremental funding, contract funding, formula-based funding, and performance-based funding (Gu, 2012).

Incremental allocation is the oldest way to allocate funds, much like the "base plus growth" model in the early times of Chinese higher education. It determines the level of funding based on the previous year's base, as well as the government's financial capacity and development needs of colleges and universities. The transparency of such grants is relatively poor, and the amount of funding that a university receives depends not only on its educational level but also on the government's background and bargaining power, which can easily lead to the Matthew effect with stronger universities getting stronger (Zhou, 2012).

Contract funding is a way of bidding, linked to the project budget, which is often used for scientific research grants. It allocates funds through contracts, which allow for a more efficient allocation of limited research funding. After the financial constraints in the United States in the 1970s, the contract allocation applied not only to the allocation of research funds, but also to the allocation of special funds for teaching, infrastructure, teaching equipment, and so on. The contract allocation model is more demanding on the technical level, involving a series of work, such as bidding and evaluation, and requires greater coordination costs.

Formula funding is based on formulas that accurately measure the amount of each item. Each state has developed different formulas according to the specific situation of its colleges and universities as well as the state's financial situation. The funding formula reduces the influence of human factors on the allocation of funds, increases the transparency of allocation, and plays a fundamental role

132 *Standard for teaching funding*

in the allocation of financial resources for higher education. Formula allocations were first used by Texas and gradually emulated by other states. In developing the funding formula, Texas divided the operational costs of colleges and universities into 16 cost items according to their functions (see Table 6.2), and each of them had a funding formula. The most complex cost items were F1 faculty and staff salaries and F2 operating funds. The final total appropriation is a sum of the funds for these 16 sections (Zhou, 2012).

For F1 faculty and staff compensation, the funding formula takes into account the factors of discipline (j) and educational level (k), sets the basis of the number of credit hours (x_{1jk}) with multipliers of the adjustment coefficient (a_{1jk}) at different disciplines and educational levels, and finally obtains the total amount appropriations for the cost item, i.e., F1 = $a_{1jk} x_{1jk}$. In general, there are 17 categories of disciplines (j): literature (1), science (2), arts (3), teacher education (4), teacher internship (5), agriculture (6), engineering (7), family economics (8), law (9), social services (10), library science (11), training (12), sports (13), health services (14), pharmacy (15), optometrist (16), and technology (17). For the educational level (k), F1 funding mainly considers five levels: four-year undergraduate (1), undergraduate of high-level college (2), master (3), special occupation (4), and doctor (5).

Similar to F1 faculty and staff compensation, the funding of F2 operational funds also considers discipline (j) and educational level (k) and sets the basis of the number of credit hours (x_{2jk}) with multipliers of the adjustment coefficient (a_{2jk}) at different disciplines and educational levels, and finally obtains the total amount appropriations for the cost item, i.e., F2 = $a_{2jk} x_{2jk}$. Slightly different from F1 faculty and staff compensation, the 17 categories of disciplines (j) are literature (1), science (2), arts (3), teacher education (4), military science (5), agriculture (6), engineering (7), family economics (8), law (9), social services (10), library science (11), training (12), sports (13), health services (14), pharmacy (15), optometrists (16), and technology (17). For the educational level, F2 funding mainly considers four levels: undergraduate (1), master (2), special occupation (3), and doctor (4).

Performance-based funding is a way to determine the direction and quantity of funding by measuring the performance of colleges and universities in teaching,

Table 6.2 Cost items of higher education appropriations in Texas, United States

F1 – Faculty and staff compensation	F2 – Operating funds	F3 – Research funds	F4 – Library funds
F5 – Teaching management	F6 – Student services	F7 – Institutional management	F8 – Administrative expenses
F9 – Campus safety	F10 – Facility support	F11 – Architecture maintenance	F12 – Cleaning service
F13 – Ground maintenance	F14 – Sealed facility	F15 – Employee benefits	F16 – Educational Opportunities Services

scientific research, and so on. The appropriated funds for universities are directly linked to their performance. The higher the evaluation score, the more funding they receive, and vice versa. The advantage of performance-based funding is that everything depends on performance, and every university competes fairly. Therefore, this funding model can allocate the government's educational resources reasonably and effectively, and make the universities reduce their costs, improve the quality of teaching and scientific research, and promote their development. However, the evaluation criteria of performance-based funding are difficult to develop, and a scientific performance indicator system needs to be determined. Since the state of Tennessee began piloting performance-based funding in 1979, this funding model was been criticized in various U.S. states even as it continued to be promoted (Dougherty et al., 2016). However, in the face of the increasingly severe financial burden in the United States, performance-based funding is still the main approach for U.S. state governments to allocate funds for higher education.

Finally, it is worth noting that each U.S. state has its own funding model. Not only that, most states use a hybrid funding model, and there is no universal mainstream model but a combination of different funding models.

6.3.2 Teaching funding and accounting in public universities in the United Kingdom

6.3.2.1 Teaching funding in public universities in the United Kingdom

In the United Kingdom, teaching funding is based on a cost-related formula funding method. Teaching funding is mainly used to share the cost of teaching in colleges and universities, such as paying teachers' salaries. It is worth noting that higher education in the United Kingdom today is not like pre-school and basic education, where every student attending a public school is guaranteed a certain amount of government funds (at least the "basic appropriation"), but universities, receive government funds only when the cost of teaching in one subject is completely beyond the financial capacity of students and their parents. At present, teaching funds in UK universities are increasingly dependent on tuition income, and teaching appropriation provided by the Higher Education Funding Council is largely a "complement" to tuition income.

The basic process and method of allocation of teaching funding are, first, to measure the national average teaching cost of different subjects and then divide all subjects into different price groups according to the levels of teaching cost. For each group, there is a standard for the average student funding, thereby determining the standard of the average student funding for high-cost subjects. Second is to measure the average student funding criteria for special students, that is, the standard for the funding of targeted students. The third step is to measure the number of all types of students in all price groups in each institution. Fourth is to multiply the standard of average student funding in each institution with their corresponding number of students in each price group and then obtain the total amount of high-cost subject funding, the total amount of targeted funding, and the grand sum of the

134 *Standard for teaching funding*

two, i.e., the total teaching funding. Last, according to the total budget provided by the government, the allocation of funds for each institution is adjusted proportionally, and then the actual total teaching funding received by each institution can be obtained.

6.3.2.2 Transparent Approach to Costing (TRAC)

In 1997, three UK funding councils formed the Joint Steering Group on Costing and Pricing (JCPSG, 2016),[3] which was commissioned to encourage and assist UK universities with costing (HEFCE, 2015a). After nearly a decade of research and practice, a set of Full Economic Cost (FEC)[4] accounting techniques, namely, the transparent approach to costing, currently used by all universities in the UK, was developed. This set includes three parts: the Annual transparent approach to costing (Annual TRAC), the Research Project Transparent Approach to Costing Full Economic Cost (TRAC FEC), and the Transparent Approach to Costing for Teaching (TRAC(T)). The three higher education funding councils in the UK determined the cost of teaching in subjects on the basis of feedback of a transparent approach to costing from universities. The number of students for each price group was obtained through the results of the Higher Education Students Early Statistics (HESES) Survey, so as to calculate the total funding for high-cost subjects available to each institution.

A transparent approach to costing is essentially an adjusted activity-based costing (ABC) based on the activity complexity and cultural specificity of the university (HEFCE, 2015a).

The transparent approach to costing applied by colleges and universities in the United Kingdom is the model of the micro-/macro-activity-based costing, which holds that British universities are mainly engaged in four macro-activities, including the following three core activities and one auxiliary activity:

Teaching (T) – Can be divided into publicly funded teaching (PFT) and non-publicly funded teaching (NPFT).
Research (R) – According to the source of funding, it can be divided into research funded by the research committee, research funded by the government, research funded by charitable organizations, and research funded by the institutions of the European Commission.
Other (O)[5] – Other activities that form income other than teaching and research, such as commercial activities, accommodation, and conferences.
Supplementary activities (S) – Examples are preparatory work, proposal writing, and administration, which individually create costs, but can be properly grouped into teaching, scientific research, and other core activities (HEFCE, 2014).

The transparent approach to costing divides three kinds of cost centers according to the functions of the internal organization of colleges and universities, namely, university-level departments, academic departments, and other departments.

Among them, the university-level departments belong to the supportive department, and the academic departments and other departments belong to the production department. Each cost center is engaged in a large number of micro-activities, and these micro-activities can eventually be directly or indirectly divided into four types of macro-activities through the cost-driven method.

From the specific operations, the annual transparent approach to costing first needs to collect data. These data include financial investment data, employee numbers and student numbers with full-time equivalent and head count, employee workload allocation data, technician workload allocation data, spatial data, other cost factors, and weighting factors. After that, two formulaic sustainability adjustments are then made to the costs recorded in the consolidated financial statements, i.e., infrastructure adjustment and return for financing and investment (RFI), so that the final accounted costs cover the full economic costs of the university. Finally, the costs are grouped into direct and indirect costs, respectively.

6.3.2.3 Accounting of subject cost and the division of price groups

Following the higher education financial reform in 2012, the Higher Education Funding Council for England (HEFCE) adjusted the way teaching funding was allocated (see Table 6.3). Based on the average teaching costs of each subject, university subjects were divided into five price groups from high to low costs: A, B, C1, C2, and D. With the assumption that the average tuition fees of undergraduate students charged by the university were £7500 per academic year, the government would make the cost compensation accordingly. To those C2 or D subjects that results of a transparent approach to costing for teaching were less than £7500 per academic year, such funds were not appropriated. To those postgraduate students in taught programs (such as postgraduate education certificates) eligible for national student loans as undergraduate students, such funds were not appropriated. Most postgraduate students in taught programswere not eligible to apply for national student loans as undergraduates, so universities typically charged them lower fees than undergraduates. Based on this, the HEFCE increased additional recurrent teaching funding of £1100 per head for postgraduate students of taught programs in groups A to C of the price groups (HEFCE, 2015b). Similar to the support to postgraduate programs, however, this additional funding ended when England extended the national student loan system to the entire postgraduate education (HEFCE, 2015c).

Unlike high-cost subject funding, which is based on subject cost, targeted allocations are additional teaching funding based on students' characteristics. Targeted allocations are essentially divided into two categories: one to facilitate the admission and successful completion of disadvantaged students (e.g., students with disabilities), and the other to subsidize the additional operational/learning costs of some special subjects or special students, such as universities located in outer London and undergraduate and postgraduate programs with courses that last 45 weeks or more within one academic year. The higher education funding councils calculate the student numbers eligible for targeted allocations for

Table 6.3 Standard of HEFCE funding for price groups per student FTE (in pounds)

Price group		Subject	Undergraduates and postgraduates in courses eligible for undergraduate student support	Postgraduate students in courses not eligible for undergraduate student support
A		The clinical years of study for medicine, dentistry, and veterinary science	10,000	11,100
B		Laboratory-based subjects (science, engineering, technology, agroforestry, non-clinical medicine, and dental science)	1500	2600
C	C1	The average cost is more than 7500 pounds	Archaeology, design and creative arts, information technology, systems sciences and computer software engineering, and media studies	250	1350
	C2	Subjects that require some experimentation and fieldwork, but cost no more than 7500 pounds on average	0	1100
D		Classroom-based subjects	0	0

Source: "Guide to funding 2015–16: How HEFCE allocates its funds", retrieved May 13, 2015, from http://www.hefce.ac.uk/media/HEFCE,2014/Content/Pubs/2015/201504/2015_04.pdf.

Table 6.4 Standard for the targeted allocations per student of HEFCE (in pounds)

Price group	Universities in London		Courses that last 45 weeks or more within one academic year
	Inner London	Outer London	
A	1105	691	0
B	470	294	1439
C	360	225	1100
D	277	173	0

Source: "Guide to funding 2015–16: How HEFCE allocates its funds", retrieved May 13, 2015, from http://www.hefce.ac.uk/media/HEFCE,2014/Content/Pubs/2015/201504/2015_04.pdf.

Note: This table is mainly used for targeted allocations relating to universities located in inner London as well as undergraduate and taught postgraduate courses that last 45 or more within one academic year.

all universities through feedback from their individualized student record data of Higher Education Statistics Agency (HESA) and further calculate the total amount of targeted allocations available to universities. Table 6.4 presents part of the standard for targeted allocations.

6.4 Basic econometric methods for average student cultivation costs

6.4.1 Accounting method

The accounting method is the basic method of accounting for the costs of various types of education at all levels. Prior to 1988, China's higher education institutions' accounting followed the accounting system of government-affiliated institutions without an independent system or regulations. In December 1988, the first independent "Accounting System for Higher Education Institutions" was formally enacted in the history of higher education accounting in China. This system did not consider the "educational costing", so there were obvious limitations. In 1998, the Ministry of Finance and the Ministry of Education jointly promulgated the "Accounting System for Higher Education Institutions (Pilot)" (hereinafter referred to as the "Pilot System"), which continued until 2013. This accounting system reflects the requirements of educational costing in accounting accounts, statements, and so on. Accounting accounts include functional classification, such as wage and welfare expenditure, goods and services expenditure, subsidy expenditure to individuals and families, and capital expenditure, and also divided expenditure into "transfer expenditure", "educational expenditure", "expenditure handed to higher authorities", "subsidy expenditure on affiliated units", "operating expenditure", and "carry-over of self-raised funds for infrastructure". Educational expenditure can be further divided into teaching expenditure, research expenditure, assistance expenditure, administration expenditure, logistical support expenditure, student affairs expenditure, retiree expenditure, and other expenses. This pilot system of higher education institution accounting plays an important role in costing and budget management.

With the deepening of the reform of the higher education system, the environment and internal structure of higher education institutions were changing greatly, and the pilot system seemed powerless with the emergence of new phenomena such as the logistics of campus services, the establishment and operation of independent colleges, the multichannel financing of operation funds, the construction of new campuses on a super-large scale, and the establishment of the compensation mechanism for educational costs. In order to meet the needs of the financial budget reform and the economic business development of colleges and universities, and to further standardize the accounting of colleges and universities, after many consultations and repeated amendments, the Ministry of Finance revised and issued the "Accounting System for Colleges and Universities" on December 30, 2013 (hereafter the "New System"), which came into effect on January 1, 2014. In terms of accounting, the new system appropriately introduced an accrual basis, was based on the principles of the accrual system, and inserted the first-level accounts of "cumulative depreciation", which were used to account for the cumulative depreciation of fixed assets in colleges and universities. The "infrastructure expenditure" was included in the overall accounting report, and the expenditure account sets up nine first-level accounts: "educational expenditure", "research expenditure", "administration expenditure", "logistics support expenditure", "retirement expenditure", "expenditure handed to higher authorities", "subsidy expenditure on affiliated units", "operating expenditure", and "other expenditure". The expenditure account was divided by expenditure category, which prepared the data for the allocation and accounting of education costs.

Many scholars in China have conducted in-depth studies of the higher education cost by the accounting method (Yuan, 2000; Gan, 2007; Wu, 2016), and pointed out that the key accounting method was how to classify the cost according to the constituent elements and the purpose of the expenditure. The cultivation cost of higher education institutions consists of four parts: personnel expenditure, public expenditure, subsidy expenditure to individuals and families, and depreciation of fixed assets. Among them, the personnel expenditure includes staff's basic salary, allowances, bonuses, social security fees, and other personnel expenditure. The public expenditure includes office expenditure, printing expenditure, utilities, heating, post and telecommunications fees, transportation fees, travel expenditure, conference expenditure, training expenditure, welfare expenditure, labor costs, hospitality expenditure, rental fees, property management fees, maintenance expenditure, special materials expenditure, and other public expenditure. Subsidies for individuals and families include retirement expenditure, pension and living subsidies, medical expenditure, stipends, housing subsidies, and other expenditures. The depreciation of fixed assets includes the depreciation of buildings and equipment.

The total number of students refers to the average number of students in a natural year, including doctoral students, master's students, undergraduate students in normal courses, second bachelor's degree students, undergraduate students in short-cycle courses, higher vocational college students, college-preparatory students, adult students, doctoral or master's degree programs for in-service personnel, overseas students, teaching by correspondence, web-based students, and other types of students. This number excludes those students in various forms of social-oriented short-term training courses (for less than six months) organized by colleges and universities. Among them undergraduates studying for a second bachelor's degree, who are not counted as second bachelor's degree students to avoid double counting; and students not listed in a category are counted as "other students", including specialized secondary school students. The total number of students is calculated on average from the total number of students at the beginning of the year to the total number of students at the end of the year. The calculation formula is [(Number of students at the beginning of the year × 8) + (Number of students at the end of the year × 4)]/12.

The standard number of students. The weights of all types of students converted into standard students are 1 for undergraduates in normal courses; undergraduates in short-cycle courses, second bachelor's degree students, in-service personnel in doctoral and master's degree programs, higher vocational college students, adult students, college-preparatory students, and in-service training students. Other weights are 2 for full-time doctoral students; 1.5 for full-time master's students; 3 for overseas students; 0.1 for students taught by correspondence and web-based programs; and 0.3 for evening university and other students.

Welfare expenditure and labor union funds are charged at 3% and 2% of the total wages, respectively, and the expenditure on wages and welfare that do not meet the requirements should be deducted accordingly, and the expenditure of wages and welfare that do not meet the standards should be increased.

General maintenance costs are accounted for on the basis of actual costs incurred, and the cost of major repairs (more than 20% of the original value of the fixed asset) is included in the fixed assets, and the depreciation is calculated on the basis of the estimated usable years of the fixed assets.

For the accounting of hospitality expenditure, locally administered colleges and universities are "2% of the total public expenditure in the current year (excluding the hospitality and maintenance expenditure)" and the centrally administered universities are "1% of the total public expenditure in the current year (excluding the hospitality and maintenance expenditure)". The overexpended amount should be reduced, and the underexpended amount should not be increased.

Other public expenditures. The total amount of other public expenditures may not exceed 15% of total public expenditures for the current year (net of hospitality and maintenance expenditure). If it does not exceed 15%, it should be filled in according to the actual amount incurred. If it exceeds 15%, the relevant expenses shall be included in the corresponding cost items according to the actual situation, and for the amount that cannot be explicitly included in any cost item, it should be excluded as unreasonable expenses.

Retirement expenditure is calculated only by the part that the universities take, excluding the retirement funding and public medical funds for retirees in the form of financial assistance income. When the difference is negative (i.e., if the funding is greater than the expenditure), the item shall be counted as 0.

Cost of scientific research. Thirty percent of scientific research expenditure is taken into the cost. If the expenditure can be separately included in the cost items, the cost will be directly deducted. Otherwise, the rule of scientific research funds accounting for 70% of the total educational expenditure is used to reduce the cost of educational cultivation accordingly.

Short-term training expenditure. For short-term training income and expenditure that can be calculated separately, they shall be excluded from the total income and expenditure of the university. For the short-term training expenditure that cannot be calculated, the total expenditure and expenditure items should be deducted as a proportion of the short-term training to total income.

6.4.2 Activity-based costing method

ABC was first proposed in 1988 by American accountants Cooper and Kaplan, and it is an important improvement in traditional accounting methods (Guo, 2010). The activity-based costing method is a cost calculation and management method that measures the cost of the activity and cost object by dynamically tracking and reflecting all the activities involved in the cost object, and evaluating the job performance and the efficiency of resource utilization.

Resources, activities, cost drivers, and activity centers are key concepts for understanding activity-based costing. Resources refer to the various elements used and consumed in the process of an activity, that is, the sum of all human, financial, and material resources invested by an organization in order to complete one or more activities. Activities refer to the main work or main business area engaged in by an organization. Under activity-based costing, activity mainly refers to the work within a specific range of resources consumed by the human subject with certain purposes, which is the general term of the various processes and work links carried out by an organization providing products or services. Each activity requires a certain amount of resources, which in turn incurs a certain cost. Cost driver refers to the cause of the increase or decrease in cost changes. Resources are consumed in the course of activities, and the consumption of resources eventually results in a change in costs. In determining the cost driver, you can directly find out the cause of the cost change, find the connections among the activity, resource, and cost; help to control the cost reasonably; and carry out effective and efficient cost management. Cost driver analysis is the core and difficulty of activity-based costing. The activity center refers to the many activities of the same nature and categories together. Because many activities are of the same nature, the costs and resources consumed by similar jobs will be the same, and the reasons for their cost changes will be the same, so the drivers of their activities will be the same because of the same nature.

In the context of higher education, the aforementioned key concepts can be interpreted in a new way. For example, resources refer to the various elements that colleges and universities consume in the process of student cultivation. Typical resources include wages, welfare, office expenditure, and fixed assets. Activity refers to the cultivation of talent at all levels. In order to cultivate qualified students, professional and refined production processes are needed. Under the activity-based costing method, the talent cultivating process of colleges and universities can be subdivided into many activities, such as enrollment, teaching, student registration and achievement management, book circulation management, canteen management, and dormitory management. Cost drivers can be broken down into resource drivers and activity drivers. A resource driver is used to calculating the cause of a change in the number of resources consumed by an activity. For example, classroom teaching is a regular "activity" in colleges and universities. Classroom teaching needs to consume specialized teaching human resources, the use of special equipment resources, and the use of certain electrical power resources, so one driver of the resources is the number of hydropower meters. The activity driver is the reason for calculating the change in the amount of activity consumed by a cost object. For example, the driver for the department of educational affairs in a university can be the type of educational level of the students, the number of hours teachers teach in each semester, and so on.

For the application of activity-based costing in higher education accounting, many scholars in China have carried out some relevant studies (Zhang, 2017; Liu & Zhang, 2015). Different scholars differ in the specific division of activities and resources, but the overall thinking is more consistent. Most of them go with the following steps (Gong, 2017):

Step 1: Identify the resources consumed by the higher education institution.
Step 2: Identify the activities of the higher education institution.
Step 3: Analyze the resource driver of higher education institutions and collect the resource costs consumed by their activities.
Step 4: Establish activity centers for higher education institutions.
Step 5: Analyze the activity driver of the higher education institution, and finally calculate the cost of higher education.

6.4.3 Econometric model method

Whether it is an accounting method or activity-based costing, its essence is based on the principle of accounting to account for the actual cost of higher education. In addition, the econometric model is also an important method. This method is to set the equation of higher education cost function, to fit the statistical or survey data of higher education expenditure, and to estimate the specific form of higher education cost function, and to further calculate the average cultivating cost of higher education students.

The key to the application of the econometric model method lies in the setting of the cost function. Cost function refers to the relationship between the cost and output under the condition that the technology level and the factor price remain unchanged (Cohn et al., 1989). For the settings of the cost function, there are mainly three forms: linear cost function, quadratic cost function, and CES cost function.

The linear cost function refers to the linear relationship between the total cost (or the average student cost) and its influencing factors, as shown in the following equation:

$$C(y) = a + \sum_i b_i y_i + \varepsilon \tag{6.1}$$

In Equation 6.1, C(y) indicates the cost function; y_i indicates the output of the *i*th product (e.g., undergraduate); *a* and b_i indicate the intercept term and regression coefficient, respectively; and ε is a random error term. In general, information about the price of resources needed for talent cultivation is more difficult to obtain in the study of higher education cost functions, so the price-related variables are usually omitted (Cheng & Sun, 2008).

The quadratic cost function is also a commonly used cost function. It mainly adds quadratic terms and interaction terms to the linear cost function, of which the complete form is as follows:

$$C(y) = \sum_{i,j} b_{ij} y_i y_j + \varepsilon \tag{6.2}$$

The CES cost function, also known as the constant elasticity of substitution cost function, can be set as the following in a general form:

$$C(y) = \left[\sum_i a_i y_i^{b_i} \right]^\rho + \varepsilon \tag{6.3}$$

The greatest advantage of this function is that it requires fewer parameters to be estimated and is suitable for econometric models with small sample sizes. However, owing to its nonlinear form, it cannot be estimated by using the traditional ordinary least squares (OLS) method, thus limiting the number of variables it can include.

6.4.4 Comparison of the econometric methods for the average student cultivation cost

The previous sections describe three econometric methods for average student cultivation cost, namely, accounting method, activity-based cost, and econometric model. The first two methods belong to the field of accounting; the difference is mainly in their separate way of cost collection. In contrast, the econometric model is a statistical method that attempts to measure costs by revealing the quantitative relationship between output and cost, relying on assumptions about the form of cost functions. Moreover, the cost function is a mathematical abstraction of cost behavior, which will inevitably lose some cost information, so there may be large errors compared to the actual cost incurred. Table 6.5 summarizes the basic concepts, main features, and limitations of the three methods, from which we can gain insight into the advantages and disadvantages.

Table 6.5 Overview of the econometric methods for average student cultivation cost

	Accounting method	Activity-based costing	Econometric model
Basic concept	Based on the accounting system of Chinese higher education institutions. The higher education cost is measured and accounted for according to the basic principles of cost accounting.	To calculate the cost of activities and the cost objects by dynamically tracking and reflecting all activities involved in cost objects.	To fit the per student cultivation cost of higher education based on the cost function.
Main features	1. Taking the accounting system of China higher education institutions as the basis, it follows a high standard of regulations. 2. It can reflect the full economic costs of colleges and universities. It is matched with the actual costs incurred.	1. Taking the modern accounting theory as the basis, it integrates cost accounting, cost tracking, and cost monitoring into one. 2. It is applicable to the multi-input, multi-output model; and can dynamically reflect the cost trend of colleges and universities.	1. It mathematically abstracts the cost behavior of colleges and universities based on the theory of cost function. 2. The data required is relatively simple and can be estimated in a variety of functional forms and algorithms.
Limitations	1. Colleges and universities are not enterprises; there are institutional obstacles in accounting. 2. The three functions (teaching, research, and social service) of colleges and universities are interwoven, making it difficult to calculate the cost of teaching alone.	1. Data for the activity cost driver is difficult to obtain, which poses a challenge to the financial system of colleges and universities. 2. The three functions of colleges and universities (teaching, research, social service) are interwoven, making it difficult to cost account for teaching alone.	1. The cost function cannot fully summarize the cost behavior of colleges and universities. 2. The cost function is highly abstract, and there are estimation errors caused by missing cost information.

6.5 Principles for the formulation of the standard of average student funding for higher education institutions in China

Since the release of the "Announcement on Reforming and Perfecting the Budget and Funding System of Central Universities" in 2015 (Jiao Cai [2015], No. 467), a new round of reform on the average student funding for colleges and universities has been brewing in China. According to our study's review of relevant domestic policies, as well as the experience of countries such as the United States and Britain in the allocation of teaching funding, in the future reform of the average student comprehensive quota of colleges and universities, it is recommended to follow the following principles.

First, the average student comprehensive quota funding mechanism for colleges and universities should be matched with the current financial and accounting system of higher education. In recent years, China's financial system and budget system have improved, as well as the financial and accounting system of higher education. In 2012, the Ministry of Finance issued a document revising the "Financial System for Higher Education Institutions" (Jiao Cai [2012], No. 488), and at the end of 2013 revised and issued a new version of the "Accounting System for Higher Education Institutions" (Cai Kuai [2013], No. 30), which standardized a range of procedures, including budgets, final accounts, and the use of funds in higher education institutions. The new accounting system will inevitably affect the use of funds in colleges and universities, but also affect the accounting of average student cultivation cost in colleges and universities. Therefore, the future setting of average student comprehensive quota standards and the funding mechanism in colleges and universities should be matched with the current financial system and the new accounting system.

Second, the base for the average student comprehensive quota in higher education institutions should be determined by a combination of various methods. Traditionally, the base of the average student comprehensive quota funding for colleges and universities was determined by using the accounting method, that is, decomposing and accounting the cultivation cost by account titles, and then finally determining the average student cost. As pointed out earlier, the accounting method can be the one that most directly reflects the cost of cultivation, but the method is also faced with many limitations, for example, the overlapping of the three functions of teaching, scientific research, and social services in universities, especially the hard-to-separate mixture of teaching and scientific research in research universities. Thus it might be difficult to rely solely on the accounting method to scientifically determine the base of the average student comprehensive quota. In the future, it is worth trying to use a variety of methods for accounting, and then weighting the results with certain proportions, in order to finalize the base of the average student comprehensive quota.

Third, the adjustment coefficient of the average student comprehensive quota of higher education institutions should not be limited to the discipline and degree-awarding level, but also take into account factors such as region and college type. After several attempts at reform, the adjustment coefficient of the average student comprehensive quota of colleges and universities has been greatly improved, but it is still mainly limited to disciplines, especially for central universities. Some local colleges and universities also take into account the type of institutions and their degree-awarding level (e.g., Henan and Tianjin). From the experience of developed countries such as the United Kingdom and the United States, higher education funding should not only take into account the disciplinary differences in the cost of student cultivation, but also take into account the type of students, the institution's geographical location, and other factors. For example, the American government funding for public colleges and universities is mainly based on a funding formula, and these funding formulas have to consider more than a dozen factors. In the United Kingdom, higher education funding is not only categorized according to subjects but also makes an adjustment to the funding rates by considering whether students receive a national student loan. In the future, setting the adjustment coefficient of the average student comprehensive quota in colleges and universities should take into account the impact of regional economic factors, quality level, institution type, and discipline on the cost of student cultivation. Therefore, it is suggested that the adjustment coefficient apply a layered design: The first layer is the region (economic factors), which includes three kinds of adjustment coefficients according to the level of economic development, and the adjustment coefficients of developed regions, moderately developed regions, and less developed areas are different. The second layer is about the institution (quality level and institution type), which sets different adjustment coefficients according to the quality level (double first-class universities and non–double first-class universities under the administration of the Ministry of Education; provincial key universities considered double first-class; and other local universities), as well as institution type (comprehensive, science and engineering, normal, finance, sports, language, nationality, and art). The third layer is discipline, which sets separate adjustment coefficients for the current 13 bachelor degree disciplines. In addition, the average student funding of master's and doctoral students also needs to be distinguished according to the disciplinary adjustment coefficient, which should be certain times the average student funding for an undergraduate student in the corresponding discipline.

6.6 Estimates of the adjustment coefficients for the funding standard based on the factors influencing the cultivation cost

From four aspects – the level of economic development, quality level, student numbers, and institution type – this section conducts modeling analysis on the factors influencing the average student cultivation cost and then calculates the adjustment coefficients of the average student funding. Specifically, this section constructs the panel data (2015–2018) of the cultivation cost of 76 universities under the administration of China's Ministry of Education, analyzes the marginal effects of the aforementioned four factors, and uses the estimated results to calculate the adjustment coefficient of average student funding for colleges and universities with different economic development levels, different quality levels, different student numbers, and different institution types.

6.6.1 Analysis of the influencing factors of the average student cultivation cost

The issue of training cost in colleges and universities has always been a critical issue in the study of educational finance, but most of the existing research is conducted from the perspective of accounting, to examine how to account for the cultivation cost (Yu, 2019; Wu et al., 2016; Pan, 2015), but studies on the influencing factors of cultivation cost are relatively rare. For example, Zhang and Wang (2007) divided the higher education cost into macro and micro aspects and used the Delphi method to verify. The macro factors include the economy, inflation, education system, infrastructure, and knowledge development. Micro factors include institution orientation, teaching force, student numbers, management level, education quality, and education structure. Similarly, Wang and Liu (2009) used the Delphi method to divide the factors affecting the higher education cost into 11 aspects: hardware, quality of education, teaching force, price, institution orientation, student numbers, management level, student structure, management system, market economy, and knowledge development. These studies only found possible factors and did not conduct empirical studies based on data. Considering the availability of data in empirical research, this study mainly takes into account the four factors of quality level, student numbers, institution type, and economic development, and examines their effects on the cultivation cost of colleges and universities.

6.6.1.1 Quality level

Colleges and universities at different levels show great differences in cultivation costs. Since the universities under the administration of the Ministry of Education (MOE) published the relevant data, each year the budget data of these MOE-administered universities caused considerable social repercussions. Even within the MOE-administered universities, entering or not entering the list of double first-class also had a great impact on their costs. In 2019, there were eight MOE-administered universities with budgets of more than 10 billion yuan, of which Tsinghua University ran ahead with 28 billion yuan (Bianjiaoyu, 2019), while the last-ranked Central Conservatory of Music had a budget of only 718 million. The difference in expenditure and cost between universities at different quality levels is of concern to researchers (Hu, 2011). For instance, Tang (2017) used the sample of the MOE-administered universities from 2006 to 2010 and the cost function for quantitative research, which showed that universities with "985" titles tended to have higher costs than other universities. It can be expected from this that, under the current policy environment, the cultivation costs of double first-class universities are higher than that of non–double first-class universities, while the cultivation costs of the world-class universities are higher, when compared with the costs of universities with only world-class disciplines.

6.6.1.2 Student numbers

Student numbers have a direct impact on university costs. In Chinese and international empirical studies on higher education costs, the student numbers of all kinds at all levels are always included as an influencing factor (Cheng & Sun, 2008; Agasisti & Johnes, 2010; Worthington & Higgs, 2011). Under the background of higher education vast expansion, the student numbers in most colleges and universities are increasing year by year, which to some extent pushes up the costs of university operation, that is, the larger the student numbers, the higher the university expenditure, as well as the cultivation cost. However, there are also studies showing that this effect is not purely linear, but presents a nonlinear trend. The numbers of undergraduate students in normal courses and short-cycle courses, and the numbers of postgraduate students have a U-shaped impact on the costs of university operation, that is, the operation costs present a trend of decrease-before-increase accompanying the expansion of student numbers (Tang, 2017). Overall, when the student numbers exceed a certain threshold, this tends to lead to a substantial increase in the cultivation cost.

6.6.1.3 Institution type

There are many kinds of divisions for institution types, including comprehensive, science and technology, normal, language, art, agriculture and forestry, and finance. However, most colleges and universities do not vary greatly in cost due to their different types, because after several rounds of reforms and transformations, most of the colleges and universities with industrial characteristics (such as science and technology universities, normal universities) have become comprehensive universities with a full range of disciplines. Nevertheless, some special types of colleges and universities still vary in cost, especially medical or art universities. Some studies have pointed out that the operation cost of a university with a medical school is not significantly different from that without a medical school (Tang, 2017). This is mainly due to the fact that medical schools often have affiliated hospitals, and most of the cultivation costs of medical students (e.g., internships) are covered by affiliated hospitals. However, it is also worth noting that art colleges often have the characteristics of small scale and high cost due to reasons like teaching mode. Therefore, its cultivation costs need to be considered by the inclusion of dummy variables.

6.6.1.4 Level of local economic development

The level of local economic development is a macro variable indicating the environment surrounding colleges and universities. Colleges and universities are small communities, so their costs are closely related to the level of local economic development. Colleges and universities in developed regions tend to be expensive in terms of commodity and land prices, and their personnel costs are also higher, whereas for colleges and universities in underdeveloped areas, these prices are relatively low. Some studies have pointed out that there is a clear regional imbalance in the allocation of financial resources for higher education in China, and investment in the developed areas of the eastern region is substantially higher than that in the underdeveloped areas of the central and western regions (Lin & Cheng, 2015; Tang, 2019). Therefore, the level of local economic development is also an important factor to be examined in this study.

6.6.2 Data, variables, and model settings

This section takes MOE-administered universities as the subject to conduct research, including a total of 76 independently operated universities (those universities that have separate campuses in other cities are considered different institutions) but not the University of International Relations. The list of sampled universities is shown in Table 6.6.

The variables involved in this study mainly include the average student cultivation cost (Cost), quality level (Class), student numbers (Size), institution type (Art), and economic development level of the province or city where the university is located (Econ). See Table 6.7 for details. Among them, the average student cultivation cost variable (Cost) is equal to the total educational expenditure divided by the FTE student numbers (undergraduate, master's, and doctoral students). These two sets of data are taken from the financial statements of the MOE-administered universities. The specific calculation formula is

$$\text{Average student cultivation cost} = \frac{\text{Total cost to be shared}}{\text{FTE student numbers per year}} \quad (6.4)$$

In this formula, the total cost to be shared is difficult to calculate. In the case of the detailed data of each MOE-administered university is not available, this study uses the concise costing method, and the calculation formula is as follows:

$$\begin{aligned}
&\text{Total cost to be shared} \\
&= (\text{total educational expenditure} - \text{infrastructure expenditure} \\
&\quad - \text{capital expenditure}) \\
&\quad + (\text{total expenditure on scientific research} \\
&\quad - \text{infrastructure expenditure} - \text{capital expenditure}) \\
&\quad \times 30\% + \text{fixed asset depreciation} \\
&\quad + (\text{administration expenditure} + \text{logistical support expenditure}) \\
&\quad \times \text{the ratio of educational expenditure to educational} \\
&\quad \text{and research expenditure}
\end{aligned} \quad (6.5)$$

In Equation 6.5, the straight-line depreciation method is used for the depreciation of fixed assets. According to the relevant regulation 8 in the supplementary

Table 6.6 List of sampled MOE-administered universities

Peking University	Hefei University of Technology	Shandong University	China University of Geology (Beijing)
Beijing University of Chemical Technology	Hohai University	Shaanxi Normal University	China University of Geology (Wuhan)
Beijing Jiaotong University	Hunan University	Shanghai University of Finance and Economics	Ocean University of China
University of Science and Technology Beijing	North China Electric Power University	Shanghai Jiaotong University	China University of Mining and Technology (Beijing)
Beijing Forestry University	North China Electric Power University (Baoding)	Shanghai International Studies University	China University of Mining and Technology (Xuzhou)
Beijing Normal University	East China University of Science and Technology	Sichuan University	China Agricultural University
Beijing Foreign Studies Universities	East China Normal University	Tianjin University	China Renmin University
Beijing University of Posts and Telecommunications	South China University of Technology	Tongji University	China University of Petroleum (Beijing)
Beijing Language and Culture University	Huazhong University of Science and Technology	Wuhan University	China University of Petroleum (East China)
Beijing University of Chinese Medicine	Huazhong Agricultural University	Wuhan University of Technology	Chinese University of Pharmacy
Dalian University of Technology	Central China Normal University	Xidian University	China University of Political Science and Law
University of Electronic Science and Technology of China	Jilin University	Xi'an Jiaotong University	Zhongnan University of Economics and Law
Northeastern University	Jiangnan University	Northwestern University of Agriculture, Forestry and Technology	Central South University
Northeast Forestry University	Lanzhou University	Northwest A&F University	Zhongshan University
Northeast Normal University	Nanjing University	Southwest University	Central University of Finance and Economics

(Continued)

150 *Standard for teaching funding*

Table 6.6 Continued

Donghua University	Nanjing Agricultural University	Southwest Jiaotong University	Central Academy of Fine Arts
Southeastern University	Nankai University	Chang'an University	Central Academy of Drama
University of International Economics and Business	Tsinghua University	Zhejiang University	Central Conservatory of Music
Fudan University	Xiamen University	Communication University of China	Chongqing University

regulations of the government accounting system, the specific formula is set as follows:

Depreciation of fixed assets

= Year-end amount of housing and building assets / 30

+ Year-end amount of general equipment assets / 6   (6.6)

+ Year-end amount of special equipment assets / 10

+ Year-end amount of furniture, appliances, equipment / 15

The quality level variable (Class) refers to the title of "world-class universities". According to the "Announcement on the Release of the List of World First-Class Universities and First-Class Disciplines" (Jiaoyanhan [2017], No.2) by the Ministry of Education, the Ministry of Finance, and the National Development and Reform Commission, released on September 21, 2017, 42 first-class universities are on the list. The student numbers variable takes the medium-sized universities (30,000–50,000 students) as the reference group and is further divided into two dummy variables: small size (below 30,000 students) and large size (more than 50,000 students) indicated by size1 and size2, respectively. The dummy variable level of economic development (Econ) uses the provincial gross domestic product (GDP) data in 2015–2018 from the National Bureau of Statistics, adjusts the data to the base period of 2015 with consumer price index (CPI) inflators, calculates and ranks the mean of 31 provinces, and defines the top 10 provinces as the economically developed regions (i.e., Beijing, Shanghai, Tianjin, Jiangsu, Zhejiang, Fujian, Guangdong, Shandong, Inner Mongolia, and Chongqing).

Based on panel data for 2015–2018, as well as the aforementioned variables, this section uses the panel data model approach to build the following panel data model:

$$\text{Cost}_{it} = a + b_1 \text{Class}_{it} + b_2 \text{Size1}_{it} + b_3 \text{Size2}_{it} + b_4 \text{Art}_{it} + b_5 \text{Econ}_{it} + e_{it} \quad (6.7)$$

Table 6.7 Variable definitions in the model of influencing factors

Variable name	Description of the variable	Note
Cost	The average student cultivation cost, in 10,000 yuan, adjusted to the base year of 2015 with CPI inflator	Financial statements of MOE-administered universities for 2015–2018.
Class	Dummy variables: 1 = first-class universities, 0 = others	Jiao Yan Han [2017], No. 2.
Size1	Dummy variables: 1 = 30,000 students or less, 0 = others	FTE student numbers in the financial statements of MOE-administered universities for 2015-2018.
Size2	Dummy variables: 1 = 50,000 students or more, 0 = others	FTE student numbers in the financial statements of MOE-administered universities for 2015–2018.
Art	Dummy variables: 1 = art college, 0 = others	Among the universities, there are only three art colleges: the Central Conservatory of Music, the Central Academy of Fine Arts, and the Central Academy of Drama.
Econ	Dummy variables: 1 = developed regions, 0 = others	Using the average real per capita GDP from 2015 to 2018 at the provincial level where universities are located. The top 10 provinces are defined as developed regions.

In Equation 6.7, all variable names are the same as in Table 6.7, a represents the intercept or constant, and e represents random error terms. The subscript i represents year i, and the subscript t represents the t university. Since the independent variables in the formula remained mostly stable during the observation period, such as quality level (Class) and institution type (Art), this study uses the mixed OLS model, the fixed effect model, and the random effect model to estimate. In the application of the panel data method, it is first necessary to compare the model fit of mixed OLS and fixed effect model. If the results of the F-test are significant at the level of 0.05, it is indicated that the fixed effect model is more appropriate, and the Hausman test can be further used to compare the model fit of the fixed effect model and the random effect model, so as to determine the most appropriate model for the final explaining model.

6.6.3 Descriptive statistical analysis

The sample data used in this study is from 76 MOE-administered universities from 2015 to 2018, resulting in a total of 304 observations. Table 6.8 presents the descriptive statistics for the main variables. The mean average student cultivation cost is 48,000 yuan, and its standard deviation is 22,900 yuan. The university with the lowest cost had an average student cultivation cost of 20,900 yuan in 2015,

152 Standard for teaching funding

Table 6.8 Descriptive statistics

	N	Mean	Standard deviation	Minimum	Maximum
Cost	304	4.80	2.29	2.09	18.45
Class	304	0.42	0.49	0	1
Size1	304	0.24	0.43	0	1
Size2	304	0.39	0.49	0	1
Art	304	0.04	0.20	0	1
Econ	304	0.68	0.47	0	1

and the university with the highest cost had an average student cultivation cost of 184,500 yuan in 2018.

Regarding the quality level, 32 (42%) of the sampled universities are world first-class universities. The remaining 43 universities are world first-class discipline universities. Only the Beijing Language and Culture University is not a double first-class university. Therefore, in the following analysis, this study will take the full sample including Beijing Language and Culture University as the main results, and the sample without Beijing Language and Culture University as the robustness check. In terms of student numbers, 24% of the sampled universities had FTE student numbers less than 30,000 (small size), 37% had FTE student numbers between 30,000 and 50,000 (medium size), and 39% had FTE student numbers higher than 50,000 (large scale). Among the small-scale universities, three art universities are the most unique, namely, the Central Academy of Fine Arts, the Central Conservatory of Music, and the Central Academy of Drama, and the student numbers for them are only about 3000–5000. In order to avoid bias to overall estimates caused by these special universities, this study sets the art universities (Art) as a dummy variable to control for the effect. Finally, the dummy variable of the level of regional economic development indicates that the actual per capita GDP at the provinces where the universities are located ranks among the top 10 in China. According to the results of the descriptive statistics, 68% of the universities are in economically developed areas due to the differences in the distribution of MOE-administered universities between the regions.

6.6.4 Model results and analysis

Based on the panel data from the MOE-administered universities for 2015–2018, as well as the model shown in formula 6.7, this study first uses the mixed OLS model and fixed effect model for regression analysis, with the results presented in Table 6.9. From the perspective of fitted results of the model, both the mixed OLS model and the fixed effect model have a high explained variance, with R^2 reaching more than 0.4, i.e., more than 40% of the variance in cultivation cost can be explained by the independent variables. However, the p-value of the F-test is

Table 6.9 Estimated results of the influencing factor model for the average student cultivation cost

	Cost (mixed OLS model)	Cost (fixed effect model)
Class (First-class universities = 1)	0.573*** (0.220)	0.573*** (0.054)
Size1 (Less than 30,000 students = 1)	−0.237 (0.181)	−0.254* (0.087)
Size2 (More than 50,000 students = 1)	1.393*** (0.278)	1.332*** (0.136)
Art (Art universities = 1)	6.075*** (0.509)	6.069*** (0.282)
Econ (Developed regions = 1)	1.685*** (0.226)	1.674*** (0.102)
Constant	2.682*** (0.238)	2.718*** (0.171)
N	304	304
R^2	0.411	0.410
F-test	$F(3,295) = 2.43$, Prob >F = 0.066	

Notes: *, **, and *** represent significance at the level of 0.1, 0.05, and 0.01, respectively. The data in parentheses are robust standard errors.

0.066 and does not meet the general requirements of the fixed effect model for the level of significance (0.05). Therefore, the fixed effect model is not appropriate and the results of the mixed OLS model should be selected as the optimal result.[6]

From the results of the mixed OLS model, the regression coefficient of the dummy variable quality level is 0.573 and is significant at the level of 0.01, indicating that the cultivation cost of world first-class universities is 5730 yuan higher than that of non–world first-class universities. In terms of the student numbers variable, the regression coefficient of small-scale universities is not significant, but the regression coefficient of large-scale colleges and universities is significant, which indicates that the cultivation cost of small-scale universities is not significantly different from that of medium-sized universities, but the cultivation cost of large-scale universities is 13,930 yuan higher than that of medium-sized universities. In terms of the institution type variable, the regression coefficient of art universities is 6.075 and is significant at the level of 0.01, indicating that the cultivation cost of art universities is 60,750 yuan higher than that of other types of universities. In terms of economic development level, the cultivation cost in developed regions is generally higher, with a regression coefficient of 1.685 and a significance level of 0.01.

Based on the results of the model, it is not difficult to find that factors of quality level, student numbers, institution type, and regional economic development level all have significant impacts on the average student cultivation cost in MOE-administered universities. Overall, the cultivation costs of world

Table 6.10 Average student cultivation costs in MOE-administered universities and the adjustment factor of the average student funding in universities with different characteristics

Average student costs of reference universities (10,000 yuan)	Adjustment factor of average student funding for non-reference universities
Non–world first-class universities 4.667	World first-class universities 1.12
Medium-scale universities 4.126	Large-scale universities 1.34
Non-art universities 4.576	Art universities 2.33
Universities in non-economically developed regions 3.703	Universities in economically developed regions 1.45

first-class universities were higher than that of non–world first-class universities, the cultivation costs of universities with more than 50,000 students were higher than that of universities with less than 50,000 students, the cultivation costs of art universities were higher than that of non-art universities, and the cultivation costs of universities in developed regions were higher than those in other regions. These findings are broadly consistent with those in the existing literature.

Based on the preceding analysis of the factors influencing the average student cultivation cost, we can further deduce the adjustment coefficients of the average student cultivation funding of colleges and universities at different levels, with different scales and types, and in different regions (see Table 6.10). The results are as follows:

(1) For colleges and universities at different quality levels, the average student cultivation costs of non–world first-class universities were 46,670 yuan, while the marginal effect of the world first-class universities was 0.573 million. Therefore, the adjustment coefficient of average student funding for world first-class universities can be set to (5730 + 46670)/46670 = 1.12, that is, the average student funding of world first-class universities is 1.12 times that of non–world first-class universities.

(2) For colleges and universities of different student numbers, the average student cultivation cost of medium-scale colleges and universities was 41,260 yuan, while the marginal effect of large-scale colleges and universities was 13,930 yuan. Therefore, the adjustment factor of the average student funding for large-scale colleges and universities can be set at (13930 + 41260)/41260 = 1.34, i.e., the average student funding of large-scale colleges and universities is 1.34 times that of medium-scale colleges and universities.

(3) For different types of colleges and universities, the average student cultivation costs in non-art universities were 45,760 yuan, while the marginal effect of art universities was 60,750 yuan. Therefore, the adjustment factor of the average student funding of art universities can be set at (60750 + 45760)/45760 = 2.33, that is, the average student funding for art universities is 2.33 times that of non-art universities.

(4) For colleges and universities located in regions with different levels of economic development, the average student cultivation costs of universities in other regions were 37,030 yuan, while the marginal effect of universities in developed regions was 16,850 yuan. Therefore, the adjustment factor of the average student funding of universities in developed regions can be set at (16850 + 37030)/37030 = 1.45, that is, the average student funding for universities located in developed regions is 1.45 times that of the universities located in underdeveloped regions.

6.6.5 Robustness check

Inside the 76 MOE-administered universities, only Beijing Language and Culture University does not enter the list of double first-class construction (neither world first-class universities nor world first-class disciplines), so its average student cultivation costs may be different from other MOE-administered universities. In order to further improve the homogeneity of the sample, this section excludes the case of the Beijing Language and Culture University and uses the sample of the other 75 MOE-administered universities for a robustness check. The results are presented in Table 6.11.

The results of the robustness check are very consistent with the results in Table 6.9. First, in terms of model fit, the change of R^2 is very small, and the results of the F-test also support the use of the mixed OLS model. From the results of each regression coefficient in the mixed OLS model, it is basically consistent with the results of the mixed OLS model in Table 6.9. Finally, for comparison

Table 6.11 Results for robustness check

	Cost (Mixed OLS model)	Cost (Fixed effect model)
Class	0.554**	0.555***
(First-class universities)	(0.220)	(0.052)
Size1	−0.169	−0.187
(Less than 30,000 students)	(0.182)	(0.093)
Size2	1.394***	1.332***
(More than 50,000 students)	(0.278)	(0.136)
Art	5.996***	5.989***
(Art university = 1)	(0.510)	(0.274)
Econ	1.694***	1.683***
(Developed regions = 1)	(0.226)	(0.103)
Constant	2.685***	2.721***
	(0.238)	(0.173)
N	300	300
Overall R^2	0.409	0.409
F-test	F(3, 291) = 2.42, Prob > F = 0.066	

Notes: *, **, and *** represent significance at the 0.1, 0.05, and 0.01 level, respectively. The data in parentheses are robust standard errors.

Table 6.12 Comparison of adjustment factors

Category	Main model	Robustness check model
Quality level	1.12	1.12
Student numbers	1.34	1.34
Institution type	2.33	2.31
Level of economic development	1.45	1.46

purposes, the adjustment coefficients of average student funding obtained from the main model (Table 6.9) and the robustness check model (Table 6.11) are presented in Table 6.12.

6.7 Summary

From the perspective of history and comparison, this chapter discusses the model of teaching funding in colleges and universities and the formulation of the average student funding. First, from the historical point of view, this chapter reviews the four stages of China's higher education funding model: "base plus growth" (1955–1985), "comprehensive quota plus special subsidies" (1986–2002), "basic expenditure plus project expenditure" (2002–2008), and "average student comprehensive quota" (2008–present). Second, taking the "Opinion on Further Improving the Level of the Average Student Funding in Locally-Administered Higher Education Institutions Offering Degree Programs" promulgated in 2010 by the MOE as the policy turning point, this chapter describes the current funding policy and the standard of average student funding in locally administered universities in four places – Tianjin municipality and the provinces of Henan, Fujian, and Hebei – as well as their standard for average student funding. In the third section of this chapter, from the perspective of international comparison, we describe the higher education funding models in the United Kingdom and the United States, as well as their standard of average student funding. The fourth section of this chapter demonstrates three calculation methods of higher education average student cultivation cost, namely, the accounting method, the activity-based costing method, and the econometric model method, and compares the three methods. Based on the summary of the higher education funding policy and average student funding model in China and other countries, section five of this chapter discusses the future trend of the average student funding of higher education in China from a theoretical perspective. The last section of this chapter uses a concise average student costing method to calculate the average student cost from 2015 to 2018 in 76 MOE-administered universities and establishes an econometric model to estimate the adjustment coefficients of the average student funding of universities at different levels of economic development, different quality levels, different student numbers, and different university types, so as to provide a reliably empirical basis for the education and financial administrations to further improve the average student funding standard and revise the adjustment factors of the comprehensive quotas.

Notes

1 The conversion coefficients: are vocational normal universities and traditional Chinese medical universities, 0.50; colleges of music or fine arts, 1.60; agricultural colleges, 1.80.
2 The conversion coefficients are philosophy/literature/history, 1.0; economics/law/education/management, 1.02; science, 1.15; engineering, 1.45; agronomy, 1.30; medicine, 1.60; and art, 1.50. Doctoral and master's students are 2 times and 1.5 times, respectively, of undergraduate students in the same discipline.
3 The group is composed of three higher education funding councils and representatives from higher education institutions.
4 This cost includes all direct and indirect costs, and appropriate investment in universities' infrastructure and future productivity.
5 Inside the "Other" category of macro-activities there is a sub-macro activity — Clinical Services (CS), which includes clinical and dental academic institutions that provide services to the National Health Service (NHS) based on knock-for-knock arrangements. During the process of cost collection, it will once again be integrated into teaching, scientific research, other, and ancillary activities.
6 Due to mixing, the OLS estimation is better than the fixed effect model, so this study does not compare the results of the fixed effect model and random effect model further.

References

Agasisti, T., & Johnes, G. (2010). Heterogeneity and the evaluation of efficiency: The case of Italian universities. *Applied Economics*, 42(11), 1365–1375.
Bianjiaoyu. (2019). 75 CMOE-administered universities' budget. Retrieved June 8, 2020, from https://baijiahao.baidu.com/s?id=1632051353400750886&wfr=spider&for=pc
Cheng, G., & Sun, Z.J. (2008). Research on Chinese higher education efficiency. *China Economic Quarterly*, 3, 1079–1103.
CMOE (China's Ministry of Education). (2014). Tianjin: Covering education of all levels and types with government funding. Retrieved February 7, 2021, from http://www.moe.gov.cn/jyb_xwfb/s5989/s6635/201509/t20150925_210766.html
Cohn, E., Rhine, S. L.W., & Santos, M. C. (1989). Institutions of higher education as multiproduct firms: Economies of scale and scope. *Review of Economics and Statistics*, 71, 284–290.
Dougherty, K.J., Jones S.M., Lahr, H., Natow, R. S., Pheatt, L., & Reddy, V. (2016). Performance funding for higher education. *Annals of the American Academy of Political & Social Science*, 655(1), 163–184.
Gan, G. H. (2007). *Research on Higher Education Cost Sharing*. Shanghai: Shanghai University of Finance and Economics Press.
Gong, X. H. (2011). *Research of Universities' Financial Allocation Mode in China*. Dissertation. Northeast University (China).
Gong, Y. L. (2017). *Research on Cost Accounting and Cost Control of Higher Education in China*. Dissertation. Jiangxi University of Finance and Economics.
Gu, Y. (2012). *A Comparative Study of the Higher Education Financial Allocation System*. Dissertation. Northwest Normal University (China).
Guo, H. L. (2010). *Research on Higher Education Standard Costing and Accounting System*. Beijing: China Agricultural and Science and Technology Press.
HEFCE. (2014). TRAC Guidance: The Transparent Approach to Costing for UK Higher education institutions (applies from 2014-15). Retrieved January 9, 2016, from http://www.hefce.ac.uk/media/hefce/content/What,we,do/Leadership,governance

,and,management/Financial,sustainability,and,TRAC/TRAC,guidance/TRAC%20Guidance%20August%202014%20Version%201.0.pdf

HEFCE. (2015a). History of TRAC. Retrieved May 8, 2015, from http://www.hefce.ac.uk/funding/finsustain/trac/history/

HEFCE. (2015b). Guide to funding 2015–16: How HEFCE allocates its funds. Retrieved May 13, 2015, from http://www.hefce.ac.uk/media/HEFCE,2014/Content/Pubs/2015/201504/2015_04.pdf

HEFCE. (2015c). Postgraduates: Policy and funding. Retrieved May 13, 2015, from http://www.hefce.ac.uk/sas/pg/

Hu, Y. Z. (2011). Analysis on financial differences of different universities. *China Higher Education Research, 11*, 17–20.

JCPSG. (2016). Transparent approach to costing (TRAC) guidance. Retrieved January 8, 2016, from http://www.jcpsg.ac.uk/guidance/foreword.htm

Li, B. (2016). *The Study on the Mechanism of the Financial Allocation for Higher Education Based on the Cost and Performance*. Dissertation. Tianjin University.

Lin, L. N. & Cheng, C. (2015). The Study of regional difference in recurrent expenditure per student between colleges and universities. *Heilongjiang Researches on Higher Education, 9*, 76–78.

Liu, X. Y. & Zhang, Z. H. (2015). Analysis of higher education cost accounting based on activity-based cost method. *Journal of Beijing University of Aeronautics and Astronautics (Social Sciences Edition), 28*(6), 86–89+94.

Pan, J. S. (2015). University cultivation costing and tuition fees: An example of 5 universities in Guangxi province. *Studies of Finance and Accounting in Education, 26*(3), 28–32.

Sun, P. Q., Su, Y. F., Chen, W. S., & Yang, L. (2015). Per *Student Cultivation Cost and Financial Allocation Model in Different Disciplines in Universities: An Example from A Science and Technology University*. Presentation at the First China Educational Finance Meeting.

Sun, Z. J. (2009). Changes in university income in a decade of expansion in China: An interpretation. *Tsinghua Journal of Education, 4*, 72–80.

Tang, Y. P. (2017). What impacts on the operating costs of universities: Empirical research based on data from MOE-administered universities. *Journal of Educational Studies, 13*(1), 93–106.

Tang, Y. P. (2019). Adequacy, equilibrium and convergence of higher education finance in China, *Heilongjiang Researches on Higher Education, 37*(10), 71–74.

Wang, S. L. & Liu, F. (2009). Evaluation and analysis of influencing factors of university education cost. *Modern Economic Information, 10*, 206.

Wang, S. M. (2012). *Research on Public Education Financing System under Public Finance Framework*. Beijing: Economic Science Press.

Worthington, A. C., & Higgs, H. (2011). Economies of scale and scope in Australian higher education. *Higher Education, 61*, 387–414.

Wu, L. (2016). *Higher Education Cost Management Theory and Practice*. Beijing: China Renmin University Press.

Wu, W. W., Zeng, G. H., & Yu, L. W. (2016). University talent cultivation quality cost: Efficiency measure and structure optimization. *Studies of Finance and Accounting in Education, 27*(6), 44–50.

Yu, F. (2019). Measuring and analyzing undergraduate cultivation cost. *Contemporary Economics, 9*, 116–119.

Yuan, L. S. (2000). *Explorations on Education Costing.* Beijing: Beijing Normal University Press.
Zhang, F. (2017). Activity-based costing in the applications of higher education costing. *Economic Research Guide, 21,* 87–88.
Zhang, H. L. & Wang, S. L. (2007). Research on influencing factors of university education cost. *Studies of Finance and Accounting in Education, 5,* 26–30.
Zhou, X. F. (2012). *Research on Higher Education Funding Model.* Hefei: Anhui Education Press.

7 Research on the standard of average teacher research funding for university teachers

7.1 Research background

Scientific research and production are of strategic importance to national development. China's premier, Li Keqiang, pointed out at the executive meeting of the State Council in 2016 that the reform of "releasing, managing and serving" in the field of scientific research would help to fully mobilize the enthusiasm and creativity of researchers, which is of great significance for cultivating innovative momentum, enhancing the development of an endogenous driver, and moving toward an innovative country and a world scientific and technological powerful country (Xinhuanet, 2016). Higher education institutions are not only places to carry out teaching and train talent but also are in important positions for scientific research. Reforming university research funds is one of the important aspects to promote the reform of "releasing, managing and serving". Therefore, how to optimize the fund structure and improve the efficiency of the use of funds is undoubtedly of great significance to the promotion of scientific research productivity in colleges and universities.

At present, the total amount of research funds invested in colleges and universities in China has been increasing. According to research by Zhang and Sun (2014), in 2009, only 11 universities in China spent more than 1 billion yuan on scientific research, but in 2015, 27 universities in China spent more than 1 billion yuan on scientific research. In just a few years, the number of universities with research funding of more than 1 billion yuan had doubled.

While the total amount of research investment in colleges and universities is increasing, the structure of university research funds has attracted much social attention. Yingsheng Zhao (Chinadaily, 2014), an office director of the Department of Comprehensive Reform of China's Ministry of Education, pointed out at the first academic seminar on university development and financing and investment, "Although the funding for scientific research has increased substantially, it does not mean that the funding structure has been optimized". A study by Xu (2013) shows that research funds are gradually concentrated in universities in economically developed areas, resulting in great differences in the level and quality of scientific research in universities in the east, central, and west. Under the unreasonable allocation of scientific research funds, the continuous growth of

DOI: 10.4324/9781003250524-7

scientific research investment has not played its due role in promoting science and research in China (Shi & Rao, 2010).

The allocation method of university research funds is considered to be an important reason for the unreasonable allocation of scientific research funds. For a long time, China has allocated scarce scientific research funds mainly in a competitive manner (Tang et al., 2011). The allocation of scientific research funds in this competitive manner, on the one hand, fully mobilizes the enthusiasm of university teachers to carry out scientific research and production activities, but on the other hand, creates the Matthew effect in the field of scientific research due to excessive competition, which is not conducive to young teachers playing the driving role in the scientific research and innovation activities of colleges and universities (Fan & Jia, 2013).

In order to change this situation, China's Ministry of Finance and Ministry of Education jointly issued "The Interim Measures for the Management of Fundamental Research Funds for Central Universities" in 2008 (CMOF, 2009) and established fundamental research funds as noncompetitive research funds allocated to universities under the administration of China's Ministry of Education (MOE). To a large extent, the fundamental research funds alleviate the situation of fierce competition for scientific research funds among MOE-administered universities and provide a certain financial guarantee for this group of university teachers to carry out scientific research work. Although the fundamental research funds for central universities are noncompetitive above the university level, in regard to distribution within a university, it is often based on methods such as annual plan, project guideline, and expert selection to provide merit-based funding, which is disguised as "competition". Moreover, in China's university research funding, noncompetitive funds are still far less than competitive funds, reflecting its unreasonable structure.

Along with the promotion of the construction of first-class universities and first-class disciplines, those non-key local universities and those non-"985 Project" and non-"211 Project" universities also hope to enter the list of "double first-class" by improving scientific research conditions, and attracting and cultivating high-level teachers. However, many teachers in non-key universities have difficulty in obtaining competitive funding for scientific research projects, and they are left behind in carrying out scientific research activities and participating in domestic and international academic exchanges, which increases their research pressure. Therefore, it is of great practical significance to give noncompetitive research funding to university teachers who have research ability to helping these teachers in non-key universities to carry out research activities and improve their research levels, and to provide decision-making reference for the formation of a long-term mechanism for double first-class construction of research funding.

The purpose of this study is to establish a noncompetitive funding mechanism for individual teachers, that is, to set up standards for the allocation of average teacher research funds in order to improve the current uneven distribution of scientific research funds in universities, so as to ensure the basic needs of university teachers engaged in scientific research activities. The main research content includes the following two aspects:

First, the analysis of the current situation of university teachers' research funds. This mainly includes the structure and distribution of the research funding type for university teachers, the distribution and concentration of the total amount of research funds, and the lack of research funds for university teachers.

Second, the design of noncompetitive research funding standards. This mainly includes the analysis of the university teachers' attitudes toward the establishment of noncompetitive research funding, the analysis of the advantages and disadvantages of the establishment of noncompetitive research funding, the analysis of university teachers' demands for noncompetitive research funding, and the design of the allocation standard for average teacher research funding by referring to experiences from research funding in universities in other countries.

7.2 Literature review

7.2.1 Clarification of concepts

7.2.1.1 Research funds

Research funds, also known as research money or scientific and technological financial resources, are the hard resources of science and technology.[1] This concept mainly refers to the funds used to carry out scientific and technological activities, that is, for scientific research and experimental development, applications and promotions of scientific research outputs, and scientific research services activities. It is the basis for scientific research activities (Zhou, 2014).

Research funding of Chinese colleges and universities comes from four main sources:

1. Government appropriations for science and technology, including funds allocated by the central government and local governments at all levels to support the development of science and technology through scientific research funds, science and technology special funds, and research foundations.
2. The scientific and technological funds of enterprises, i.e., the research and development funds invested by enterprises in order to improve the level of research and development, and innovate products.
3. Financial institutions' research loans to scientific research institutions.
4. Reserved funds of various institutions other than enterprises.

The nature of scientific research funds is very complex. Competitive research funds are similar to private goods in economics, which are highly competitive and exclusive. But noncompetitive research funds are similar to quasi-public goods (such as institutional-level scientific research funds), which are noncompetitive and nonexclusive to some degree. The essence of scientific research funds is resources, and therefore it shares the same characteristics of any other resource: scarcity, demand, and selectivity.

7.2.1.2 Noncompetitive research funds

There is relatively little research on noncompetitive research funding inside and outside China. For instance, academic earmarks in the United States mainly refer to academic appropriations that universities receive from Congress by lobbying, rather than going through peer review (Figueiredo, 2002). This kind of funding is typical noncompetitive research funding that does not require an application from someone else (unrequested), need for authorization (unauthorized), or need for discussion (undiscussed) (Weiner, 1999).

In China, the clarifications of noncompetitive research funding are inconsistent. Tian and Xiao (2014) summarized the characteristics of noncompetitive research funding, and concluded that noncompetitive research funding, on the one hand, did not need peer review, but on the other hand, there was a relationship with the project guidelines. Kang (2007) summarizes the system of government funding for university research as follows, as shown in Table 7.1.

It is rather clear from Table 7.1 that there is almost no noncompetitive research funding for the individual researcher. The purpose of this study is to set up noncompetitive scientific research funds for individual university teachers. Therefore, the noncompetitive scientific research funds for individual teachers are defined as the research funds obtained directly by university teachers without any competition (e.g., the selection mechanism of peer review).

7.2.2 Investment system of higher education research funding inside and outside China

7.2.2.1 Investment system of higher education research funding in the United States

The United States has long adhered to the concepts of "market regulation" and "state intervention" in the allocation of research funds, and advocated the value of "who benefits, who pays". As a result, government and nongovernment investment have become the main channels of research funding for colleges and universities in the United States, with government investment for U.S. colleges and universities accounting for about 60% of the total higher education research funds in the United States (Duan & Zhang, 2016). Colleges and universities in the United States receive research grants almost entirely through "peer-review" methods. Studies have shown that 90% of the federal government's research projects are funded on merit using peer-review methods (Chen & Wang, 2009).

At the federal level, there is no science and technology authority in the United States, and the overall coordination of science and technology management is the responsibility of the Office of Science and Technology Policy (OSTP) in the

Table 7.1 The Chinese government's funding system for scientific research in colleges and universities

Funding nature/ subject	University level	Science platform level	Individual level
Competitive research funding	Research infrastructure construction plan	The start-up funds of national engineering centers; the start-up funds of the national engineering and technology research centers; and the project funding of other ministries and provincial key laboratories	National Natural Science Foundation of China; National Social Science Foundation of China; National Subjective Science and Technology Plan (973 Plan, 863 Plan, Science and Technology Support Program, etc.); Humanity and social sciences projects of China's Ministry of Education
Noncompetitive research funding	Fundamental research funds for central universities	Recurrent funds for National key laboratories, and provincial/municipal key laboratories	Almost none
Quasi-competitive research funding	The research part of special funds of 211 Project or 985 Project; research funds allocated in forms of projects	Research funds allocated to various science platforms in forms of projects	Local governments and state ministries entrust university researchers with funding for research projects

White House, the National Science and Technology Council (NSTC), and the President's Council Advisors on Science and Technology (PCAST). There are nearly 30 departments responsible for the management of research and development (R&D) funds inside the federal government, of which the National Science Foundation, the Department of Commerce, the Department of Energy, the Ministry of Health, the Department of Defense, the National Aeronautics and Space Administration (NASA), and the Department of Agriculture managed about 96% of the total federal government's R&D funds. The division and cooperation between these departments and institutions reflect the diversified allocation of federal research funds in the United States.

The National Science Foundation is the only dedicated agency for scientific and technological management in the U.S. administration. Through funding for basic research projects and other programs, it improves science education, develops and applies scientific knowledge, and enhances international scientific cooperation to promote the development of science in the United States. Its plan is divided into five categories: basic research plan, science education plan, applied research plan, science policy plan, and international cooperation plan (Gu, 2013), which is the main channel for American colleges and universities to obtain basic research funding.

7.2.2.2 Investment system of higher education research funding in the United Kingdom

The United Kingdom's science and technology management system is mainly composed of two levels, namely, administration and affairs management. The administration level consists mainly of the British government's Department for Business, Innovation and Skills (BIS); the Ministry of Defence; and the Department of Energy. These departments allocate science and technology funds from their own departmental budgets and are only responsible for developing macro-development strategies for the research councils. The affairs management level consists of the research councils and the higher education funding councils. The research councils have independent rights on policymaking, use of funds, and management. The money used by research councils to fund science and technology projects is mainly from the government's "science budget", and they determine the direction, plans, and projects for R&D in the research areas that they take charge of (Gu, 2013).

The UK government uses a "dual support system" for university research funding (Wang & Zhang, 2015) known as the Higher Education Funding Council for England (HEFCE) and the British Research Council. The HEFCE provides financial support for the construction of scientific research infrastructure, which accounts for about 28% of the government's total R&D expenditure. With the support of the Department for Education and the BIS, the HEFCE determines the standard for research allocation based on the research quality assessment of higher education institutions [Research Assessment Exercise (RAE)/Research Excellence Framework (REF)] with assessment indicators for subject scale, subject cost, and subject level. As a result, the funding is also known as quality-related funding (Ma, 2018). The British Research Council funds research projects or research initiatives, also known as project-related funding, which accounts for about 32% of the government's total R&D expenditure. The funding model is mainly through the seven research committees under the guidance of the Research Council.

7.2.2.3 Investment system of German higher education research funding

Germany mainly implements a "dual funding system" of research funding. The research funds of colleges and universities are received, on the one hand, from the federal government's basic funding, consisting of about 75% and, on the other hand, from third-party contract funding, consisting of about 25% (Yang, 2007).

166 *Average teacher research funding*

At the federal level, the Federal Ministry of Education and Research (Bundesministerium für Bildung und Forschung, BMBF) is generally responsible for the preparation, coordination, and aggregation of the draft of annual scientific research budgets throughout the country. The budget for research funds is discussed and approved by the Cabinet and submitted to Parliament, which reviews the budget and financial accounts of research funds in accordance with strict procedures before they can be implemented. Other parts of the federal government also have certain funds for scientific research, such as the Federal Ministry of Economy and Energy, which is responsible for innovation policy and industry-related research, research management in the energy and aviation fields, and the science and technology projects of small- and medium-sized enterprises. This amount of research money accounts for about 20% of the total (Zhao & Wang, 2018). The Federal Ministry of Agriculture, the Federal Ministry of Transportation, and the Federal Ministry of Environment are responsible for science and technology plans for their own ministries, accounting for 8% of total research funds.

7.2.2.4 Investment system of higher education research funding in Japan

Japan's research funds are largely managed by different ministries. As the main government administration of science and technology, education, and culture in Japan, the Ministry of Education, Culture, Sports, Science and Technology (MEXT) manages about 64% of the national science and technology budget and is responsible for formulating a unified science and technology policy and R&D plan to ensure the coordination and comprehensiveness of academic and scientific research.

Japan implements a dual structure funding system that treats noncompetitive and competitive research funds with equal weight (Bai & You, 2018). Noncompetitive research funds mainly refer to the general funds that ensure the basic funding needs of researchers and the basic operating funds of research institutes. After the reform of the national university in Japan, the government allocated a large number of basic funds to support educational and scientific research activities, creating a relatively free academic environment for researchers. Competitive research funding comes from a variety of sources, but is primarily managed by the Cross-Ministerial R&D Management System to coordinate and communicate the management of different departments. The Cross-Ministerial R&D Management System is led by the MEXT, and the routine works are undertaken by the Office of Research Funding Administration (ORF). The Science and Technology Policy Committee coordinates the development priorities submitted by various departments, formulates the key directions and areas of national research, and submits them to the Cabinet for review.

7.2.2.5 Investment system of higher education research in China

At present, China's research funding allocation uses a four-level management system, as shown in Figure 7.1. The research funds obtained by colleges and universities are mainly through a competitive or guaranteed way.

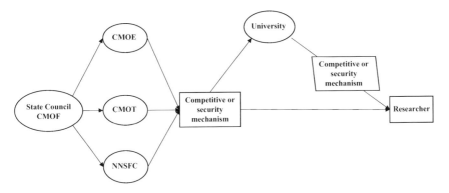

Figure 7.1 China's university research funding system.

After the Ministry of Finance allocates research funds to the Ministry of Education, the Ministry of Science and Technology, and the foundation committees (National Natural Science Foundation of China, the National Office for Philosophy and Social Sciences), each unit allocates the funds to individuals or universities in a competitive or guaranteed manner. For example, the fundamental research funds for central universities are allocated by the Ministry of Education to central universities in a guaranteed (noncompetitive) manner, while the soft science projects of the Ministry of Education, and key scientific and technological innovation projects are allocated to individuals in a competitive manner. The Ministry of Science and Technology and the foundation committees allocate research funds to individuals or universities mainly in a competitive manner.

As a result, China's higher education research funds mainly come from government finance, and the ratio of guaranteed research funds to total funds is relatively small. According to relevant research, in 2011, the noncompetitive research funds of China's colleges and universities accounted for about 20% of the total higher education research funds (Xi et al. 2014), revealing the serious imbalance between guaranteed funds and competitive funds.

7.2.3 The noncompetitive research funding standard inside and outside China

7.2.3.1 The performance-based noncompetitive research funding allocation standard outside China

Across the world, the practice of determining noncompetitive research funding based on performance has become a trend, but it is not universal. An early study by Liu (2004) summarized the patterns of the relationship between higher education performance and government funding in various countries and divided these countries into four types, namely, very high correlation (United Kingdom), high correlation (Poland), low correlation (Finland), and very low correlation (France). Next, we will describe them one by one.

Very high correlation country, United Kingdom. The United Kingdom relies heavily on third-party assessment bodies to evaluate the research activities in higher education institutions. The HEFCE plays an important role and conducts research assessments every four to five years. The HEFCE is always pursuing a mature research assessment framework (the Research Assessment Exercise, or RAE) and continuously improving on the assessment. In 2014, the HEFCE proposed a new framework for evaluating research funding – the Research Excellence Framework, or REF. Its main highlights are that it divided university research funding into three subprofiles, namely, the research outputs subprofile, the impact subprofile, and the environment subprofile. Among these three subprofiles, the proportion of research outputs accounted for 65%, the proportion of research impact accounted for 20%, and the proportion of research environment accounted for 15%. Each subprofile is evaluated primarily through expert review. This formularized allocation model of research funds based on performance assessment has three important features, namely, taking into account the differences in disciplines, the differences between institutions, and focusing on performance. Through the REF evaluation framework, the UK government is able to allocate research funding to every discipline in every university step by step, with a high degree of transparency and equity.

High correlation country, Poland. Poland established the Committee on Scientific Research (CSR) in 1991 to develop and implement policies that include the allocation of funds through several competitive channels. The chairman of the committee was appointed by Parliament, and one-third of its members were ministers and two-thirds were researchers elected by scientific organizations. Research funds of the CSR were an important source of funding for universities. The committee provided noncompetitive research funding to universities through statutory grants. Each year, the universities submitted applications to the committee, including a record of the previous year's results and a research program for the coming year. A panel of scientists evaluated all applications and assigned a grade from A (best) to C (worst) to each institution. Finally, the basic and applied research committees in the CSR made decisions on the allocation of funds.

Low correlation country, Finland. The Finland Ministry of Education provides recurrent funding for universities, including research funds. The research funds are provided by a contract between the university and the Finland Ministry of Education known as the performance management contract. University research funds include basic funding (90%), project funding (7%), and performance-related funding (3%). The performance-based allocation emphasizes the quality and impacts indicators of research and teaching, including centers of excellence in research and education, funding for the Academy of Sciences, international funding and cooperation, graduate employment rates, whether the university targets have been met, and the special evaluation of university strategic planning. All these materials are included in a database, and this database is based on annual reports submitted by universities. Beyond this, there is no specific evaluation system to determine the allocation of funds.

Very low correlation country, France. In France, the National Committee for the Evaluation of Public Scientific, Cultural and Professional Establishments (CNE) conducts a comprehensive evaluation of French higher education institutions. The committee evaluates the teaching, research, management, and environment of universities and also examines the implementation of contracts between universities and the Ministry of Education. Although the evaluation results are closely related to policy development, they do not directly determine the allocation of funds, but rather a public report is given to university administrators.

7.2.3.2 The average student teaching funding standard in China

There is no Chinese literature on the standard for the allocation of noncompetitive scientific research funds, but in China, higher education teaching funding is allocated through the way of average student funding, which is typically a noncompetitive method to allocate funds by the government, and is of worthiness to be drawn from.

The method of average student funding is mainly based on the number of all kinds of students in colleges and universities, and the formula of the current average student comprehensive quota funding used by China's Ministry of Education is as follows:

$$\text{Total Fund} = \text{People Fund} + b \times \text{Public Fund} \tag{7.1}$$

Total Fund indicates the number of appropriations, People Fund indicates overhead funds (6000 yuan/student/year for undergraduates in normal or short-cycle courses; 22,000 yuan/student/year for master's students; 28,000 yuan/student/year for doctoral students); Public Fund indicates the public funds (6,000 yuan/student/year); and b is the conversion coefficient for public funds of different disciplines.

This allocation method has aroused heated discussion in academic circles. On the one hand, basic public goods are provided with government support to strongly promote social equity and embodies the connotation value of public finance (Yan, 2011); on the other hand, scholars think that this way of allocation is considerably unreasonable, because it does not fully take into account the differences between institutions and disciplines (Li et al., 2011).

As a result, Chinese scholars have conducted a lot of research on the measure of average student cultivation cost. But there is a common idea in the existing research to obtain the average student cultivation cost by utilizing the total cultivation cost of higher education as well as the student numbers.

Calculating the total cultivation cost of higher education generally utilizes the principle of cost-sharing and the accrual system in colleges and universities to clarify various expenses related to the cultivation of students, and then add them up (Yao, 2011). For the calculation of the number of students, one approach is to calculate the numbers of master's students, doctoral students, and undergraduate students separately; the other approach is to add then up after assigning different weights to the numbers of master's students and doctoral students (Xuan et al., 2014).

To sum up, the noncompetitive research funding systems for universities in the United Kingdom, Poland, and other countries fully take into account subject differences and institution differences. However, although the current higher education teaching funding in China belongs to a typical noncompetitive funding model, it does not fully consider the difference between the disciplines and the higher education quality provided by the institutions, resulting in a large gap with the actual cultivation costs.

7.2.4 Current allocation of competitive and noncompetitive research funding inside and outside China

Whether inside or outside China, there is not much research on noncompetitive research funding. Noncompetitive is relative to competitive, so when we are exploring the research progress of noncompetitive research funding inside and outside China, it is also necessary to review the current situation of competitive research funding inside and outside China.

7.2.4.1 Current allocation status of competitive and noncompetitive research funding in the United States

The United States is a powerful country in science and technology. As always, the system of innovation in the United States has long been considered the most productive system in the world. Moweryr (1994) believes that the federal government's financial support is an important reason for the continued increase in U.S. scientific productivity. There are two main ways in which U.S. colleges and universities can receive funding: one is to obtain government funding through a competitive way; the other is through government-allocated academic earmarks to conduct research.

Competitive research funding accounts for 90% of the total higher education research funding, and the most important part of the competition is to determine the allocation of research funds through peer review. Researchers submit applications to government-established research projects, which are evaluated by experts in the relevant fields. This approach to obtaining competitive research funding through peer review was considered the most effective way for scientific institutions to receive scarce scientific resources (Nelson & Rosenberg, 1993). But with the increase of the competitiveness of scientific research, the method of peer review also brought great disadvantages. Because some faculty members of elite universities served as members of the review group, peer review became a tool for elite universities to compete for competitive research funding, making the competition for projects lose its fairness. Most of the projects approved by peer review were often the "safe" projects with traditional beliefs, crowding out research funding for breakthrough research, and resulting in a structural imbalance in research funding. Competition for scientific research also resulted in a high concentration of scientific research funds going to a small number of elite schools resulting in a monopoly phenomenon in research funds. According to the statistics in 2001, the top 20% of U.S. colleges and universities had 33% of the total higher education research funding, and the top 50% of colleges and universities had 60% of the total higher education research funding.

Competition has led to the phenomena of structural imbalances and excessive concentration in research funds, which has led to a growing demand for noncompetitive research funding, and "academic earmarks" have received increasing attention from the government and universities. According to the 2003 U.S. Annual Financial Report, there were 1964 academic earmarks included in the government budget, with total funding of $2 billion, accounting for 10% of total higher education research funding (Brainard & Borrego, 2003). The international common view on academic earmarks is that these earmarked projects effectively alleviate the imbalance in the structure of research funds caused by competition. Figueiredo (2004) pointed out in a study that the establishment of academic earmarks would help the government to redistribute the allocation of research funds for universities, thus effectively safeguarding universities' research infrastructure services. Some universities disadvantaged in competitive projects were able to improve the infrastructure of their research activities and also ensure their conduction of normal scientific research processes to some degree (Ferrin, 2003). In the United States, as financial support for university research declined, academic earmarks made up to the shortage of research funds in non-elite colleges and universities to some degree.

7.2.4.2 Current allocation status of competitive research funding in the United Kingdom

The United Kingdom's competitive funding is funded mainly by seven research committees under the British Research Council (BRC): the Arts and Humanities Research Council (AHRC), the Biotechnology and Biological Sciences Research Council (BBSRC), the Engineering and Physical Sciences Research Council (EPSRC), the Economic and Social Research Council (ESRC), the Medical Research Council (MRC), the Natural Environment Research Council (NERC), and the Science and Technology Facilities Council (STFC). Almost all the funds of the seven research committees come from the government's science and technology budget, with most of the funds allocated to research projects in universities and the rest going to research institutions of the research committees, large international scientific cooperation projects, and independent research organizations.

The seven research committees conduct a fair and rigorous review of colleges and universities to determine whether the projects can be applied and conducted. After an independent, expert peer review of the researchers' applications for funding, the support system will select research projects with the greatest research potential to fund. According to the research characteristics of their respective subject areas, the seven research committees set up different standards for evaluation. This method is more objective and closer to reality, so it can evaluate the research projects well.

7.2.4.3 Current allocation status of competitive and noncompetitive research funding in Germany

The federal government, state governments, the economic sector, and the European Union are the four main sources of research funding in Germany. The total research spending in 2015 was approximately EUR62.4 billion, of which approximately 65% came from enterprises and approximately 32% from the federal and state governments. For universities, most of the research funds came from the federal and state governments and can be mainly divided into institutional funds and project funds. The former is mainly government appropriations, mainly used for indirect costs such as personnel wages, the purchase and operation of large equipment and public service equipment, and infrastructure construction (mainly management fees), which belongs to noncompetitive funds. The latter is mainly used to pay for the direct costs of research projects (pay of the temporary staff and the purchase of small specialized equipment), which belongs to competitive funds.

The Federal Ministry of Education and Research (BMBF) is the German government's scientific research authority, which manages about 70% of the research funds. After providing the recurrent funding for universities and other public research institutions, the remaining funds are used as competitive research project funds. Research projects in Germany are divided into three main categories: direct project funding, indirect project funding, and cooperation project funding. Direct project funding is direct government funding for major research areas with the aim of ranking at the international advanced level. Indirectly funded projects are generally targeted at facilities and equipment and are designed to safeguard the conditions of research platforms. Cooperation projects are joint government research projects to solve a certain problem, so that universities, research institutions, enterprises can form a research group to conduct research (Ma, 2018).

7.2.4.4 Current allocation situation of competitive research funds in Japan

In 2017, the Japanese government provided a budget of 427.9 billion yen for competitive research, supporting all disciplines, from natural sciences to humanities and social sciences, and providing greater funding for basic research. There are five categories of research funds: scientific research supplementary funds (research funds), strategic research project, research output extension project, international scientific and technological cooperation research promotion project, and national research promotion project. Among them, the scientific research supplementary funds (research funds) are the competitive funds of the largest amount with the widest coverage from the Japanese government allocation, accounting for more than 50% of all competitive research funds. The scientific research supplementary funds are appropriated by the MEXT and managed by the Japan Society for the Promotion of Science (JSPS). The scientific research supplementary funds consist mainly of three categories: young scholar research funds, basic research and special promotion research, and new academic fields and challenging research (Xia & Zhong, 2016).

7.2.4.5 Current allocation situation of competitive research funds in China

China's research funds are also divided in two ways: competitive and noncompetitive. In the opinion of Xiao (2010), taking a competitive way to allocate research funds led universities to form an all-around and multilevel competitive situation, which played a key role in improving the efficiency of scientific research. Compared with research institutions, universities spent less than half of the money than did research institutions but produced several times more outputs than those research institutions. However, this high efficiency did not bring about the high quality of research output. According to the statistics, compared with the highly efficient university research, the overall research quality of research institutions was higher than that of universities (CERNET, 2015). Wen et al. (2013) explored the relationship between research funding and research outputs of public research institutions and found that the competition mechanism did not have a significant positive impact on outputs of patents and papers. On the contrary, the competitive allocation model has led to the following disadvantages in scientific research and production.

First, the competitive funding model leads to an overconcentration of research funds. The allocation of competitive scientific resources based on academic contributions and performance is a principle of spontaneity (Liu, 2015). Based on this principle of spontaneity, funding flows undoubtedly toward individuals with strong research capabilities and academic impact. For example, in the applications of some interdisciplinary projects and the applications of some key projects, the applications can only get approved through the building of research teams under the "celebrity effect" (Fan & Jia, 2013). And this celebrity effect puts young university teachers at a disadvantage when applying for such projects. According to the relevant research, China's research funding allocation is currently highly centralized, with 90% of the research funds concentrated in the hands of 20% of the researchers (He et al. 2014). According to the principle of diminishing marginal benefits, excessive concentration will lead to the inefficiency of research funding (Li et al., 2011).

Second, the competitive funding model makes researchers seek quick success and instant benefits. The emphasis on competition can fully improve the efficiency of research production, but overemphasis on competition will lead university teachers to have the mentality of quick success and instant benefits in research. Chinese scholar Zhou (2013) stated that the competition mechanism made it difficult for researchers to concentrate on research, but dispersed researchers' energies, making them conduct research activities with a strong utilitarian mind. This utilitarian and competitive mind made university teachers overseek the symbolic significance of "research", which is not conducive to producing high-quality and high-level research outputs (Fang, 2009).

7.2.4.6 Current allocation situation of noncompetitive research funds in China

In 2008, the Ministry of Education and the Ministry of Finance issued the "Interim Measures for the Management of Fundamental Research Funds for Central Universities" (henceforth "Fundamental Research Funds"), and established fundamental research funds for central universities as noncompetitive research funds among central universities. And in 2016, the "Measures for the Management of Fundamental Research Funds for Central Universities" further strengthened the stable support of the central universities to carry out independent research. Fundamental Research Funds is a noncompetitive research investment, its original intention being to alleviate many problems in scientific research and production caused by excessive competition.

Since the pilot of 14 universities in 2008, now nearly 92 central universities have been granted the funds. And the investment has been continuously increased from 100 million yuan to 3 billion yuan in 2014 (Liu, 2014). In the view of most university teachers, fundamental research funds are conducive to scientific research and production in colleges and universities. For example, Zhang et al. (2011) analyzed the management modes and the funding efficiencies of fundamental research funds for central universities and concluded that the fundamental research funds were effectively combined with the university characteristics, which not only provided a good research environment for young teachers and researchers, but was also conducive to the promotion of the independent innovation ability of universities. Cui et al. (2013) conducted statistics on the execution of fundamental research funds at Northwest University of Agriculture, Forestry and Technology, and found that the approval rate of independent research projects was high and the research outputs were very great. Cao (2016) conducted statistics on the execution of the fundamental research funds at East China University of Technology, and found that, whether in disciplines of natural sciences or humanities, the funding effect was significant, the research innovation ability levels of young teachers were greatly improved, and the research outputs supported by the funds were rated as excellent in evaluations.

Through sorting the management measures of fundamental research funds in some universities, we obtained Table 7.2. The management measures of fundamental research funds of these universities can be found in Table A7.1 in the Appendix.

Comparing the management measures of fundamental research funds in the aforementioned universities, it can be seen that when universities implement fundamental research funds for internal funds allocations, competitive funding is still the major choice, and funding is still based on the merit of applications.

7.2.4.7 Summary

Through the review of Chinese and international literature, it can be seen that the overall proportion of noncompetitive research funds is very low inside and

Table 7.2 Management measures for the fundamental research funds for central universities, selected cases

Institution name	Funded projects	Funding management agency/ measures	Funding channel
Peking University	The funds are used for the independent research at Peking University, including institutional independent research funds; start-up funds for researchers; students' research and innovation ability enhancement funds; excellent scientific research team construction funds; cultivation funds for basic, frontier, and interdisciplinary research.	Office of Discipline Construction	
Zhejiang University	Youth scientific research and innovation special funds (for individuals); scientific research and development special funds (for individual in a team), president special funds (for individuals recommended by departments); researchers in STEM disciplines under 40 years old; researchers in SSH disciplines under 45 years old; Overseas-returned young researchers under 45 years old; project term 1–3 years.	The leading group of independent scientific research plan; young researcher and research innovation special funds are managed by the faculties, and the rest is managed by the university research management office.	The selection is organized according to the annual plan.

(*Continued*)

Table 7.2 Continued

Institution name	Funded projects	Funding management agency/measures	Funding channel
Nanjing University	Key projects (for the team, up to 15 projects, each project up to 500,000 yuan); foreign experts and scholars special funds (for the introduction of experts, up to 20 projects, each project up to 300,000 yuan); general projects (for individuals, up to 80 projects, each project up to 100,000 yuan); small projects (for cooperative projects, each up to 50,000 yuan); the MOE key laboratories (for laboratories under construction, each around 0.5–1 million yuan according to the evaluations); special construction funds for key science and technology; special construction funds for humanities and social sciences; project term 2–3 years.	"Fundamental research funds" management leading group, office of scientific research, and office of humanities and social sciences are responsible for management.	Annual assessment; the selection is organized according to the annual plan.

Average teacher research funding 177

China University of Science and Technology	Young researcher innovation funds (for individuals), cultivation funds for innovative team (for teams), cultivation fund for key direction project (for individuals), international exchange and cooperation funds (for individuals). Young researcher innovation fund cannot be funded twice for the same person; the International Exchange and Cooperation Fund can be applied once a year, but one person can only apply for two projects in one year; the term for the young researcher innovation project is 2 years; the terms for innovation team and key direction projects are 3 years.	"Fundamental research funds" management leading group, young researcher innovation projects are arranged by the departments, the innovation team and the key direction projects are arranged by the office of scientific research.	Submission, evaluation, and selection are organized according to the annual guidelines.
Southwest University	Express projects (for newly recruited PhDs); general projects; student projects; key projects; great projects; innovative team projects; cultivation projects; acceptance check system is rigorous.	The setup of a special fund leading group; research management office is responsible for review and arrangements.	Express projects are funded directly; other projects are funded through applications, and the academic committee is responsible for review and selection.

(*Continued*)

Table 7.2 Continued

Institution name	Funded projects	Funding management agency/measures	Funding channel
Northwestern University of Agriculture, Forestry and Technology	Young researcher science fund projects; the cultivation special projects of great project; agricultural science innovation special key projects; project term is 3 years.	Office of research and office of finance are responsible for the management.	Application, review, and selection are organized according to the annual guidelines.
South China University of Technology	Young teacher projects of natural sciences (frontier science projects, interdisciplinary projects, free exploration projects, and university-city cooperative special projects); young teacher project of social sciences; recruited talent projects (for foreign teachers); student science and technology innovation projects; project term 2 years.	"Fundamental research funds" management leading group.	Experts are responsible for the review and selection.
Jinan University	Youth funds; cultivation projects of outstanding talents; team projects; perspective and technological innovation projects; cultivation projects of national project; soft science projects.	The setup of a special fund leading group; office of research is responsible for review and arrangements.	The cultivation projects of national project is noncompetitive project; the applications and reviews of other projects are organized according to the annual guidelines.

outside China. The most common manner is to allocate funds in a competitive way. Since the establishment of the Natural Science Foundation of China, researchers have the opportunity to freely select their research topics based on the guidelines, compete for funds by peer review, and obtain research funds of more independent utilization. This approach introduces competitive mechanisms and merit-based funding, so that funds are allocated to the most capable researchers, thereby improving the efficiency of the use of funds. This efficiency-first competitive distribution method can, on the one hand, fully mobilize the enthusiasm of researchers, while on the other hand, bring researchers into research dilemmas due to too many competitive funds and too few guaranteed funds (Xie, 2011). As a result of excessive competition, the Matthew effect in the research field is becoming more intense, resulting in an excessive concentration of research funds, as well as a serious waste of research resources. Driven by internal and external factors such as professional title evaluation and administrative intervention, young teachers and some academically competent teachers cannot fairly participate in the competition of research projects, resulting in the increase of unfair competition in the research field (Zhang, 2003).

The principle of fairness first means emphasizing the place of fairness. Setting up noncompetitive funding is to safeguard teachers' needs for basic research such that every teacher can have the basic right to engage in normal research activities, which is to a certain extent, conducive to the realization of research fairness. Whether it is the academic earmarks in the United States or the fundamental research funds in China, it plays a protective role in the basic research operation of universities and provides good research conditions for university teachers.

But academic earmarks in the United States rely more heavily on university lobbyists. They bypass the peer review and avoid the brutal debate over research funding, providing some research safeguards for those universities that could not get funded in by way of competition. However, this practice also prompts those universities with strong research capacities to join the army of lobbying politicians, which creates another competitive situation. Although the fundamental research funds for central universities in China are not competitive funds at the university level, when the funds are distributed within the university, the allocation is also subject to the traditional competitive thinking, which is still selected based on the results. This makes the fundamental research funds, which are noncompetitive research funds from the central financial budget, gradually deviate from their original intention during the process of university internal allocation.

Therefore, the establishment of noncompetitive research funds emphasizes the principle of fairness first. To a certain extent, this can alleviate the monopoly of research resources brought about by competition, which is of great significance to protect the basic research needs of university teachers, especially young teachers. Therefore, this study investigates the university teachers' need for basic research funds in China, so as to provide a decision-making reference for the policy establishment of fundamental research funds covering all university teachers.

7.3 Design and implementation of the survey on university teachers' needs for noncompetitive research funding

In order to understand the current situation of university teachers' research funds and to understand the university teachers' needs for noncompetitive research funds from their questionnaire responses, this study designed the "Questionnaire on University Teachers' Needs for Noncompetitive Research Funds", and carried out a large-scale questionnaire survey in more than 100 colleges and universities in the eastern, central, and western regions of China.

7.3.1 Questionnaire design and survey implementation

Through sorting out literature and understanding the basic research needs of university teachers, we initialized the design of the questionnaire framework, drafted a questionnaire, and discussed several times with higher education scholars and university research administrators the preparation of the preliminary questionnaire for the pilot survey. In September 2016, the questionnaire was distributed to 60 university teachers for the pilot survey. According to the feedback from university teachers, the preliminary questionnaire was revised to form the formal version of the "Questionnaire on University Teachers' Needs for Noncompetitive Research Funds" (see Appendix).

The formal questionnaire is divided into three parts containing 19 questions.

The first part is the investigation of the basic information of university teachers. This part contains a total of nine questions. Questions 1 to 6 mainly investigates the university teachers' institution type, age and title, and questions 7 to 8 investigate the university teachers' income and satisfaction. Question 9 is an investigation of university teachers' research outputs in Chinese and international journals.

The second part of the questionnaire is about the current situation of university teachers' research funds. This part contains a total of five questions. Questions 10 to 11 mainly investigate whether the performance bonus of research funds allocated by universities to teachers is reasonable and whether university teachers can obtain reasonable rewards. Questions 12 to 14 investigate university teachers' research funds and their shortages. Question 13 asks whether the university has established noncompetitive research projects.

The third part of the questionnaire is about the demand for the setup of noncompetitive research funds. There are five questions in this part. Questions 15 to 18 mainly investigate the attitude and demand of university teachers toward research funds. Questions 15 and 16 are true or false items. If the answer to question 15 is yes, the respondent should move on to question 16. Question 16 mainly investigates university teachers' demand for each expenditure item in the noncompetitive funds. Question 19 is an open-ended one that asks for university teachers' suggestions for setting up noncompetitive research funds.

In October 2016, the first round of online questionnaires was distributed by manually retrieving teachers' mailboxes on the official websites of universities.

From the end of 2016 to the beginning of 2017, a field study was conducted in one selected province each from the eastern, central, and western regions. In October 2016, researchers went to Hunan University and Hunan Normal University to conduct a field survey, distributed more than 300 hard-copy questionnaires, and held talks with the heads of research management and representatives of university teachers. In December 2016, researchers went to Xiamen University to conduct a field survey, distributed more than 200 hard-copy questionnaires, and held talks with research managers. In early 2017, researchers went to Tarim University in Xinjiang to conduct a field survey and distributed more than 200 hard-copy questionnaires. In the end, 847 teacher questionnaires were obtained through field surveys and online questionnaires.

7.3.2 Sample distribution and representativeness

The sample of university teachers obtained in this study involved 154 universities, and a total of 847 valid teacher questionnaires were collected. Considering that this study mainly focuses on the relevant investigation of university teachers' research funds, it is necessary to exclude the sample of higher vocational college teachers (20) as well as the sample of non-full-time teachers (18); the final sample size used in the analysis is 809. The survey data also collected descriptive statistics of the university teachers, such as the age distribution, research field distribution, university type, and job title distribution (see Table 7.3).

According to Table 7.3, in terms of discipline distribution, the proportion of teachers of humanities and social sciences (henceforth HSS) in the sample is 50.9%, and the proportion of teachers of science, engineering, agriculture, and medicine (henceforth SEAM) is 49.1%. The two proportions are quite similar. Thus, the sample is evenly distributed across the broad disciplinary categories. In terms of university type, the ordinary universities (among the "211 Project") and "985 Project" universities account for the highest proportion in the samples, 44.9% and 37.9%, respectively. The proportion of "211 Project" universities is 17.4%.

Table 7.3 Sample distribution

Discipline distribution	Humanities and social sciences (HSS)		Science, engineering, agriculture, and medicine (SEAM)		
Percentage (%)	50.9		49.1		
Institution type	985 Project universities	211 Project universities	Ordinary universities		
Percentage (%)	37.9	17.2	44.9		
Age structure	35 years and below	36–40 years old	41–45 years old	46–50 years old	Over 51 years old
Percentage (%)	28.4	27.2	16.1	11.4	16.9
Title distribution	Senior title		Sub-senior title	Middle title	
Percentage (%)	35.0		36.1	28.9	

182 *Average teacher research funding*

In terms of the age distribution of university teachers, the majority are young teachers aged 30–40 years old, accounting for 55.6% of the total sample. Compared with the results of the 2016 education statistics from the Department of Development Planning of China's Ministry of Education (CMOE, 2016) (see Figure 7.2), the age structure distribution of our sample is, overall, quite consistent. Some slight differences exist in the age groups of 35 years old and below and 36–40 years old. The proportion of university teachers aged 35 years old and below in the statistics of the Ministry of Education (33.3%) is about 5% larger than that of this study (28.4%); while the proportion of university teachers aged 36–40 years old in this study (27.2%) is about 6% larger than that of statistics from the Ministry of Education (21.6%). Therefore, in terms of age distribution, the sample of university teachers in this survey is of certain representativeness.

From the distribution of teachers' professional titles, the proportion with senior titles (full professor) is 35.0%, the proportion with sub-senior titles (associate professor) is 36.1%, and the proportion with middle titles (assistant professor) is 28.9%. A comparison with the 2016 educational statistics from the Department of Development Planning of the Ministry of Education (see Figure 7.3) shows that, overall, the job titles of our sample are distributed somewhat differently in the middle and senior titles, and are basically the same in the sub-senior titles. The proportion of university teachers with middle titles (48.6%) in the statistics of the Ministry of Education is 19.7% larger than the proportion of university teachers with middle titles in this study (28.9%); while the proportion of university teachers with senior titles in this study (35.0%) is 19.8% larger than the proportion of university teachers in the statistics of the Ministry of Education (15.2%). Therefore, in terms of job title distribution, the representativeness of the teacher sample in this study is low.

Through further cross-table analysis between job titles and ages (Table 7.4), teachers with middle titles are mainly young teachers (62%). Among teachers

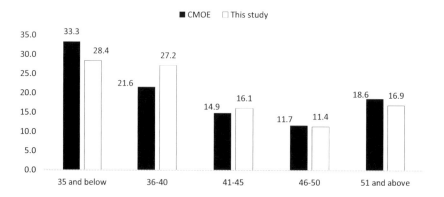

Figure 7.2 Comparison of the teacher age structure between the statistics of China's Ministry of Education (MOE) and the sample of this study.

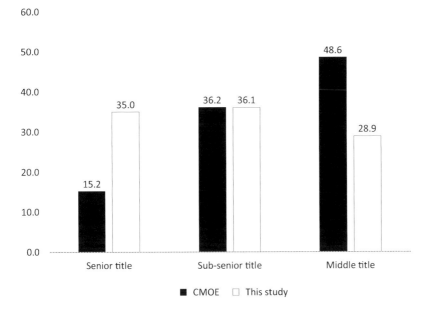

Figure 7.3 The comparison of the teacher title structure between the statistics of China's Ministry of Education (MOE) and the sample of this study.

Table 7.4 Age distribution of teachers with different titles

	35 years old and below	36–40 years old	41–50 years old	51 years old and above	Total
Senor title	6.4%	13.1%	39.2%	41.3%	100.0%
Sub-senior title	22.9%	42.1%	29.8%	5.1%	100.0%
Middle title	62.0%	25.6%	10.3%	2.1%	100.0%

with sub-senior titles, the highest proportion of teachers is aged 36–40 years old (42.1%). Among teachers with senior titles, the highest proportion of teachers is aged above 51 years old (41.3%).

In China, there are also some scholars conducting empirical research by collecting university teachers' data through fieldwork or online surveys, such as the studies from Hong Shen and her team on the survey of university teachers' development. Their study manually retrieved the e-mail addresses of teachers in 88 universities, distributed an online questionnaire with the support of the WWW. WJX.CN platform, and obtained a total of 5186 valid cases. Table 7.5 compares the basic characteristics of sample distribution between the data of Hong Shen's team and the data of this study. As can be seen from Table 7.5, the sample distribution of this study is basically consistent with the sample distribution of Hong

Table 7.5 Comparison of distribution characteristics of the two samples

		Proportion of teachers in this survey sample	Proportion of teachers in the survey sample of Hong Shen's team
Total sample size		809	5186
University type	985 Project universities	38%	38%
	211 Project universities	17%	25%
	Ordinary universities	45%	37%
Title type	Senior title	35%	38%
	Sub-senior tile	36%	42%
	Middle title	29%	20%
	<35 years old	28%	26%
	36–40 years old	27%	25%
Age structure	41–50 years old	28%	32%
	51–60 years old	15%	15%
	>60 years old	2%	2%

Shen's team in terms of university type, job title, and age structure. Although the sample size of this study is smaller than their sample size, the sample used in this study is still of certain representativeness.

7.4 Current distribution of university teachers' research projects

Research projects are important avenues for university teachers to conduct research activities. This section mainly analyzes the ability of university teachers to obtain research projects. As can be seen from Figure 7.4, the distribution of different types of projects varies greatly among the sample teachers. In this study, 46.9% of university teachers have national-level research projects, and 44.4% of university teachers have provincial-/ministerial-level research projects. Thus, national-level and provincial-/ministerial-level projects are the main project support for university teachers to engage in research activities. In addition, university-level projects are also an important source for university teachers, and 38.5% of them have university-level research projects. It is worth noting that the proportion of municipal-level and district-/county-level projects and other projects [with international cooperation or nongovernmental organizations (NGOs)] is not high, but there are still many university teachers with nongovernment projects (19.6%). Therefore, from the full sample, national-level projects, provincial-/ministerial-level projects, university-level projects, and nongovernment projects are the main types of research projects for university teachers. Also, these four types of projects are the focus of the following analysis of this section.

Average teacher research funding 185

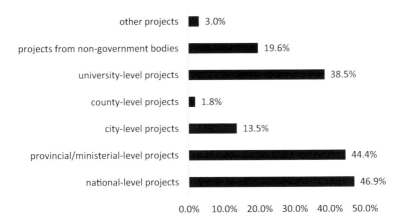

Figure 7.4 The distribution of the types of research projects obtained by teachers in the survey sample, 2013–2015.

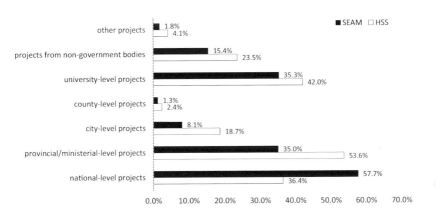

Figure 7.5 The distribution of the types of research projects obtained by teachers in samples of different disciplines, 2013–2015.

7.4.1 Distribution of research projects for university teachers in different disciplines

The sample teachers are divided into humanities and social sciences (HSS) and science, engineering, agriculture, and medicine (SEAM), and we statistically analyzed the type distribution of university teachers' research projects according to different disciplines. The results are shown in Figure 7.5.

As shown in Figure 7.5, for HSS teachers, the proportion of teachers holding provincial-/ministerial-level projects is the highest, at 53.6%, followed by university-level projects at 42.0%, and then national-level projects at 36.4%; projects

Table 7.6 Distribution of national-level projects among teachers in different disciplines and different age groups

	35 years old and below	36–40 years old	41–50 years old	51 years old and above
Humanities and social sciences (HSS)	18.7%	30.0%	30.0%	21.3%
Science, engineering, agriculture, and medicine (SEAM)	27.1%	28.8%	27.1%	17.0%

from nongovernment bodies is only at 23.5%. For SEAM teachers, 57.7% of them hold national-level projects. The proportions of those with provincial-/ministerial-level projects are almost the same as the proportion of those with university projects, about 35%. The lowest proportion is projects from non-government bodies at only 15.4%.

As one of the most important types of government-funded projects, national-level projects play a very important role in the promotion and career development of university teachers. Therefore, this study further statistically analyzed the proportion of HSS or SEAM teachers holding national-level projects by age group. The results are shown in Table 7.6.

As can be seen from Table 7.6, on the whole, HSS teachers with national-level projects are relatively older compared to SEAM teachers. For HSS teachers with national-level projects, most of them are mainly concentrated in the age group of 36–50 (60%). For SEAM teachers, the holding of national-level projects is more evenly distributed in terms of age, with little difference among the group of teachers under the age of 35, the group of teachers aged 36–40, and the group of teachers aged 41–50. However, for teachers older than 51 years, the proportion holding national-level projects is significantly lower.

7.4.2 Distribution of research projects for university teachers at different institutional levels

In China, university teachers at different institutional levels vary in the obtaining of scientific research projects. This study divides the institutional level of the sample teachers into 985 Project universities, 211 Project universities, and ordinary universities, and analyzes the distribution of different research projects in these three categories of university teachers. As can be seen from Figure 7.6, there are substantial differences among teachers at different levels in the obtaining of research projects. For teachers in 985 Project universities, the proportion of those with national-level projects reaches 65.3%. For teachers in 211 Project universities, the proportion of those with national-level projects is 53.2%. For teachers in ordinary universities, the proportion of those with national-level projects is only

Average teacher research funding 187

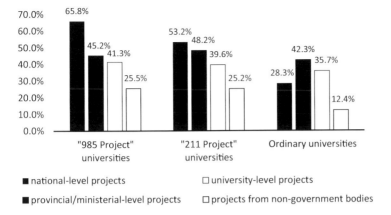

Figure 7.6 The type distribution of research projects obtained by university teachers at different institutional levels, 2013–2015.

28.3%. In contrast, the proportions of teachers with provincial-/ministerial-level projects are very similar in the three types of universities, namely, 45.2% for 985 Project universities, 48.2% for 211 Project universities, and 42.3% for other institutions. This demonstrates teachers in high-level universities have great advantages in obtaining national-level projects, while teachers in ordinary universities have greater difficulty in obtaining national-level projects.

There is no obvious gap in the proportion of teachers holding university-level projects in the three institutional types, but the pattern is still clear that the proportion of 985 Project universities is larger than that of 211 Project universities, and the proportion of 211 Project universities is larger than that of other universities. Combined with the details of the previous description on China's university research funding system, 985 Project universities and most 211 Project universities belong to the group under administration of the Ministry of Education. They can obtain the support of "Fundamental Research Funds for Central Universities" allocated by the Ministry of Education, providing funds for their teachers to conduct independent research projects. Therefore, teachers in these two types of universities have higher advantages in holding university-level projects than the other ordinary institutions.

The differences in research between SEAM and HSS disciplines may have an impact on the analysis. In order to better present the type distribution of research projects of teachers in different disciplines and at different institutional levels, this study makes a comparative analysis of the research project distribution of teachers in different disciplines based on the divisions of HSS and SEAM, as shown in Table 7.7.

As can be seen from Table 7.7, in terms of the comparison of research project distribution obtained by teachers in different disciplines within the same institutional

Table 7.7 The type distribution of research projects obtained by teachers in different disciplines at different institutional levels

Project type	University level 985 Project universities — Humanities and social sciences (HSS)	University level 985 Project universities — Science, engineering, agriculture, and medicine (SEAM)	211 Project universities — Humanities and social sciences (HSS)	211 Project universities — Science, engineering, agriculture, and medicine (SEAM)	Ordinary universities — Humanities and social sciences (HSS)	Ordinary universities — Science, engineering, agriculture, and medicine (SEAM)
National-level projects	51.6%	80.3%	40.0%	68.8%	22.0%	34.8%
Provincial-level projects	54.8%	35.5%	52.0%	43.8%	53.3%	31.5%
University-level projects	46.5%	36.8%	46.7%	31.3%	36.3%	35.4%
Projects with nongovernment bodies	29.0%	21.7%	28.0%	21.9%	17.0%	7.7%

level, for 985 Project universities, 211 Project universities, or ordinary universities, the proportion of SEAM teachers with national-level projects is generally higher than that of HSS teachers, while the proportion of HSS teachers with provincial-/ministerial-level projects is the highest in terms of the comparison of the research project distribution obtained by teachers at different institutional levels. For either HSS or SEAM disciplines, the proportion of 985 Project universities is higher than that of 211 Project universities in obtaining national-level projects, and the proportion of 211 Project universities is higher than that of ordinary institutions. With regard to the proportion of provincial-/ministerial-level projects, the proportion of HSS teachers with provincial-/ministerial-level projects are almost the same in all three levels of universities. However, the proportions of SEAM teachers with provincial-/ministerial-level projects in these three levels of universities are quite different: teachers from 211 Project universities are considerably higher than those teachers from 985 Project universities and other institutions.

7.4.3 Distribution of research projects obtained by teachers with different job titles

For university teachers, job title is another important factor in determining the ability to obtain research projects. So, this section uses job title as the division criteria, and analyzes the statistics of national-level projects, provincial-/ministerial-level projects, university-level projects, and projects from nongovernment bodies obtained by university teachers with different titles. The results are presented in Figure 7.7.

As can be seen from Figure 7.7, for teachers with senior titles, the proportion of those holding projects show an increasing trend according to the project levels. The

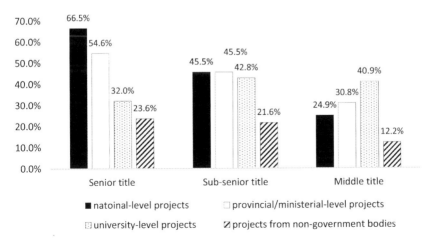

Figure 7.7 The type distribution of the research project obtained by teachers with different titles, 2013–2015.

proportions of teachers with national-level, provincial-/ministerial-level, university-level, and projects from nongovernment bodies are 66.5%, 54.6%, 32.0%, and 23.6%, respectively. For teachers with sub-senior titles, research projects are distributed roughly even on government-funded projects, that is, 45.5% for national level, 45.5% for provincial level, and 42.8% university level. But the proportion of nongovernment projects is significantly lower, only 21.6%. For teachers with middle titles, their situation is different from those with senior titles. The proportions of middle-titled teachers holding projects show a decreasing trend according to the project levels. The proportions of teachers with national-level, provincial-/ministerial-level, and university-level projects are 24.9%, 30.8%, and 40.9%, respectively. The proportion of nongovernment projects is about 12.2%, substantially lower than the proportion of government-funded projects. Overall, the higher the title of teachers, the higher the proportion of teachers with high-level projects; the higher the title of teachers, the higher the proportion of teachers with nongovernment projects. The proportion of teachers obtaining nongovernment projects is relatively low in all title groups, especially those teachers with middle titles whose proportion of obtaining nongovernment projects is less than 15%. This is probably because of the short research years and relatively low social influence of middle-title teachers, so they are at a disadvantage in the competition of nongovernment projects.

Further statistics are made on the distribution of research projects of teachers with different titles by the HSS and SEAM disciplines, as shown in Table 7.8. Among the group of HSS teachers, those with the senior or sub-senior titles have advantages in obtaining national-level and provincial-/ministerial-level projects. The proportions of senior title teachers obtaining national-level and provincial-/ministerial-level projects are 55.7% and 63.4%, respectively. The proportions of sub-senior title teachers obtaining national-level and provincial-\ministerial-level projects are 33.1% and 58.4%, respectively. Regarding university-level projects, the opposite trend is shown. This phenomenon is also evident with SEAM teachers. The proportions of senior-title teachers receiving national-level and provincial-/ministerial-level projects are 75.7% and 47.4%, respectively, while the proportions of teachers with sub-senior titles receiving national-level and provincial-/ministerial-level projects are 59.4% and 31.2%, respectively, which are substantially higher than the proportions of middle-title teachers receiving national-level and provincial/ministerial-level projects. It can be seen that teachers with senior or sub-senior titles have prominent advantages in the applications and approvals of national-level and provincial-/ministerial-level projects. This is related to the fact that senior title teachers usually have relatively longer years of research and are more experienced in applying for research projects. However, some scholars found that this was related to the Matthew effect in the allocation of competitive research projects. The Matthew effect refers to the relationships between scholars' achievements and their position in the academic system. Those scholars in the dominant position often use a high platform to obtain more highly competitive projects, while disadvantaged scholars are often left behind, being placed at the bottom of the academic system (Zhang, 2014; Wang and Du, 2014). For example, outstanding academic leaders, "Jie Qing", and "Changjiang Scholars"

Table 7.8 Type distribution of research projects obtained by teachers in different disciplines and with different titles

Discipline type	Humanities and social sciences (HSS)			Science, engineering, agriculture, and medicine (SEAM)		
	Senior	Sub-senior	Middle	Senior	Sub-senior	Middle
Project type						
National-level projects	55.7%	33.1%	20.5%	75.7%	59.4%	29.9%
Provincial-/ministerial-level projects	63.4%	58.4%	37.8%	47.4%	31.2%	22.4%
University-level projects	37.4%	42.9%	45.7%	27.6%	42.8%	36.4%
Projects from nongovernment bodies	29.0%	26.0%	15.0%	18.4%	16.7%	9.3%

in universities often have many competitive projects and a huge amount of funds, but ordinary teachers without academic titles receive very little competitive funds.

7.5 Distribution of research funds for university teachers

Research projects are important opportunities for university teachers to conduct research activities. Whether the funds for research are sufficient is directly related to the development and progress of the projects. This section mainly examines the distribution of the research funds of sample university teachers by aggregating the total amount of funds from various types of projects obtained by the university teachers in the years 2013–2015. Table 7.9 shows the overall situation of university teachers' research funds. As can be seen from Table 7.9, the average research funds of sample university teachers are 598,000 yuan, and the average research funds of SEAM teachers are 911,000 yuan, which is about three times the average of HSS teachers. In terms of institution type, the gaps between different levels of universities are very obvious. The teachers at 985 Project universities have the maximum average of research funds, reaching 1,114,000 yuan. The teachers at 211 Project universities are ranked second, reaching 460,000 yuan. Those teachers of ordinary universities have the minimum average, only 214,000 yuan. In terms of the teacher's title, the gaps are also very obvious. The average research funds of senior-title teachers are as high as 1,240,000 yuan, while the average research funds for teachers with sub-senior titles are halved (approximately 339,000 yuan), and the average research funds for middle-title teachers are only half of the teachers with sub-senior titles (approximately 145,000 yuan).

Observing Figure 7.8 we can find that in the group of sample teachers, the distribution of research funds is basically a step type, that is, the larger the proportion of a group of teachers, the fewer research funds that group obtains, while a large number of research funds are in the hands of a small number of teachers. As can be seen from Figures 7.8, 29.6% of teachers have research funds less than 50,000 yuan, making them the largest group in the sample. The proportion of teachers with research funds from 50,000 to 100,000 yuan is slightly lower, about 10% of the total. Also, 95% of university teachers have research funds of less than 2 million yuan. Less than 5% of teachers have more than 2 million yuan research funds,

Table 7.9 Overall situation of university teachers' research funds (10,000 yuan)

Discipline	Humanities and social sciences (HSS)		Science, engineering, agriculture, and medicine (SEAM)
	29.6		91.1
University type	985 Project universities	211 Project universities	Ordinary universities
	111.4	46.0	21.4
Job title	Senior	Sub-senior	Middle
	124.0	33.9	14.5
Overall		59.8	

Average teacher research funding 193

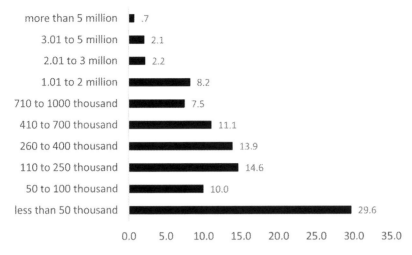

Figure 7.8 The distribution of research project funds received by sample university teachers.

and teachers with more than 5 million yuan research funds are even less. The following section will examine the distribution of university teachers' research funds from the aspects of different disciplines and different types.

7.5.1 *Distribution of research funds for university teachers in different disciplines*

To a large extent, the nature of the disciplines determines the amount of research funds. For example, disciplines such as engineering and medicine often receive a larger amount of research funds because of their need for experimental equipment. In contrast, the cost of research in the humanities and social sciences is lower, so the amount of research funds is also lower. This section is classified according to the two broad disciplines of HSS and SEAM, and analyzes the distribution of university teachers' research funds in different broad disciplines. The results are presented in Table 7.10.

As can be seen from Table 7.10, for HSS teachers, the proportion of those with research funds less than 50,000 yuan is the highest (31.3%), and the proportion of those with research funds ranging from 110,000 to 200,000 yuan is 20.9%. The sum of these two categories of teachers accounts for more than 50% of the sample. The proportion of teachers with funds between 260,000 and 400,000 yuan is 14.6%, and the proportion of teachers with funds between 50,000 and 100,000 yuan is 13.3%. It can be seen that teachers with funds under 400,000 yuan account for about 80% of the HSS sample teachers, becoming the absolute main body. By contrast, the number of teachers with funds above 400,000 yuan

Table 7.10 Distribution of research funds for teachers in different disciplines (%)

Research funds (yuan)	Humanities and social sciences (HSS)	Science, engineering, agriculture, and medicine (SEAM)
Less than 50 thousand	31.3	27.7
50 thousand to 100 thousand	13.3	6.5
110 thousand to 250 thousand	20.9	8.1
260 thousand to 400 thousand	14.6	13.4
410 thousand to 700 thousand	9.5	12.8
710 thousand to 1000 thousand	4.4	10.8
1.01 million to 2 million	4.6	12.1
2.01 million to 3 million	1.0	3.3
3.01 million to 5 million	0.5	3.8
More than 5 million	0	1.5

is relatively small, and almost no teacher can reach the research funding level of above 5,000,000 yuan.

For SEAM teachers, the proportion of teachers with research funds less than 50,000 is also the highest, accounting for 27.7%. The second-highest proportion is those teachers with research funds ranging from 260,000 to 400,000 yuan, accounting for 13.4%. The proportion of teachers with research funds ranging from 410,000 to 700,000 yuan is almost the same as the proportion of teachers with research funds ranging from 1,010,000 to 2,000,000 yuan, accounting for 12.8% and 12.1%, respectively. By contrast, the proportion of teachers with research funds of 50,000–100,000 and 110,000–250,000 is lower, accounting for 6.5% and 8.1%, respectively. Overall, the amount of funds for SEAM teachers is generally higher than that of HSS teachers. Even more, there are a few SEAM teachers having more than 5 million yuan in research funds, accounting for 1.5% of the total teachers.

Through the preceding analysis we can find that, whether it is HSS disciplines or SEAM disciplines, those teachers with research funds under 50,000 yuan occupy a considerably large proportion. Therefore, in the next step, this study focuses on this group of teachers to examine the basic characteristics of these teachers with more limited research funds. The statistical results are presented in Table 7.11.

As can be seen from Table 7.11, teachers with research funds under 50,000 yuan have some common characteristics.

First, young teachers are the main group. Among teachers with funds under 50,000 yuan, those in HSS disciplines are dominated by teachers aged 35 years old and below and 36–40 years old, accounting for 38% and 21.7%, respectively; those in SEAM disciplines are dominated by teachers aged 35 years old and below and 36–40 years old, accounting for 39.1% and 29.1%, respectively. The results are shocking because the group of teachers aged 40 years old and below are right at their young and energetic time, which enables them to strive for more resources from research projects and conduct high-level scientific research.

Table 7.11 Distribution of age and title structures of teachers with research funds under 50,000 yuan (%)

		Humanity and social sciences (HSS)	Science, engineering, agriculture, and medicine
Age structure	35 years old and below	38	39.1
	36–40 years old	21.7	29.1
	41–45 years old	14.0	17.3
	46–50 years old	10.1	7.3
	51 years old and above	16.2	7.3
Title structure	Senior	14.7	14.5
	Sub-senior	28.7	35.5
	Middle	56.6	50.0

However, teachers in this age group are unexpectedly in the highest proportion of teachers with funds under 50,000 yuan. This needs to attract the attention of research project management agencies. How to provide this age group of teachers with guarantees of research funding and help them continue to conduct high-level scientific research work is the issue that should be thought of by policymakers in relevant departments such as the Ministry of Education, Ministry of Science and Technology, the National Natural Science Foundation of China, and the National Office for Philosophy and Social Sciences.

As for job titles, teachers with middle titles are the largest group. Those teachers whose research funds are less than 50,000 yuan usually face more difficulties in applying for projects with larger funds, as a result of their low ranking. For example, among the teachers with a national-level project, the proportions of those with middle titles are 20.5% (HSS) and 29.9% (SEAM). For middle-title teachers with research funds under 50,000 yuan, the proportion of those holding national-level projects is even lower (1.4% for HSS and 1.8% for SEAM).

It is worth pointing out that the reason why teachers with research funds under 50,000 yuan cannot obtain research projects may not be due to their insufficient research capabilities. The growing "title wall" in China makes young teachers face "more applicants but fewer positions" competition when they get promoted from middle to sub-senior titles. Many young teachers with strong research capabilities are also unable to enter the ranks of senior titles because of the reality of brutal competition.

Research funds are a scarce resource. The review of research projects is based on the standard of "academic capacities" measured by job titles and merit-based funding. On the one hand, this is good to ensure the efficiency of the use of research funds. But at the same time, it is unfair for teachers who have strong research capacities but do not get promoted to senior or sub-senior titles due to the title wall. Therefore, it is of great significance to establish noncompetitive research funds to ensure that this group of teachers can conduct basic research activities.

7.5.2 Distribution of research funds for university teachers in different institution types

This section divides the institutions with which the sample teachers are affiliated into 985 Project universities, 211 Project universities, and ordinary universities out of the 211 Project, and analyzes the distribution of teachers' research funds in three categories of institutions. The statistical results are shown in Table 7.12.

As can be seen from Table 7.12, for HSS disciplines, the research funds of 985 Project university teachers mostly range from 110,000–250,000 to 260,000–400,000 yuan, accounting for 22.6% and 21.9%, respectively. There are also some 985 Project university teachers having research funds between 3,000,000 to 5,000,000 yuan, accounting for about 1.3%, but there is no one having research funds of more than 5,000,0000 yuan. Among 211 Project universities, teachers' research funds are concentrated at the level of 50,000 yuan and below, accounting for 29.3%, and there is no teacher having research funding of more than 2,000,000 yuan. Among ordinary institutions, the proportion of teachers with research funds of less than 50,000 yuan is even higher, reaching 47.3%, which indicates that nearly half of the teachers in these ordinary institutions have research funds of less than 50,000 yuan.

For SEAM disciplines, the amount of research funds is one step higher, but the gaps between different levels of universities are more obvious. Among 985 Project universities, the teachers' research funds range mostly from 710,000–1,000,000 yuan to 1,010,000–2,000,000 yuan, and the proportions are both 19.7%, adding up to about 40% of the total. Among the 211 Project universities, the research funds of most teachers range from 260,000–400,000 yuan to 410,000–700,000 yuan, accounting for 23.4% and 17.2%, respectively, which added up to about 40%. Among ordinary institutions, up to 50.8% of teachers' research funds are under 50,000 yuan.

Overall, there is a huge gap in the research funds of teachers at different levels of universities. For HSS teachers in the distribution of those funding levels above 100,000 yuan, there exists an obvious phenomenon of increasing proportion with higher university levels. For SEAM teachers, the same pattern exists in the distribution of those funding levels above 700,000 yuan. This is likely to be relevant with the fact that the HSS or SEAM teachers in higher-level universities have greater opportunities to obtain national-level projects, or key/great projects.

7.5.3 Concentration of research funds for university teachers

Through the preceding analysis, it has been found that the difference of research funds between teachers with different titles and working at different levels of universities is very obvious. For this reason, this section focuses on the concentration of research funds for university teachers. This study measures the concentration of research funds by ranking sample teachers from low to high according to the total amount of individual teachers' research funds, and calculating the group of teachers' total funds at different quantiles (5%, 10%, 20%, 80%, 90%, and 95%) as a percentage of the grand total funds.

Table 7.12 Distribution of research funds for teachers in different types of universities (%)

Discipline type	Humanities and social sciences (HSS)			Science, engineering, agriculture, and medicine (SEAM)		
Funding group	985 Project universities	211 Project universities	Ordinary universities	985 Project universities	211 Project universities	Ordinary universities
Less than 50 thousand	13.5	29.3	47.3	6.6	12.5	50.8
50 to 100 thousand	10.3	6.7	18.7	4.6	7.8	7.7
110 to 250 thousand	22.6	21.3	19.2	6.6	9.4	8.8
260 to 400 thousand	21.9	24.0	4.4	9.2	23.4	13.3
410 to 700 thousand	13.5	12.0	4.9	15.8	17.2	8.8
710 to 1000 thousand	7.7	4.0	1.6	19.7	10.9	3.3
1.01–2 million	7.1	2.7	3.3	19.7	10.9	6.1
2.01–3 million	1.9	0	0.5	5.9	3.1	1.1
3.01–5 million	1.3	0	0	7.9	4.7	0
More than 5 million	0	0	0	3.9	0	0
Total	100	100	100	100	100	100

It can be seen from the calculations that in the subsample of HSS teachers, the quantiles of research funds distribution are 0 (5%), 0 (10%), 20,000 (20%), 402,000 (80%), 785,000 (90%), and 1,200,000 (95%). In the subsample of SEAM teachers, the quantiles of research funds distribution are 0 (5%), 0 (10%), 9,600 (20%), 1,044,000 (80%), 2,000,000 (90%), and 3,372,0000 (95%). Accordingly, the concentration of research funds for HSS and SEAM teachers can be further calculated. See Table 7.13.

The results of Table 7.13 show that among HSS teachers, the sum of the research funds of the teacher group at the bottom 20% accounts for only 0.1% of the total, while the sum of the research funds of the group of teachers at the top 20% accounts for 83.29% of the total. Among SEAM teachers, the situation is very similar. The sum of research funds of the teacher group at the bottom 20% accounts for only 0.01% of the total, while the sum of research funds of the teacher group at the top 20% accounts for 84.13% of the total. As a result, it can be seen that 20% of teachers, whether in HSS or SEAM disciplines, control more than 80% of the total funds, and those top scholars (95%) control nearly half of the research funds. Through further calculation, it can be seen that the Gini coefficient of research funds for HSS teachers is 0.65, and the Gini coefficient of research funds for SEAM teachers is 0.72. It shows that the uneven degree of the distribution of university teachers' research funds is relatively high, and the uneven degree is higher in SEAM disciplines than in HSS disciplines.

What are the characteristics of the teacher group with low research funding? Table 7.14 presents the statistical results of the group characteristics in terms of age, job title, and university type.

Through the analysis of Table 7.14, it can be seen that for the teacher group with the smallest research funds in HSS disciplines, 40.74% of them are under 35 years old, 60.49% of them have middle titles, and 67.90% of them work in ordinary institutions. For SEAM disciplines, the situation is very similar. Inside the group of teachers with the smallest research funds, 43.00% of them are under the age of 35, 51.90% of them have middle titles, and 84.81% of them work in ordinary institutions.

Table 7.13 Concentration of research funds for teachers in different disciplines (%)

Concentration of funds	Humanities and social sciences (HSS)	Science, engineering, agriculture, and medicine (SEAM)
Top 5%	48.27	59.52
Top 10%	64.70	67.97
Top 20%	83.29	84.13
Bottom 20%	0.10	0.01
Bottom 10%	0.00	0.00
Bottom 5%	0.00	0.00
Gini coefficient	0.65	0.72

Table 7.14 Distribution of teacher characteristics at the bottom 20% of funds (%)

Age group	35 years old and below	36–40 years old	41–50 years old	51 years old and above
Humanities and social sciences (HSS)	40.74	19.75	20.99	18.52
Science, engineering, agriculture, and medicine (SEAM)	43.00	22.78	27.85	6.30

Title type	Senior	Sub-senior	Middle
Humanities and social sciences (HSS)	12.35	27.16	60.49
Science, Engineering, Agriculture, and Medicine (SEAM)	16.46	31.65	51.90

University type	985 Project universities	211 Project universities	Ordinary universities
Humanities and social sciences (HSS)	16.05	16.05	67.90
Science, engineering, agriculture, and medicine (SEAM)	8.86	6.33	84.81

7.6 Analysis of university teachers' attitudes toward noncompetitive research funding

7.6.1 Overall attitude toward the establishment of noncompetitive research funding

As can be seen from Figure 7.9, from the full sample, more than sixfold (67.4%) of teachers agreed with noncompetitive research funding, 20.5% of teachers disagreed, and 12.1% of teachers were neutral. So, what is the attitude of teachers in different disciplines, different types of universities, and with different titles toward noncompetitive research funding? The results of the statistics are presented in Table 7.15.

As can be seen from Table 7.15, in terms of difference among disciplines, there are 69.17% of teachers in HSS disciplines supporting the establishment of noncompetitive research funding, slightly higher than the 65.57% in SEAM disciplines. In terms of the university types, the proportion of teachers in 985 Project universities

200 *Average teacher research funding*

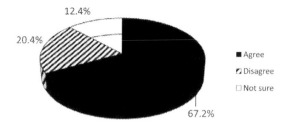

Figure 7.9 The distribution of university teachers' attitudes toward noncompetitive research funds.

Table 7.15 Percentage of teachers with different characteristics who agreed with the establishment of noncompetitive research funding (%)

Discipline type	Humanities and social sciences (HSS)		Science, engineering, agriculture, and medicine (SEAM)	
Proportion	69.17		65.57	
University type	985 Project universities	211 Project universities	Ordinary universities	
Proportion	64.84	64.03	70.99	
Title type	Middle	Sub-senior	Senior	
Proportion	69.20	72.51	60.78	
Age group	35 years old and below	36–40 years old	41–50 years old	51 years old and above
Proportion	66.80	66.97	72.85	60.60

and 211 Project universities who supported the establishment of noncompetitive research funding is about the same, about 64.84% and 64.03%, respectively. The teachers in ordinary institutions held a more positive attitude toward noncompetitive research funding, with 70.99% of them agreeing. In terms of job titles, teachers with sub-senior titles were the most positive in their attitude toward the establishment of noncompetitive research funding, with 72.51% of them agreeing. Next are middle-title teachers, with 69.20% of them agreeing. Among teachers with senior titles, the proportion of those who agreed with the establishment of noncompetitive research funding is relatively low (60.78%), but the proportion also surpasses one-half. Finally, in terms of age structure, teachers aged 41–50 years old are the most positive in their attitude toward the establishment of noncompetitive research funding, with a high proportion of 72.85% of teachers agreeing. Young teachers aged under 35 years old and 36–40 years old also had a positive attitude, with the agreeing proportions of 66.8% and 66.97%, respectively. The proportion of agreeing teachers aged 51 years old and above was relatively low (60.60%).

7.6.2 *Factors affecting the attitude toward the establishment of noncompetitive research funding*

As can be seen from the aforementioned results, teachers with different job titles, working in different levels of universities, and in different age groups generally agree to the establishment of noncompetitive research funding, but there are still some differences. In order to further examine which factors influence university teachers to support the establishment of noncompetitive research funding, the following logistic model is built for empirical analysis:

$$Ln(p/(1-p)) = b_0 + b_1 age + b_2 ZG + b_3 FG + b_4 paper \\ + b_5 grant + b_6 XK + b_7 U985 + b_8 U211 + e \quad (7.2)$$

In the equation, p indicates the proportion of teachers who agree with the establishment of noncompetitive research funding. age indicates the age dummy variable of university teachers (the reference group is 50 years old and older). ZG and FG indicate the senior (full professor) and sub-senior (associate professor) titles in the university system, respectively. $paper$ indicates the number of papers published. Grant indicates the number of research funds. XK indicates whether the teacher belongs to HSS disciplines or not (HSS = 1). $U985$ indicates whether the teacher works in at a 985 Project university (985 Project university = 1). $U211$ indicates whether the teacher works at a 211 Project university (211 Project university = 1), and e is a random error term.

Considering the needs of modeling, this study processed the sample data by deleting those cases responding "not sure" in the item regarding the establishment of noncompetitive research funding, and a total of 713 cases with the responses of "yes" and "no" were kept. The clarifications and descriptive statistics for variables are shown in Table 7.16.

As can be seen from Table 7.16, the explanatory variables are divided into three main categories: the first category is the characteristics of individual teachers, the second category is the characteristics of teacher research, and the third category is the characteristics of the universities. The teacher's individual characteristics variables include age and job title. The age variables are set to be four dummy variables with 51 years old and above as the reference: $age1$ (35 years old and below), $age2$ (36–40 years old), $age3$ (41–45 years old), and $age4$ (46–50 years old). Teachers with senior titles account for 35% of the total, and teachers with sub-senior titles account for 36% of the total. The average value of academic papers published by teachers is 3.55, with a minimum of 0 and a maximum of 12. The average value of teachers' research funds is 597,700 yuan, with a minimum of 0 yuan and a maximum of 65 million yuan. The mean of discipline types is 0.51, indicating that 51% of teachers belonged to the HSS disciplines. In addition, 38% of the teachers in the sample worked at 985 Project universities, and 17% of them worked at 211 Project universities.

Table 7.17 presents the basic results of the logistic model. Unlike ordinary linear regressions, the results of the logistic model do not represent the marginal effect of the independent variables on the dependent variable, but the probability that the variations of the independent variables will change the individual's choice. From the results of the logistic model, it can be seen that, among the teacher characteristics variables, teachers of different age groups held different attitudes toward the establishment of noncompetitive research funding. Referencing with the group of

Table 7.16 Description of the main variables and their descriptive statistics

Variable name	Variable description	Values	Mean	Standard deviation	Minimum	Maximum
age1	Whether a teacher is younger than 35 years old	0 = No; 1 = Yes	0.28	0.45	0	1
age2	Whether a teacher is aged between 36 and 40 years old	0 = No; 1 = Yes	0.27	0.45	0	1
age3	Whether a teacher is aged between 41 and 45 years old	0 = No; 1 = Yes	0.16	0.37	0	1
age4	Whether a teacher is aged between 45 and 50 years old	0 = No; 1 = Yes	0.11	0.32	0	1
ZG	Whether a teacher is a full professor	0 = No; 1 = Yes	0.35	0.48	0	1
FG	Whether a teacher is an associate professor	0 = No; 1 = Yes	0.36	0.48	0	1
paper	Academic publications	Continuous variables	3.55	2.09	0	12
grant	Research funds	Continuous variables	59.77	244.85	0	6500
XK	Discipline type	0 = Science, engineering, agriculture, and medicine; 1 = Humanities and social sciences	0.51	0.50	0	1
U985	Whether the institution is included in 985 Project	0 = No; 1 = Yes	0.38	0.49	0	1
U211	Whether the institution is included in 211 Project	0 = No; 1 = Yes	0.17	0.38	0	1

Table 7.17 Results for logistic models

Variable	Odds ratio	Standard error	z Value	P > z	95% Confidence interval	
age1	0.773	0.281	−0.710	0.478	0.379	1.575
age2	0.758	0.248	−0.850	0.396	0.399	1.438
age3	1.292	0.446	0.740	0.459	0.656	2.542
age4	1.418	0.504	0.980	0.325	0.707	2.844
ZG	0.491**	0.163	−2.140	0.032	0.256	0.941
FG	0.954	0.262	−0.170	0.863	0.557	1.632
paper	0.912*	0.046	−1.850	0.064	0.827	1.006
grant	1.001	0.001	0.740	0.462	0.999	1.002
XK	1.211	0.243	0.950	0.340	0.817	1.796
U985	0.997	0.225	−0.010	0.989	0.640	1.552
U211	0.785	0.205	−0.930	0.353	0.471	1.309
constant	6.011	2.590	4.160	0.000	2.584	13.985

teachers 51 years old and above, teachers in the groups of 41–45 years old and 46–50 years old were more likely to support the establishment of noncompetitive research funding, while the groups of 35 years old and under and 36–40 years old were less inclined to agree with the establishment of noncompetitive research funding. This may be due to the fact that most teachers over the age of 41 were already mature researchers and had their own research directions and research teams, thus they needed more stable financial support. Whereas young teachers more needed to obtain competitive projects at the provincial-/ministerial-level and national level because of the requirement of promotion, resulting in their less preference to agree with the establishment of noncompetitive research funding. Teachers with senior titles were less inclined to agree with noncompetitive research funding, and the effect of senior title was significant at the 0.05 level. Some studies show that there are differences in the professional development motivation of teachers at different age groups (Lei, 2018; Wang & Feng, 2018). Young teachers often face greater pressure for promotion and evaluation, and some universities even implement tenure track policies, most of which set requirements for obtaining national-level and provincial-/ministerial-level projects. So young teachers will be more inclined to pay attention to competitive research funding. For middle-aged teachers, although they have been promoted to senior or sub-senior titles, they also face certain evaluation pressure from the job contract, so they will also tend to support competitive research funding. However, for elder teachers, most of them have made some achievements in research, and their evaluation pressure is relatively small, so they are more inclined to support their own research through noncompetitive research funding. The different attitudes of teachers with different titles toward noncompetitive research funding reflect the differences in teachers with different titles when competing for research projects, since the higher the teacher's title, the higher their scientific research productivity (Liang & Zhou, 2016). Teachers with senior or sub-senior titles have an advantage in applying for competitive research projects.

In the application criteria of some national-level projects (such as National Social Science Funds), it is required that qualified applicants should be of senior or sub-senior titles. Therefore, teachers with the senior title are more inclined to support competitive research funding than noncompetitive research funding.

In the variables of teachers' research characteristics, HSS teachers were more inclined to support noncompetitive research funds, while teachers with high outputs were less inclined to support noncompetitive research funds, and the effect was significant at the 0.1 level. In the current national research funding system, compared with SEAM disciplines, the research funding channels for HSS disciplines are very limited, which also makes HSS teachers more inclined to support noncompetitive research funding, so as to provide necessary financial support for their own research work. For teachers with high outputs, their research productivity is substantially higher than that of other teachers, and they also have comparative advantages in all kinds of competitive project evaluations, resulting in their much higher probabilities of obtaining funding for competitive research projects than other teachers. So this group of teachers will not be in the trap of a shortage of research funds and will not support the establishment of noncompetitive research funding.

In the university characteristics variables, teachers in 985 Project universities were less willing to support noncompetitive research funding than teachers in ordinary institutions, and teachers in 211 Project universities were less inclined to support noncompetitive research funding. However, neither effect is of statistical significance. This result reflects the different emphasis of different levels of universities on the evaluation criteria of teachers' research performance (Li et al., 2018). For 985 Project universities, teachers have strong research capacities and higher research levels, so the evaluation of teachers' research performance focuses on their contribution to solving the country's major needs and solving the real problems of socioeconomic development, rather than simply a competitive research project or output. Moreover, 985 Project universities themselves are a high research platform. Those teachers in 985 Project universities have a lot of opportunities to obtain competitive funds, and thus pay more attention to competitive research funding. Therefore, their willingness to support establishment of noncompetitive research funds supporting freewill exploration is relatively low. For 211 Project universities, their evaluations of research performance pay more attention to the performance in competitive projects and high-level publications, while noncompetitive research funding accounts for a smaller weight in the performance evaluation. So teachers in these universities are usually not inclined to support noncompetitive research funds.

7.7 The standard of average teacher research funds

From the preceding analysis, it can be seen that the university teachers' demand for noncompetitive research funds is very obvious. In terms of competitive research funding, China has formed a comprehensive funding system, but there is no mechanism and standard for noncompetitive research funding. To this end, this section first takes the United Kingdom as a case study to introduce its non-competitive research funding standards, and then based on the data of our survey, as well as the actual situation of the higher education development in China, to reasonably design the standard of average teacher research funds for different disciplines.

7.7.1 Research funding in UK universities

The Higher Education Funding Council for England (HEFCE) was the main functional body for higher education funding in England. Overall, the expenditure of England universities consists of four main aspects: personnel expenditure, other operating expenses, depreciation and interest, and other financial expenditure. Among these, personnel expenditure accounts for the largest proportion (about 55% of total university expenditure), followed by other operating expenditure (about 37% of total university expenditure), and the fixed asset depreciation (approximately 6% of total university expenditure). In terms of expenditure sectors, the academic sectors (i.e., schools, departments, institutes) account for the largest proportion of expenditure. For example, in the academic year 2013–2014, England's universities spent about 11.4 billion pounds on the academic sectors, accounting for 39% of total expenditure for that year.

In the United Kingdom, all government funding for higher education must be based on the results of a third-party assessment, and the Research Excellence Framework (REF)[2] is rightly an important assessment project to determine the eligibility and funding level for universities. HEFCE's research grants do not cover all higher education institutions in England, but are only for research institutions with outstanding research quality in colleges and universities. Therefore, it is called quality-related (QR) funding. In addition to the mainstream quality-related funding used to share the recurrent research expenditure of university research institutions, the QR funding also includes other funds such as the QR research degree program supervision fund, the QR charity support fund, the QR business research element, and the QR funding for National Research Libraries. The contents of these research funds are detailed in Table 7.18.

Of the various research funds provided by the HEFCE, whether it is mainstream QR funds or several other QR funds, the amount of research funds received by universities depends on their research performance. In practice, the HEFCE calculates the quality score based on the percentage of REF quality thresholds and their corresponding weights for each research institution, and uses the quality score to measure the research performance of the research institution and to distribute research funds. Among all channels of funds, the mainstream QR funds are the largest share of allocations. For example, in the 2015–2016 academic year, the research funds taken charge by HEFCE totaled 1.5 billion pounds, of which more than 1 billion pounds were mainstream QR funds, accounting for more than 60% of all QR-related funds. Next, this study takes mainstream QR funding as an example to introduce the specific implementation process of noncompetitive research funding in the United Kingdom.

Table 7.18 Classification and content of HEFCE research grants

Classification	Funding content
Mainstream QR funding	The main basis is the results of research assessment, and it allocates the grant money through a particular formula based on the grades of assessment.
QR research degree program supervision fund	This part of funds is allocated to all departments receiving mainstream QR funding. It is calculated on the basis of the number of FTE postgraduate students in all departments.
QR charity support fund	Many charities support university research, especially in medical discipline, but they do not fully meet the economic costs of research. Therefore, HEFCE provides supporting funds. The allocation of this part of the funds is in proportion to the charitable funds received by universities, and this part of the allocation of funds does not have a minimum quality threshold requirement.
QR business research element	This part of the funding supports higher education institutions to undertake business or industrial research. The allocation of this part of the funds is in proportion to the funds received by universities from business or industry, and this part of the allocation of funds does not have a minimum quality threshold requirement.
QR funding for National Research Libraries	This part of funds is allocated to support five research libraries in the United Kingdom.

Note: This table is compiled from the study of Liu and Zuo (2016).

7.7.1.1 REF assessment and mainstream QR funding

The REF was the seventh large-scale assessment of research quality in UK universities. The REF system had three main elements: research outputs (65%), research impact (20%), and research environment (15%). The entire assessment consisted of a total of 4 main expert panels (A, B, C, and D) and 36 units of assessment (UoAs). Panel A was about medical discipline and life sciences, including six UoAs such as clinical medicine, public health and health service, and life sciences. Panel B was about physical sciences, including nine disciplines such as earth systems and environment, physics, chemistry, and computer engineering. Panel C was about social sciences, including 11 disciplines such as architecture, geography and environmental archaeology, economics, law, and sociology. Panel D was about humanities, including ten disciplines such as regional studies, modern languages and linguistics, English language and literature, history, and classical literature. The REF divided the quality of research into five levels: 4* indicated the world's leading, 3* indicated internationally excellent, 2* indicated recognized internationally, 1* indicated recognized nationally, and unclassified indicated quality below the nationally recognized level. The allocation of mainstream QR funds was based on the REF assessment results, with considerations of research volume and subject cost weights in different disciplines, to determine the respective allocation share of 36 UoAs, and then the appropriated funds of each

Average teacher research funding 207

UoA were distributed to the universities on the basis of their research volume and quality weights.

7.7.1.2 Allocation methods for mainstream QR funds

Step 1: Separating the total into three indicator pots. The total amount of mainstream QR funds is first separated into three pots according to the proportion weights of the three indicators – research outputs (65%), research impact (20%), and research environment (15%) – and then each pot gets distributed according to the weights (HEFCE, 2015).

Step 2: Distributing between the four main assessment panels. This is the ratio of the research volume rated 3* or 4* to the total research volume for each panel. The research volume is determined by the following measure: the number of full-time equivalent (FTE) researchers in the assessment multiplied by the proportion of 3* and 4* in the quality profile. Taking research outputs as an example, the quality subprofile and corresponding research volume in the UoA X_1 of three universities are shown in Table 7.19.

Step 3: Determining the shares for each UoA. Each main panel consists of several UoAs, so the next step is to determine the allocation that a single UoA of each panel in the previous stage can obtain. The appropriated funds for each UoA are distributed within the panel according to a certain proportion, and the proportion is measured by the ratio of the volume reaching 3* and 4* quality levels multiplied by subject cost weights to the whole panel. Among them, the principle of determining the subject cost weights is 1.6 for high-cost laboratory and clinical subjects, 1.3 for intermediate-cost subjects, and 1 for other subjects. Table 7.20 shows the research volume of three universities – A, B, and C – in three UoAs [X_1 (high cost), X_2 (intermediate-cost),

Table 7.19 Quality and research volume in UoA X_1 in REF

	FTE	4*	3*	2*	1*	0	Research volume of 3* and above
University A	164.15	17.0	55.7	24.6	1.1	1.6	119.34
University B	84.45	13.5	56.7	28.2	1.3	0.3	59.28
University C	192.05	39.4	45.0	13.7	0.6	1.3	162.09

Table 7.20 Research volume of three universities in units of assessment X_1, X_2, X_3

	UoA X_1	UoA X_2	UoA X_3
University A	119.34	15.92	10.63
University B	59.28	15.07	10.93
University C	162.09	25.35	12.41
Total	340.71	56.34	33.97

208 *Average teacher research funding*

Table 7.21 Allocation shares of each unit of assessment (UoA)

	UoA X_1	UoA X_2	UoA X_3	UoA X_t
The total volume of 3* and above	340.71	56.34	33.97	431.02
Subject cost weights	1.6	1.3	1	
Cost-weighted volume	545.14	73.24	33.97	653.02
Percentage of allocation	88.57%	11.23%	5.2%	100%

and X_3 (other)]. The shares of appropriations received on the basis of the aforementioned research volume are shown in Table 7.21.

Step 4: Determine the number of funds that each university obtains. Once the total allocation for each UoA (subject) has been determined, the final stage is to proportionally allocate the funds for each UoA between universities. This proportion is the ratio of the quality-weighted research volume of one university to the total quality-weighted research volume of that subject. The principle for determining the weights of quality ratings is 4 for 4*, 1 for 3*, and 0 for other ratings. Table 7.22 presents the final allocation for the three universities.

7.7.2 The standard of average teacher research funds in Chinese universities

7.7.2.1 The basic idea of allocating average teacher research funds

Unlike current competitive research funding projects, the allocation of average teacher research funds belongs to noncompetitive research funds, the aim of which is to alleviate the negative effects caused by excessive competition, and at the same time to protect teachers needs for basic research funds and stimulate their internal research motivation. Through a questionnaire survey and international comparison, this study shows that noncompetitive average teacher research funds should form a regular process for allocation, with "cultivation" and "guarantee" as the basic purposes, to become an effective complement to the competitive research projects. The allocation of average teacher research funds should be included in the national budget and led by the Ministry of Education in practice. The basic ideas for their allocation and distribution are as follows.

First, establish a national system of average research funding for university teachers, with central finance as the main funding source and local finance as the supplementary funding source. The allocation of average teacher research funds can draw from the experience of the new mechanism for guaranteeing the rural compulsory education funds, which are shared proportionally by the central and local finances (e.g., 8:2 in west China, 6:4 in central China, and 2:8 in east China). The allocation of average teacher research funds in central universities shall be carried out by the Ministry of Education, and the allocation of average teacher

Table 7.22 Allocation results for mainstream QR funding

University	UoA X_1 Weighted volume of 3* and above	Percentage	Percentage of allocation	UoA X_2 Weighted volume of 3* and above	Percentage	Percentage of allocation	UoA X_3 Weighted volume of 3* and above	Percentage	Percentage of allocation	Total
University A	203.05	29.62	24.75	21.44	18.11	2.03	26.17	35.96	1.87	28.65
University B	93.49	13.64	11.40	27.45	23.19	2.61	20.11	27.63	1.44	15.45
University C	389.09	56.74	47.42	69.50	58.70	6.59	26.50	36.41	1.89	55.90
Total	685.63	100	83.57	118.39	100	11.23	72.78	100	5.20	100

research funds in local universities shall be implemented by the department of education in the provinces.

Second, adhering to the quality orientation, determine the shares of allocation based on the results of the discipline assessment. The average teacher research funds should adhere to the orientation of quality and the results of the latest round of discipline assessment, and the funds distributed to universities according to their proportions of disciplines rated A, B, and C. The colleges and universities should open accounts for average teacher research funds, and count the teacher numbers by discipline (excluding those retired and transfer teachers). Then colleges and universities should use the standard of average teacher research funds to calculate the total amount, add it into the annual budget, and then submit the budget to the administrative departments for examination and approval. The research funds are appropriated by the department of finance, and then administered by the administrative departments. The account balance is reviewed annually and can be transferred to the next year.

Third, establish the "application and performance evaluation" mechanism to ensure the efficiency of the average teacher research funds. The purpose of setting up noncompetitive research funds is to "cultivate" and "guarantee". On the one hand, the average teacher research funds can provide basic research conditions for young teachers in colleges and universities, which can help to improve their academic norms and broaden their academic horizons. On the other hand, noncompetitive research funds can provide basic protection for older teachers and avoid the phenomenon that they cannot get adequate funds because of a "research gap year" and "job title evaluation". Its obvious difference with competitive research funds is that noncompetitive research funds do not need complex review procedures. It uses the academic reporting system, which empowers university academic committees to be responsible for reviewing the research progress of teachers who obtain the funds every year, to safeguard university teachers' enthusiasm for research and receive the maximum benefit of average teacher research funds.

7.7.2.2 The measure of standard of the average teacher research funds

Scientific research is a very complex knowledge-production activity. As a result of the huge differences in different disciplines, it is difficult to directly measure its costs, so this study uses a questionnaire survey to obtain the amount of various research expenditure in different disciplines, in order to calculate university teachers' basic needs for research projects.

The specific procedures were as follows.

Step 1: The questionnaire data were classified into two broad categories according to the HSS and SEAM disciplines, and further narrowed to the sample with the response of "agree" to the question "Do you agree with the establishment of a noncompetitive 'average teacher research funding system' (i.e., to provide all full-time teachers with funds for basic research activities in accordance with the annual allocation)?" A total of 522 samples were included, of which 288 were HSS teachers and 234 were SEAM teachers. We calculated the basic funding standard for the two broad disciplines separately.

Step 2: The data of teacher research funds was separated into HSS and SEAM disciplines, and university teachers' basic needs for research funds were calculated.

$$X_i = \sum_{i=1}^{n} (a_{1i} + a_{2i} + \cdots + a_{ki}) \tag{7.3}$$

where i indicates a case in the data; and $a_{1i} \ldots a_{ki}$ indicates k kinds of research expenditure items, e.g., testing and processing fees (excluding labor fees).

Step 3: To avoid the impact of outliers on the calculation results, this study sorted each teacher's basic needs for research funds X_i from minimum to maximum, calculated the percentiles at 5% and 10%, then deleted the cases larger than the 5% and 10% percentiles.

Step 4: The average of the remaining cases were calculated to obtain the funding standard.

Through these four steps, it is possible to calculate the standard of average teacher research funds in HSS and SEAM disciplines, as shown in Table 7.23.

In order to match the standard of average teacher research funds with the current national funding policy, this study did further calculations by drawing from the data of the young researcher funds of the Natural Science Foundation of China. The department of management can be seen as HSS disciplines inside the young researcher funds, with an average funding level of 191,100 yuan (2010–2016). Other departments can be seen as SEAM disciplines, with an average funding level of 224,700 yuan. It can be calculated that, according to the current funding standards of national-level projects, the average teacher research funding for HSS and SEAM disciplines is 637,000 yuan/year and 749,000 yuan/year, respectively. Combined with the calculation results of Table 7.23, the amount of noncompetitive research funds in HSS disciplines is about 50,000–60,000 yuan,

Table 7.23 Standard for the average teacher research funds (10,000 yuan/year)

Treatment	Humanities and social Sciences (HSS)			Science, engineering, agriculture, and medicine (SEAM)		
	No deletion	5% deletion	10% deletion	No deletion	5% deletion	10% deletion
Mean	6.40	5.33	4.87	12.68	9.91	8.45

and the amount of noncompetitive research funds in SEAM disciplines is about 80,000–90,000 yuan.

7.8 Conclusion and recommendations

7.8.1 Main conclusions

Based on the investigation of the current situation of teachers' research funds in a number of colleges and universities and the analysis of the demand for noncompetitive research funds, the following main research conclusions are drawn.

1. There exists some unequal phenomena in the allocation of university research funds. There might exist some phenomena of unfair competition in the applications of research projects for university teachers. On the one hand, the university level has a significant impact on teachers' applications for national-level projects. Compared with ordinary universities, 985 Project and 211 Project universities had a relatively higher proportion of funding, while teachers in ordinary universities were at a disadvantage by applying for national-level projects and their funding proportion was relatively low. On the other hand, job title, as a standard measurement of academic capacity, plays a key role in funding allocation. Considering that the quota of title promotion is strictly controlled in Chinese universities, and the increasingly high title wall makes it impossible for teachers with certain research capacities to successfully get promoted, some teachers are at a disadvantage when applying for research funds, making it difficult to obtain adequate research funds.
2. The Mathew effect is significant in the allocation of competitive research funds in universities. As a result of the substantial effects of university level and job title on the allocation of funds, the phenomenon of the Matthew effect on competitive research funds in universities is very serious. This is reflected, on the one side, in the high concentration of university research funds, where 10% of researchers obtained about 60% of the total research funds. The Gini coefficient reached 0.65, revealing the existence of a serious distribution imbalance. Compared with 985 Project or 211 Project universities, ordinary universities constituted the main group at the bottom 20% of research funds, whose teachers account for 70% of the bottom 20%. On the other side, teachers with low titles and young ages tended to be at a low funding level. Statistics show that the main body of teachers with research funds under 50,000 yuan is the group of teachers aged 36–40 with a middle title.
3. University teachers generally agreed that there is a lack of research funds. University teachers as a whole perceived the lack of research funds. The data showed that 52.2% of university teachers agreed that there is a lack of research funds, 57.9% of teachers with middle titles agreed that there is a lack

of research funds, and 53.7% of young teachers under the age of 35 agreed that there is a lack of research funds. Therefore, university teachers generally agreed that there is a lack of research funds.
4. University teachers generally agreed with the establishment of noncompetitive research funds, but teachers of different ages have different attitudes, and teachers with low job titles and weak research capacities are more inclined to support noncompetitive research funds. Attitudes toward noncompetitive research funding among different age groups were different. With teachers aged above 51 years old as a reference group, two teacher groups (aged 41–45 years old and 46–50 years old) were more inclined to support noncompetitive research funding, while the two groups aged under 35 years old and 36–40 years old were relatively less willing to set up noncompetitive research funding. Compared with teachers with middle titles, teachers with senior or sub-senior titles were less inclined to support noncompetitive research funds, because teachers with senior or sub-senior titles had an advantage in competitive research projects. Those teachers with stronger research capacities less agreed with the establishment of noncompetitive research funding, because the stronger research capacity means that the independent ability and willingness to undertake a project are also stronger, which enables these teachers to be at an advantaged position in competitive research funds.
5. The appropriate amount of noncompetitive research funds for HSS disciplines is about 50,000–60,000 yuan, and the appropriate amount of noncompetitive research funds for SEAM disciplines is about 80,000–90,000 yuan. From the perspective of demand, university teachers generally agreed that the set of funding amounts should be based on differences in disciplines and the actual needs of university teachers, which rules out the phenomena of egalitarianism and enjoying the "research bonus". After calculating the aggregated data of the actual demand, the reasonable funding amount for HSS disciplines is about 50,000–60,000 yuan, and the reasonable funding amount for SEAM disciplines is about 80,000–90,000 yuan.

7.8.2 Policy recommendations

1. Increase investment in noncompetitive research and fully understand the significance and function of the allocation of average teacher research funds. As for noncompetitive research funding, average teacher research funds cannot only alleviate the negative externality brought about by competition, but also effectively protect the basic research funding needs of young teachers, and stimulate their endogenous research power while perfecting the investment mechanism of research funding. However, at present, university research is mostly a competitive project. For example, in the total amount of research funds in Shanghai Jiaotong University in 2008–2013, less than 3% was noncompetitive research funds (Zhang & Bai, 2015). Limited management and

small funding amounts make noncompetitive research funds hard to emphasize in the competitive context of "survival of the fittest, merit-based funding". Therefore, it is necessary to increase the investment of noncompetitive research funds, reasonably allocate the shares between the competitive and noncompetitive fund, and fully understand the significance and functions of average teacher research funds.

2. Take "cultivation" and "guarantee" as the basic goals to form a regular allocation process for average teacher research funds. These principles take into account any differences and reflect actual needs. The national finance is responsible for the funds, and the Ministry of Education is responsible for the management. Universities should open accounts of noncompetitive research funds for individual teachers and allocate funds annually. The universities should count the teacher numbers by discipline excluding those retired and transfer teachers. Then universities should use the standard of average teacher research funds to calculate the total amount, add it into the annual budget, and then submit the budget to the administrative departments for examination and approval. The research funds are appropriated by the department of finance, and then administered by the administrative departments. The account balance is reviewed annually and can be transferred to the next year.

3. Establish and perfect the "application and performance evaluation" mechanism for average teacher research funds. Noncompetitive research funds are set up for the purpose of "cultivation" and "guarantee". For young teachers, noncompetitive research funds can provide basic conditions for their initial research and to carry out independent research with the aim of "cultivation". Therefore, we propose that in the applications of this kind of funds, adhering to the project application system would help to improve young teachers' academic norms; adhering to the academic reporting system would also help young teachers to broaden their academic horizons, which could prepare them for future applications for competitive research projects. For teachers with research capabilities, noncompetitive research funds mainly play a protective role in avoiding the phenomenon of not being able to obtain adequate funds due to a research gap year and low job title. Scientific and reasonable performance evaluation mechanisms cannot only mobilize teachers' enthusiasm to use noncompetitive research funds to conduct research work, but also maximize the efficient use of such research funds. The biggest difference with competitive research funds is that noncompetitive research funds do not require a complex application and examination procedures. Using the system of project application and academic reporting, university departments are responsible for the management and use of funds. Expert groups could provide suggestions to the teachers who received the funds on the design of their research projects every year, and evaluate the progress and outputs of their research work at year-end academic report meeting.

Appendix: Questionnaire on the current situation and demand of research funds of university teachers

Dear Teacher:

Greetings! In order to better understand the current situation of research funds for teachers in colleges and universities, and to clarify their actual needs, our project team is conducting this investigation. Completing this questionnaire will take you approximately 5 minutes, and your recommendations will provide an important reference for setting up noncompetitive research funds for colleges and universities. We are committed to keeping the information you fill in confidential, and please fill it out carefully. The choice questions in the questionnaire are all single-choice questions; please check the options according to your actual situation. Thank you very much for your cooperation!

Faculty of Education, Beijing Normal University

"Post-4% era" China's higher education financial investment scale and configuration structure research

October 10, 2016

Part I Basic Information

1. What discipline does your research field belong to?

(1) Philosophy   (2) Economics   (3) Law   (4) Education

(5) Literature   (6) History   (7) Science   (8) Engineering

(9) Agronomy   (10) Medicine   (11) Military   (12) Management

(13) Art

2. The name of your current institution is _____

3. The type of your institution belongs to

(1) Comprehensive   (2) Science and engineering   (3) Finance   (4) Normal
(5) Medicine   (6) Politics and law   (7) Language   (8) Agriculture and forestry
(9) Ethnicity   (10) Art   (11) Sports

4. The level of your current institution is

(1) 985 Project university   (2) 211 Project university
(3) Not 211 Project university   (4) Other, e.g., public vocational
                                       colleges or adult colleges

5. What is your current title?

(1) Full senior title (professor)   (2) Associate senior title (associate
                                            professor)

(3) Middle-level title (lecturer/assistant professor)   (4) Other (teaching assistant/
    administrative/experimental personnel)

6. Your age is

(1) 30 years old and below   (2) 31–35 years old   (3) 36–40 years old   (4) 41–45 years old   (5) 46–50 years old   (6) 51 years old and above

7. Your annual pre-tax income in your institution is (including basic salary, post allowance, overtime pay, research bonus, housing funds, benefits, etc.)

(1) 50,000 yuan and below   (2) 60,000–100,000 yuan   (3) 110,000–150,000 yuan
(4) 160,000–200,000 yuan   (5) 210,000–250,000 yuan   (6) 260,000–300,000 yuan
(7) 310,000–400,000 yuan   (8) 410,000–500,000 yuan   (9) 510,000 yuan and above

8. Are you satisfied with your annual income?

(1) Very satisfied   (2) More satisfied   (3) Not satisfied   (4) Very dissatisfied

9. Your total number of papers published in 2013-2015:

1) Published in Chinese journals

(1) More than 3   (2) 2–3   (3) 1   (4) 0

2) Published in international journals

(1) More than 3   (2) 2–3   (3) 1   (4) 0

Of which SCI:

(1) More than 3   (2) 2–3   (3) 1   (4) 0

Of which EI:

(1) More than 3   (2) 2–3   (3) 1   (4) 0

Of which SSCI:

(1) More than 3 articles   (2) 2–3   (3) 1   (4) 0

Part II The Current Situation of Competitive Research Funds

10. Do you think the research performance bonus is properly distributed in your institution?

(1) Very reasonable   (2) Reasonable   (3) Unreasonable   (4) Very unreasonable

11. Do you think your research efforts have been reasonably rewarded?

(1) Reasonably rewarded   (2) Not reasonably rewarded

12. **In 2013–2015, as the principal investigator, you received research funds amounted to _____ yuan, of which (please fill in 0 if none):**

(1) National-level project funds _____ yuan

(2) Provincial- and ministerial-level project funds _____ yuan

(3) City-level project funds _____ yuan

(4) District/county-level project funds _____ yuan

(5) Institution-level project funds _____ yuan

(6) Cooperative projects with industry or government _____ yuan

(7) International organizations, NGOs, and nonprofit organizations (e.g., World Bank, Ford Foundation, etc.) projects _____ yuan

13. **Does your institution set up noncompetitive research funding projects (i.e., 100% granted projects, regardless of submitting applications, such as the Research Start-up Funds for new teachers)?**

(1) Yes, projects like young teachers' research start-up funds or research funds for teachers under 40 years, which are limited to certain groups of teachers.

(2) Yes, the institution allocates a certain amount of research funds to all teachers.

(3) No.

(4) Do not know.

14. **Your current funding situation is (please tick the box ☐):**

(1) Total research funds	☐ very lacking	☐ lacking	☐ adequate	☐ very adequate	☐ no need
(2) Funds for purchase of equipment	☐ very lacking	☐ lacking	☐ adequate	☐ very adequate	☐ no need
(3) Material fees	☐ very lacking	☐ lacking	☐ adequate	☐ very adequate	☐ no need
(4) Testing and laboratory processing fees	☐ very lacking	☐ lacking	☐ adequate	☐ very adequate	☐ no need
(5) Fuel power fees	☐ very lacking	☐ lacking	☐ adequate	☐ very adequate	☐ no need
(6) Travel expenses	☐ very lacking	☐ lacking	☐ adequate	☐ very adequate	☐ no need
(7) Meeting fees	☐ very lacking	☐ lacking	☐ adequate	☐ very adequate	☐ no need

218 *Average teacher research funding*

(8) International cooperation and exchange fees   □ very lacking □ lacking □ adequate □ very adequate □ no need

(9) Publication/documentation/information dissemination/intellectual property fees   □ very lacking □ lacking □ adequate □ very adequate □ no need

(10) Labor fees   □ very lacking □ lacking □ adequate □ very adequate □ no need

(11) Expert consultation fees   □ very lacking □ lacking □ adequate □ very adequate □ no need

(12) Indirect fees (management fees, performance fees, etc.)   □ very lacking □lacking □ adequate □ very adequate □ no need

Part III The Demand for Noncompetitive Research Funds

15. **Do you agree with the establishment of a noncompetitive "teacher-average research funding system" (to fund basic research activities for all teachers in an annually allocative way)?**

(1) Agree   (2) Disagree   (3) I don't know

16. **If you agree to the establishment of a noncompetitive "teacher-average research funding system", the funding amount allocated to every teacher in your discipline should be _____ yuan/year, the expenditure should be (please fill in 0 if none)**

(1) The purchase of small equipment _____ yuan/year   (2) Material fees_____ yuan/year

(3) Testing and laboratory processing fees _____ yuan/year   (4) Fuel power fees _____ yuan/year

(5) Domestic travel expenses_____ yuan/year   (6) Meeting fees _____ yuan/year

(7) International cooperation and exchange fees (including international travel expenses) _____ yuan/year   (8) Publication/documentation/information dissemination/intellectual property fees _____ yuan/year

(9) Labor fees _____ yuan/year   (10) Expert consultation fees _____ yuan/year

17. **If a noncompetitive basic funding account of teacher average research funds is set up for every teacher (annually allocated), are you in favor of not returning the remaining year-end funds to a higher authority, but for continued use in the coming year?**

(1) Agree (2) Disagree (3) It's not clear

18. **If you feel the need for a long-term growth mechanism is necessary, which will be the more reasonable way?**

(1) Linked to GDP growth (2) Linked to inflation indices (e.g.. CPI) (3) Linked to the growth rate of government appropriations

19. **What other suggestions do you have for the establishment of noncompetitive research funding?**

Table A7.1 Management methods for basic research funds in some universities

Institution name	Website
Peking University	http://xkb.pku.edu.cn/docs/20161223143513597582.pdf
Zhejiang University	http://www.zju.edu.cn/c1421921/content_2024166.html
Nanjing University	http://scit.nju.edu.cn/Item/133.aspx
China University of Science and Technology	https://wenku.baidu.com/view/c1d38af64693daef5ef73d7b.html
Southwest University	http://kjc.swu.edu.cn/s/kjc/xxzc/20131203/784362.html
Northwestern University of Agriculture, Forestry and Technology	http://jcc.nwsuaf.edu.cn/gzzd/jyjfgl/115284.htm
South China University of Technology	http://www2.scut.edu.cn/socialsci/2013/0929/c929a17570/page.htm

Notes

1 Hard resources are relative to the soft resources, including knowledge, organization, system, information, innovation policy, and intermediary services and innovation culture.
2 Since 1986, the Research Assessment Exercise (RAE) was used for evaluating the quality of research in universities through peer review on a regular basis, and only those institutions reaching a certain level were eligible for QR funds. Since 2015, the Framework for Research Excellence has taken the place of RAE.

References

Bai, X., & You, D. Y. (2018). Comparative research and enlightenment on the system of scientific research funding between China and Japan. *Technology and Industry, 18*(4), 100–104.

Brainard, J., & Borrego, A. M. (2003). Academic pork barrel tops $2 billion for the first time. *Chronicle of Higher Education, 50*(5), 18–20.

Cao, X. (2016). Discussion on the implementation of basic scientific research business expenses in central universities. *Contemporary Educational Practice and Teaching Research: Electronic Journal, 1*, 74–74.

CERNET (China Education and Research Network). Why is the quality of university research publications is lower than research institutions? Retrieved April 2, 2017, from http://www.edu.cn/rd/zui_jin_geng_xin/201511/t20151105_1334950.shtml

Chen, X. L., & Wang, C. P. (2009). The implications of the funding method of research funding for American universities to China. *World Education Information, 9*, 48–51.

Chinadaily. (2014). The country's first academic seminar on the development and investment of college students was held at Beijing Normal University. Retrieved May 2, 2017, from http://www.chinadaily.com.cn/hqcj/xfly/2014-11-26/content_12786234.html

CMOE (China's Ministry of Education). Age of full-time teachers (Higher education institutions offering degree programs). Retrieved January 5, 2019, from http://www.moe.gov.cn/s78/A03/moe_560/jytjsj_2016/2016_qg/index_1.html

CMOF (China's Ministry of Finance). (2009). Announcement on the issue of the "Temporary Measures for the Management of Fundamental Funds of Basic Research for Central Universities". Retrieved April 20, 2017, from http://jkw.mof.gov.cn/zhengwuxinxi/zhengcefabu/200908/t20090818_194961.html

Cui, W. F., Liu, X., Zhao, L., & Wang, Z. G. (2013). Review and reflection on the implementation of basic scientific research business expenses in central universities: Taking Northwest Agricultural and Forestry University of Science and Technology as an example. *Science and Technology Information, 27*, 159–160.

Duan, C. Y., & Zhang, Y. B. (2016). Source composition, expenditure distribution and resource allocation implications: Research on research funding for higher education in the United States. *Modern Education Management, 6*, 119–123.

Fan, G. Q. & Jia, X. R. (2013). Study on the influence of "Matthew effect" on the development of young teachers in the field of scientific research in colleges and universities. *Journal of Higher Education Management, 2*, 70–74.

Fang, H. (2009). Consumerist tendencies in educational research. *Journal of Dali University, 1*, 83–84.

Ferrin, S. E. (2003). Characteristics of in-house lobbyists in American Colleges and Universities. *Higher Education Policy, 16*(1), 87–108.

Figueiredo, J. D. (2004). *How Does the Government (Want to) Fund Science? Politics, Lobbying and Academic Earmarks*. Cambridge: Massachusetts Institute of Technology (MIT), Sloan School of Management.

Figueiredo, J. M. D. (2002). *Academic Earmarks and the Returns to Lobbying*. Cambridge, MA: National Bureau of Economic Research, Inc.

Gu, Q. (2013). *The Reference Research of Financial Science and Technology Input Management in Typical Developed Countries to Our Country*. Dissertation. China: Southwest Jiaotong University.

He, G. X., Zhao, Y. D., & Yang, Q. Q. (2014). The degree of unequal distribution of scientific research resources in China: An analysis of the concentration of funds for scientific research personnel. *China Soft Science, 6*, 58–66.

HEFCE. (2015). Guide to funding 2015–16: How HEFCE allocates its funds. Retrieved May 13, 2015, from http://www.hefce.ac.uk/media/HEFCE,2014/Content/Pubs/2015/201504/2015_04.pdf

Kang, X. M. (2007). Research on the Chinese government's funding system for university research. Retrieved May 12, 2020, from http://ciefr.pku.edu.cn/xmykt/gdjy/gdjy-8337.shtml

Lei, W. (2018). The characteristics, current situation and strategy of the professional development of young teachers in colleges and universities. *Educational Theory and Practice, 38*(24), 41–43.

Li, B., Li, Z. F., & Cui, Y. H. (2011). Problems and countermeasures in the management of research funds for research on the subject system. *Forum on Science and Technology in China, 7*, 5–11.

Li, C., Lin, H. X., & Su, Y. J. (2018). An empirical study on the relationship between performance appraisal, knowledge sharing and scientific research and innovation of college teachers. *Modern Education Management, 9*, 56–62.

Li, G. J., Ren, W. J., Bian, Y., Gao, H., Zhang, Z. L., & Gao, Y. X. (2011). Analysis of the composition of the training cost of both science and engineering and humanities students: Take higher education institutions under Beijing Municipal administration as an example. *China Higher Education Research, 1*, 37–40.

Liu, X. K., & Zuo, X. J. (2016). Model and enlightenment of research quality grants for universities in the United Kingdom based on the framework of excellence (REF). *Journal of Dalian University of Technology (Social Sciences Edition), 37*(3), 6–11.

Liang, W. Y., & Zhou, Y. X. (2016). Social capital, cooperation and "the mystery of scientific research productivity": Based on the empirical analysis of Chinese research university teachers. *Peking University Review of Education, 14*(2), 133–156+191–192.

Liu, B. (2014). The management and funding results of special funds for basic scientific research business expenses in central universities. *Science & Technology Review, 2*, 129–132.

Liu, K. (2015). The dialectical test of the "Matthew effect" of university research funding. *Studies of Finance and Accounting in Education, 2*, 25–28.

Liu, L. (2004). Relevance of research evaluation and grants at European universities. *Fudan Education Forum, 3*, 70–74.

Ma, L. L. (2018). *The Enlightenment of Research Fund Management to Foreign Universities in China*. Dissertation. Hebei University of Science and Technology.

Mowery, D. C. (1994). *The U.S. National Innovation System: Origins and Prospects for Change*. Amsterdam: Springer Netherlands.

Nelson, R. R. (1993). *National Innovation Systems*. Oxford: Oxford University Press.

Shi, Y., & Rao, Y. (2010). China's research culture. *Science, 329*(5996), 1128.

Tang, M. H., Ma, L., Yu, S. X., & Li, W. (2011). Research on the management mode of basic scientific research business expenses in central universities. *Science and Technology Management Research, 10*, 77–81.

Tian, H., & Xiao, Y. (2014). Research on the relationship between competitive funding and noncompetitive financing: Taking examples of national key laboratories in university Y. *Science & Technology Progress and Policy, 15*, 19–23.

Wang, M., & Zhang, G. B. (2015). Research and reflection on the "double funding system" of research funding for universities in the UK. *Science and Technology Management Research, 24*, 29–34.

Wang, W. Y., & Du, Y. H. (2014). "Mathew effect" in the academics and its implications. *Qilu Journal, 3*, 103–107.

Wang, Y. F., & Feng, Y. (2018). Research on the characteristics and influencing factors of internal and external career development of older teachers in colleges and universities. *China Adult Education, 19*, 53–56.

Weiner, T. (1999). Lobbying for research money: Colleges bypass review process. *New York Times*, Aug 24.

Wen, K., Zhang, J., & Song, Q. (2013). Research on the relationship between the allocation mechanism of scientific research funds and scientific research output: Taking some public research institutions as an example. *Science of Science and Management of S.& T.*, *4*, 10–18.

Xi, Y. M., Li, H. J., & Guo, J. E. (2014). Research on the optimal allocation of scientific research funds in universities in China. *Science and Technology Progress and Policy*, *3*, 103–107.

Xia, H. H., & Zhong, B. L. (2016). On the enlightenment of Japan's competitive fund allocation mechanism to China's innovative scientific research management. *Journal of Higher Education Management*, *10*(3), 87–93.

Xiao, G. L. (2010). Multi-level all-round competition is the key to the high efficiency of scientific research in our country's colleges and universities. *Science of Science and Management of S.& T.*, *9*, 21–24.

Xie, S. Q. (2011). *Research on the Management of Scientific Research Funds in Higher Education Institutions*. Dissertation. Wuhan University of Science and Technology.

Xinhuanet. (2016). The State Council issued the "2016 key points of the reform work of promoting the decentralization in conjunction with optimizing service". Retrieved April 2, 2017, from http://news.xinhuanet.com/2016-05/24/c_1118924776.htm

Xu, Y. (2013). The formation mechanism and its review of the unbalanced development of regional higher education: A framework for the interpretation of "national action". *Research in Educational Development*, *19*, 18–25.

Xuan, J., Wang, J., Xu, N., & Du, M. C. (2014). Study on the training cost of college students based on basic running indicators: Take university Y as an example. *Friends of Accounting*, *19*, 22–27.

Yan, C. B. (2011). System design and reflections on the establishment of the standard for the average student funding. *Modern Education Management*, *9*, 43–45.

Yang, M. (2007). On the current situation, problems and countermeasures of research financing in German higher education institutions. *International and Comparative Education*, *12*, 71–75.

Yao, L. H. (2011). Analysis of the cost burden of college accrual system and student cultivation. *Communication of Accounting and Finance*, *32*, 63–64.

Zhang, B., Chen, G. S., & Fan, D. L. (2011). The management mode and the effectiveness of the special funds for basic scientific research business expenses of the central universities. *R&D Management*, *6*, 105–109.

Zhang, J. G., & Sun, J. (2014). The current situation, reason and solution of the management of research funds in colleges and universities. *Journal of Jiangsu University of Science and Technology (Social Science Edition)*, *3*, 98–103.

Zhang, L. P. (2003). The existence and prevention of unfair competition in scientific research work. *Studies in Science of Science*, *S1*, 165–169.

Zhang, Y. F., & Bai, J. (2015). Noncompetitive funding to support the optimization of independent scientific research paths in colleges and universities. *Scientific and Technology Progress and Policy*, *2*, 19–23.

Zhao, Q. H., & Wang, J. H. (2018). The characteristics of the allocation and management of research funds by the German federal government. *Global Science, Technology and Economy Outlook*, *33*(4), 40–45.

Zhou, W. (2014). *Research on Evaluation of Provincial Science and Technology Resource Allocation Efficiency*. Hefei: China University of Science and Technology Press.

Zhou, C. (2013). The government needs to further increase the investment of research funds in colleges and universities. *Studies in Science of Science, 10,* 1450–1452.

Index

Page numbers in **bold** denote tables, those in *italic* denote figures.

211 Project 2, **11**, 68, 161, **164**, 181, **184**, 186–187, **188**, 189, 192, 196, **197**, **199**, 200–201, **202**, 204, 212

985 Project 2, **11**, 68, 98, 161, **164**, 181, **184**, 186–187, **188**, 189, 192, 196, **197**, 199, **200**, 201, **202**, 204, 212

2011 Collaborative Innovation Plan **11**, 68

academic: appropriations 163; capacities 195, 212; circles 1, 169; committee **177**, 210; contributions 173; departments 134–135; earmarks 163, 170–171, 179; environment 166; fields 173; horizons 210, 214; impact 173; international exchanges 161; leaders 190; norms 210, 214; papers 201; publications **202**; reporting system 210, 214; research 166; sectors 205; seminar 160; system 190; titles 192; value 5; year 82, 135, **137**, 205

accounting 99, 122, 126, 133, 137–141, 144; field of 142; methods 10, 137–138, 140–141, **143**, 144, 156; perspective 146; principle of 142; report 138; of subject cost 135; system 81, 137–138, 144, 150; techniques 134

activity-based costing (ABC) 134, 140–141, **143**, 156

adaptivity 69

Agasisti, T. 147

allocation: advance 80; budget 11, 16, 123; contract 131; differential 8–9; education 130; efficient 131; external 15, 98; financial 1–13, 15–20, 55–56, 59, 65, 82, 97, 121, 132, 147; formula 9, 12, 132; imbalance 116; incremental 9, 131; internal 4, 16, 179; investment 1–2, 4, 15, 21, 98, 101, 104, 117; mode 13, 19, 120; optimal 9; policy 21; principles 19; quota 6, 9, 12, 16, 21; ratio 19, 104; rational 16; resource 15, 55, 100; scientific research 9, 160–161, 169, 173; standard 12, 22, 162; structure 1, 6, 15, 17–21, 98, 101, 103; targeted 135, 137; teaching 9; transparency 131; workload 135

Arts and Humanities Research Council (AHRC) 171

Asia-Pacific Economic Cooperation (APEC) 97

Atkinson index 58–59, **60**, *61*, 65

augmented Dickey–Fuller (ADF) 111

augmented mean group (AMG) 36, **44**, 84

autocorrelation 108, 111

autoregression integrated distribution (ARID) model 36

autoregressive (AR): coefficient 40–41; integrated moving average (ARIMA) 21, 36, 41, **45**, 98, 105, 109; models 40–41, **45**, 106

Bai, X. 166, 213
Baldwin, N. 23
Bao, C. 1, 68
Barro, R. J. 59, 69
Basic Requirements for Entrepreneurship Education for Undergraduate Students 4, 97
Bates, J. 42
Becker, G. 12
Beijing Guide 5
best linear unbiased estimation (BLUE) 30
Bi, X. Y. 13, 16
Bianjiaoyu 146

Index

Biotechnology and Biological Sciences Research Council (BBSRC) 171
Brainard, J. 171
British Research Council (BRC) 165, 171
budget 2, 75, 91; allocation 11, 16; annual 2, 82; expenditure 3–4, 10–11, 15–16

Cao, S. J. 12
Cao, X. 174
Carnoy, M. 12
Carpentier, V. 12
CERNET (China Education and Research Network) 173
Chapman, B. 12
Chatfield, C. 38
Chen, X. L. 163
Chen, X. Y. 12
Cheng, G. 12, 142, 147
Chinadaily 160
China Educational Finance Statistical Yearbook 72
China Statistical Yearbook 71–72, 104
Chowdry, H. 12
coefficient 17, 31–32, 34, 39, 88; adjustment 6, 22, 107, 109, 132, 144–146, 154; autoregressive 40; conversion 12, 122–124, **125**, 127–130, 169; correlation 56–59, 65, 88; elasticity 57, 59, 65; estimated 86; Gini coefficient 58, 198, 212n2; median 17; model 14, 17; regression 31–33, 57, 61–62, 109, 142, 153, 155; Theil 58; unchanged 31–32
Cohn, E. 12, 141
Cointegrated Augmented Dickey-Fuller (CADF) test 86
cointegration model 36
Collaborative Innovation Plan 68
colleges: adult 215; advanced vocational 118; art 147, **151**; central 2; general 15; higher vocational (HVC) 15–16, 18–19, 21, 43, 72, 97, 101, 104, 116–118; independent 138; large-scale 153–154; local 1–3, 14, 21, 126–127, 139, 145; medium-scale 154; non-elite 171; ordinary 3, 21; private 10, 49; province-administered 129–130; public 3, 48, 130–131, 145; research-oriented 21; undergraduate 15–16, 21, 43, 104; vocational 16, 118, 128, 215
common correlated effects mean group (CCEMG) 36, 84
Communist Party of China 20, 68
convergence 56, 59, 61–62; absolute 61–62, **63**, 65; conditional 61–62, **64**, 65;

concept of 5; degree of 62; existence of 61; rate of 61–62, 65
Cui, W. F. 174

deviation 75; average forecast 76; individual 33; magnitude of 75; negative double standard 111; positive double standard 111; standard 72, **114**, 151, **152, 202**
Dickey–Fuller test 37
Ding, X. H. 12, 14
Dougherty, K.J. 133
Du, Y. H. 56
Duan, C. Y. 163
Durbin–Watson (DW) statistic 108

Eberhardt, M. 36, 84
econometric model 6, 13–14, 17–18, 36, 59, 62, 69, 71, 74, 103–104, 116, 141–142, **143**, 156
Economic and Social Research Council (ESRC) 171
Education Commission 121, 128
elasticity coefficient 57–59, 65
Engineering and Physical Sciences Research Council (EPSRC) 171
enrollment 73, 85, 99, 101, 104, 116, 123–124, 141; expansion of 122; forecast 71, 76; full-time equivalent 73, 85; gross rate 48, 71–73, 76–78, 80–81, 85, **93**; higher education 70, 72–73, 76, 85, 99, 101, 105, 117; opportunities 3; postgraduate 75–76; scale 21; size 71–72, 75–76; total 73, 85; undergraduate 70
error components model 33
estimation 6, 21, 30, 32, 84, 121, **143**; bias 31–32, 37; methods 17, 76, 86; model 107; model parameter 112; over- 81; results 34–35; robust 37; technique 34; uniform 34
evaluation 131, 171, 174, **176—177**, 179, 203–204; competitive project 204; comprehensive 169; criteria 133, 204; financial performance 129; framework 168; job title 210; performance 204, 210, 214; pressure 203; results 169; score 133; special 168; system 168
Excellent Engineer Education and Cultivation Plan (2010) 4, 97
expenses 8, 138–139, 169; administrative 120, **132**; business 4, 16; education 121; infrastructure 18; living 8; medical 127; miscellaneous 8; official **11**; operating **11**, 18, 120, 205; private 8; research 4;

travel **217**, 217; unreasonable 139; welfare 4
external balance 56, 58–59, 65; analysis of 59, 65; indicators 65

Fan, G. Q. 161
Fan, X. Z. 12
Fang, F. 48
Fang, H. 173
feasible generalized least squares (FLGS) 33
Federal Ministry of Agriculture 166
Federal Ministry of Economy and Energy 166
Federal Ministry of Education and Research (BMBF) 166, 172
Federal Ministry of Environment 166
Federal Ministry of Transportation 166
Feng, W. Q. 30
Ferrin, S. E. 171
Figueiredo, J. D. 171
Figueiredo, J. M. D. 163
Finance Bureau 128
financial: allocation 1–4, 6–13, 15–20, 59, 65, 82, 121; capacity 10, 20, 22, 131, 133; expenditure 14, 205; forecasting 36, **43**; funds 1, 4, 14, 19–21, 55–56, 68, 104, 122; guarantee 8, 49, 161; investment 1, 6, 12–22, 43, 52, 54, 104, 135, 215; policy 6; resources 5–7, 12, 15–18, 20, 22, 52, 56, 97, 101, 123, 132, 147, 162; revenue 10; situation 123–124, 127–128, 131; support 3, 8, 48–49, 68–69, 73, 81, 85, 93, 117, 123, 131, 165, 170–171, 203–204; system 3, 54, **143**, 144
finite distributed lag (FDL) model 36
first difference (FD) estimator 32, 34, 37
first-order self-regressive model 40
fiscal: balance 55, 59; expenditure 1, 20, *52–53*; input 68; neutrality 55–56; policy 1, 68, 80; revenue 8; spending 68
Five-Year Plan: 13th 43, 83, 97, 112, 115–117; 14th 78, 81
fixed effect model 30–35, 43, **44**, **115**, 151–152, **153**, **155**
Fudan consensus 5
Full Economic Cost (FEC) 134–135, **143**

Gan, G. H. 138
Gardner Jr., E. S. 38, 106
global financial crisis 51–52, 75
Global University Rankings (2018) 68
Gong, X. H. 123

Gong, Y. L. 141
government: expenditure 49, **50**, 51–59, **60**, 61–62, **63–64**, 65, 69–70, 76, 79, 86, 88, 90, 97–99, 101, 117; investment 1–2, 13, 52, 54, 69, 163
Greene, W. 33, 35
gross domestic product (GDP) 1, 49, 68, 150
gross enrollment rate 48, 71–73, 77, 80–81, 85, **93**
Gu, J. F. 61
Gu, Q. 165
Gu, Y. 120, 131
Guo, H. L. 140

Han, C. L. 12
Harbin Institute of Technology 5
Hausman test 43, **44**, 151
He, G. W. 7
He, G. X. 173
heterogeneities 31
heteroscedasticity 31, 35
Higher Education Funding Council for England (HEFCE) 134–135, **136–137**, 165, 168, 205, **206**, 207
higher education institutions (HEIs) 6, 8, 10, 12, 49, 54, 70, 72–74, 82, 85, 97–98, 101–102, 104, 113, 115, 120–121, 123–130, 137–138, 141, **143**, 144, 156, 160, 165, 168–169, 205, **206**
Higher Education Statistics Agency (HESA) 137
Higher Education Students Early Statistics (HESES) 134
Hill, R. C. 31
Hillman, N. W. 12
Holt–Winters method 38, 76; nonseasonal model 21, **43**, 98, 106, 109, 112, 116; non-seasonal smoothing **45**, **110**; seasonal smoothing **45**; smoothing 38, **110**
Hou, L. L. 12
Hu, R. W. 30
Hu, S. 16
Hu, Y. M. 1, 12, 68, 97
Hu, Y. Z. 13, 15, 48, 146
humanities and social sciences (HSS) 172, **176**, 181, 185, **186**, 187, **188**, 189–190, **191**, 192–196, **197**, 198–199, **200**, 201, **202**, 204, 210–211, 213

idiosyncratic error 33, 39
industrial upgrading 4
innovation 97; ability 174, **175**; activities 161; funds **177**; independent 174;

policy 166; project **177–178**; science 78; special funds **175**; system of 170; technological 4, 167, **178**
Innovation Platform for Advantageous Disciplines 2
institutions 15, 98, 102–104, 108, 116, 145, 148, 162, 164, 168–170, 187, 189, 196, 198, 200, 204; cooperative 128; financial 162; government-affiliated 120, 137; higher education 6, 8, 10, 12, 49, 54, 70, 72–74, 82, 85, 97–98, 100–101, 104, 113, 115, 120–121, 123, 126–127, 129–130, 137–138, 141, **143**, 144, 160, 165, 168–169, 205, **206**; local 100, 114; locally administered 98; ordinary 187, 189; public 48–49; pure art 124; research 171–173, 205; scientific 162, 170; special 124; tertiary 49; undergraduate 104; vocational education 6

Jin, F. Y. 3
Jin, X. B. 13, 69–70
Jin, Y. H. 31
Johnes, G. 12
Johnstone, D. B. 7, 12, 16
Joint Steering Group on Costing and Pricing (JCPSG) 134

Kallison, J. M. 13
Kang, X. M. 163
Kharas, H. 85
Khor, N. 85
Krueger, A. B. 69

Lang, Y. F. 12–13, 69
least squares dummy variable (LSDV) 32
Lei, W. 203
Li, B. 126, 169
Li, C. 204
Li, F. L. 12
Li, G. J. 173
Li, P. S. 4
Li, W. L. 3, 16, 48
Li, Y. N. 12–14, 69–70
Li, Y. X. 12
Liang, W. Y. 203
Lin, L. N. 148
linear additive relationship 39
Liu, B. 174
Liu, K. 173
Liu, L. 167
Liu, T. Z. 98–99
Liu, X. K. **206**

Liu, X. Y 141
Liu, Z. W. 58
Liu, Z. Y. 12, **43**, 70, 86
longitudinal data 18, 30
Luo, J. P. 24n2, 98
Luo, L. Q. 30

Ma, L. L. 165, 172
Maria, T. D. 13
Mathew effect 212
maximum likelihood (ML) estimator 33, **44**
mean absolute percentage error (MAPE) 112
mean group (MG) estimator 36, 84
Measures for the Management of Fundamental Research Funds for Central Universities (2016) 161, 174
Mi, H. **43**
Ministry of Education, Culture, Sports, Science and Technology (MEXT) 166, 172
moving average (MA) 40–42, **45**, 106; coefficients of 41–42; filter 37–38; models 40–41; smoothers 37; weighted 106
Mowery, D. C. 170

Nagy, S. G. 13
National Development and Reform Commission 2, 82, 150
National Education Commission 121
National Science Foundation 164
National Statistical Bulletin on the Implementation of Education Funds 68
National Symposium on University Development, Fund Raising and Investment 4
Nelson, R. R. 170
NETEASE 99
neutrality 56; aspects of 56; financial 57; fiscal 55–56

Office of Science and Technology Policy (OSTP) 163
Overall Plan for Promoting the Construction of World-Class Universities and First-Class Disciplines 2

Pan, J. S. 146
Pesaran, M. H. 36, 84, 86
population-averaged (PA) method 62, 65
President's Council Advisors on Science and Technology (PCAST) 164
Public Finance Balance Project Team (PFBPT) 55

quality-related (QR) 165, 205–207, **209**

random effect model 30–31, 33–35, 43, **44**, 151
random sampling process 34
regional imbalance 58, 148
regression 33, 75, 78, 83, 91; analysis 152; auto- 36, 41–42, **45**; coefficient 31–33, 57, 61–62, 109, 114, 142, 153, 155; dynamic **45**; error 33; first-stage 75–76, 91; group-specific **44**; linear 31, 43, 201; models 13, 22, **45**, 69; pooled 31
Research Assessment Exercise (RAE) 165, 168
Research Excellence Framework (REF) 165, 168, 205–206, **207**
Research on Reforming and Improving the Funding Input Mechanism of Central Universities (RRIFIMCURG) 11, 13, 16
Riseqi Think Tank 2
root-mean-square error (RMSE) 75–76, 84, **87**, 88, **89**, 92, *99*, 108–109
Rossi, R. J. 70

science, engineering, agriculture, and medicine (SEAM) 181, 185, **186**, **188**, **191–192**, **194–195**, **197–200**, **202**, **211**
Shanghai Academy of Educational Sciences 9
Shen, H. 12
Shi, Y. 161
smoothers 37; moving average 37; nonlinear 37; recursive 37
smoothing 38: constant 38; double-exponential 38–39, **44**, 98, 106, 109, 112, 116; exponential 21, 36–38, 43, 106, 109, **110**; Holt–Winters (H–W) 38, **45**; multiparameter exponential 106; non-seasonal 38, 43; optimal parameters 106; parameter 38–39, **44**, 106; recursive 76; seasonal 38; secondary 38; single-exponential 38, **44**, 106; triple-exponential 106
Song, F. J. 104
subsidies 127, 138; equipment **11**; financial 10; housing 138; living 138; project **11**; special 10–11, 120–122, 156
Sun, P. Q. 124
Sun, Z. J. 10, 12, 14, 48, 70, 105, 127

talent 70, 80, 88, 113, 118; cultivation 4–5, 10, 21, 97, 140–142; demand for 97; dividends 4; high-quality 81, 86; innovative 4, 80, 118; outstanding **178**; projects **178**; skilled 118; specification 1, 5, 80; supply 13, 70; training 70, 80, 118, 130, 160
Tandberg, D. A. 12
Tang, H. W. V. 70
Tang, M. H. 161
Tang, X. W. 107
Tang, Y. P. (2017). 30, 43, 70, 146–148
Tao, C. M. 10
teaching 8, 10, 104, 131–132, 134, 141, **143**, 144, 147, 160, 168–169; allocation 9; appropriation 133; classroom 141; conditions 81; correspondence 139; cost 8, 133–135; equipment 131; expenditure 137; force 146; functions of 144; funding 10, 130, 133–135, 144, 156, 169–170; management **132**; non-publicly funded (NPFT) 134; practical 21, 104; publicly funded (PFT) 134; research 133; shortage of 122; specialized 141; staff **11**, 81; undergraduate 123, 130
technological progress 4
Tian, H. 163
Tianda Action 5
Transparent Approach to Costing (TRAC) 134–135
Trow, M. 81
tuition 8; fees 3, 7–8, 49, 54, 70–74, 76–77, 82, 85, **93**, 101, 128, 135; funding 9; income 15, 133; policies 82; pricing 8; standards 3, 8, 81–82; system 82
two-stage least squares (2SLS) 74, 91

UNESCO Institute for Statistics (UIS) 49

variance 33, 152; explained 152; forecast 42, 107; larger 42, 107; reciprocal of 109, 112; smaller 34, 42, 107
vector autoregression 36
vector error correction 36
vocational: colleges 15–16, 18–19, 21, 43, 72, 97, 101, 104, 116–118, 128, 138–139, 181, 215; development 117; education 6, 16, 18, 21–22, 101, 104, 117–118

Wang, D. 12
Wang, J. H. 12
Wang, M. 165
Wang, S. L. 146
Wang, S. M. 10, 12, 20, 30, 120
Wang, S. Y. 2, 30
Wang, W. Y. 190
Wang, Y. F. 203

Weiner, T. 163
Wen, K. 173
Woodbridge, J. M. 34
world-class discipline construction (WCDC) 2
world-class universities construction (WCUC) 2
World Conference on Higher Education (2009) 3
Worthington, A. C. 147
Wu, L. 138
Wu, W. W. 146
Wu, X. 85
Wu, Y. L. 8

Xi, Y. M. 167
Xia, H. H. 173
Xiao, G. L. 173
Xie, S. Q. 179
Xinhuanet. 160
Xiong, J. H. 3
Xu, Y. 160
Xu, Z. Q. 2
Xuan, J. 170

Yan, C. B. 169
Yang, L. J. 12

Yang, M. 165
Yao, J. J. 14, 70
Yao, L. H. 169
Ye, J. 48
Yu, F. 146
Yuan, L. S. 12, 16, 23n1, 138
Yue, C. J. 12, 14, 20, 30, 48–49, 70–71, 86

Zeng, X. D. 1
Zhang, B. 174
Zhang, F. 141
Zhang, H. F. 10, 12
Zhang, H. L. 101, 146
Zhang, H. W. **43**
Zhang, J. G. 160, 190
Zhang, L. P. 179
Zhang, X. M. 1, 68
Zhang, Y. F. 213
Zhao, L. N. 10
Zhao, Q. H. 166
Zhao, R. 30, 43, 70
Zhao, Y. 4
Zhou, C. 16, 173
Zhou, J. W. 117
Zhou, W. 162
Zhou, X. F. 130–132
Zhu, C. F. 10, 13, 69

Printed in the United States
by Baker & Taylor Publisher Services